THE POWER AND THE PAIN

The Power and the Pain

Transforming Spiritual Hardship into Joy

Andrew Holecek

SNOW LION PUBLICATIONS
ITHACA, NEW YORK

Snow Lion Publications
P.O. Box 6483
Ithaca, New York 14851 USA
(607) 273-8519 www.snowlionpub.com

Printed in USA on acid-free recycled paper.
Designed and typeset by Gopa & Ted2, Inc.

ISBN-10: 1-55939-331-9
ISBN-13: 978-1-55939-331-7

Library of Congress Cataloging-in-Publication Data

Holecek, Andrew, 1955-
 The power and the pain : transforming spiritual hardship into joy
/ Andrew Holecek.
    p. cm.
Includes bibliographical references and index.
ISBN-13: 978-1-55939-331-7 (alk. paper)
ISBN-10: 1-55939-331-9 (alk. paper)
 1. Spiritual life--Buddhism. I. Title.
BQ5670.H65 2010
294.3'4442--dc22

                                                    2009036846

This book is dedicated to my parents,
Frank and Maria,
whose love continues to sustain me.

And to Chögyam Trungpa Rinpoche,
whose genius continues to destroy me.

Contents

Foreword by the Dzogchen Ponlop Rinpoche

IN HIS BOOK, *The Power and the Pain,* Andrew Holecek directs our attention to two key points of the Buddhist spiritual journey: suffering and the obstacles and opportunities that suffering presents us with as we try to understand and transcend it. Essentially, it is a book about the hardships of the journey that sometimes take us by surprise, wear us down, or even discourage us from continuing. At the same time, it is an intelligent, clear, even humorous look at just those states, coupled with some very good advice from someone who knows the ins and outs, and highs and lows, of this trip firsthand. I have had the pleasure of knowing Andrew and working with him for over fifteen years. I am delighted to be able to offer a few words of recommendation for his excellent first book. As usual, he knows his topic, and the message he delivers comes from the heart. He is a respected teacher, philosopher-scholar, and a committed veteran of the Buddhist path. It is often said that the signs of success in practice are a clear, peaceful mind and a kind heart; in others words, wisdom and compassion. I think you will find both in this book.

Certainly many books have been written about suffering, and there will be many more to come. In fact, the topic of suffering pervades all Buddhist literature. It was the subject of the Buddha's first discourse millennia ago, and that little chat with that very small audience was so successful that we are still talking about it. We have heard about it so much by now, it's like a tune we can't get out of our head or a background noise that we no longer pay attention to. Yet the topic of our human distress will never be exhausted or our understanding of it complete until we are awakened like the Buddha. When we are getting along well, we like hearing descriptions of our buddha nature and all the wonderful qualities we'll possess in the future. Suffering sounds boring. But for someone facing real hardships, nothing could be less boring or more worth getting to know. When we take the time to look into it more deeply, as Andrew helps us to do here, we see that our suffering is not just misery; it is full of potential for not only pain but also power and joy.

As the Buddha taught, our path to enlightenment isn't perfect from the start; our experience is always mixed. The very nature of the path consists of ups and downs, happiness and suffering, clarity and confusion. That's what the path is all about—transforming negative states into positive ones and adverse conditions into circumstances that are conducive to our awakening. Still, the spiritual hardships that each of us face along the way can be hard to bear, whether these are purely psychological pressures or events that affect us on a physical level as well. Yet they can be ameliorated when we see their connection to our path as a whole. That is the distinctive gift of *The Power and the Pain* for contemporary Buddhist practitioners. It helps us make sense of our individual experiences, which, as unique as they are, have been challenging practitioners in different ways since the time of the Buddha.

Ordinarily, when you are faced with a painful experience, you might conclude that you (or someone else) are doing something wrong and that that wrongness needs to be righted. *The Power and the Pain,* however, explores the hardships of the spiritual path from the perspective of the acceptance of hardship, first, followed by an increasing understanding of its causes and its relationship to the process of transformation. There is hardship, yes, but there is also a cause for it that we can understand. On the other hand, there is an end to hardship ultimately, and there is also a cause for that ending that we can understand. If we can look at our experiences as we progress along the path with this view, then we can, as described here, begin to see patterns of hardships and patterns of becoming free of them. If we see only the way we fall into suffering without seeing any way out, then we might as well just cross our fingers and hope for some good luck.

Although we may associate words like transformation and transmutation with blissful states and heavenly realms, they imply change at the very core of our being, which is a very personal and sensitive matter. In some sense, it's a surgical process; we are going under the knife—the knife of our own intelligence, which we are sharpening all the time with our studies and meditation. We can't count on simply rising above our pain without changing at all.

When we move beyond our theories about the spiritual path into the actual practice of it, that is when the insights and methods offered in this book will become truly useful. Although the map of our journey is laid out in logical steps—we go from here to there, getting closer to our goal every step of the way—it doesn't always feel like we are following a perfect ABC kind of pattern. To say that there is a thread that runs through all of our experiences from most confused to fully awakened means that our journey doesn't have to be linear. Wherever we are, we are connected to both the beginning and end, to confusion and wisdom.

If we say that confusion is like a territory fixed within certain boundary lines and wisdom is that same territory without any boundary lines, then we can see how our path is simply a process of bringing down this fence. In fact, we don't have to take it down all at once. The minute we cut through one place, the fence can't do its job of being a fence anymore. A sense of spaciousness and openness enters our mind. It is just at such points that we might experience a sense of heightened neurosis or groundlessness. We might feel more confused than ever because our experience of who we are is in flux. The old ego model doesn't quite work anymore, and we are still too shy to see our buddha nature nakedly. So in some sense, spiritual hardships can be the result of our very successes on the path: it's only when we see something clearly that we can be shocked by it or be faced with the task of living with and up to a new understanding.

Although we are fundamentally alone on the path, the Buddha emphasized three refuges, reliable sources of wisdom, knowledge, and comradeship. While these are all ultimately within us, aspects of our own mind and heart, they also exist in the world in the form of teachers, teachings, and fellow practitioners. This means that we always have someplace to go when we are struggling. Andrew's book is in this sense a compassionate refuge for troubled times. It is also a kind of beacon or lighthouse that shows the way and illuminates the sometimes rocky ground we are walking on.

Such a book is an indispensable resource for the journey of brave pioneers who want to explore the path of discovering genuine enlightenment in everyday life. May this book fulfill the compassionate intentions of the author and become a true source of support to countless practitioners of the Buddhist path, now and in the future.

Dzogchen Ponlop Rinpoche
Nalanda West
October 25, 2009
Seattle, Washington

Acknowledgments

No book stands alone. This one was aided by the friends who gave so generously of their time and the spiritual masters whose influence saturates every page. I am deeply grateful to Jeremy Hayward, Dan Hessey, Elizabeth Namgyal, Tim and Glenna Olmstead, and Irini Rockwell for their penetrating comments. Thank you to Sharon Adams, Marc Bekoff, Frank Berliner, Elizabeth Callahan, Cindy Shelton, Ari Goldfield, Jules Levinson, Will Johnson, Mark Mathews, and Kimberly Roberts. Thank you to Daia Gerson, who was always willing to drop her projects and answer my endless questions when I needed her the most.

Special thanks to Janine Kotre, teacher and heart-friend, whose presence and open heart was of inestimable benefit. I am grateful for the courage of Steven Rhodes and the kindness of Sidney Piburn at Snow Lion Publications. Thank you to my editor at Snow Lion, Michael Wakoff, whose precision and caring did much to polish this book. Very special thanks to Laurie Mathews, who spent countless hours giving detailed feedback and offered unflagging encouragement in the face of my doubt. This book would not have happened without her.

A deep thank you to the Dzogchen Ponlop Rinpoche, an extraordinary teacher whose wisdom and warmth has graced and shaped my life for nearly twenty years. His ability to transport the brilliance of the East into the culture and vocabulary of the West is benefiting countless beings.

The biggest influence in my life, and a presence felt in every page of this book, is my teacher Chögyam Trungpa Rinpoche. He faced hardship and obstacles beyond comprehension and taught me how to transform darkness into light. The Western spiritual world, and my life, will never be the same because of his boundless love.

Introduction

Chaos should be regarded as extremely good news.
— CHÖGYAM TRUNGPA

Easy, comfortable practice won't get you anywhere!
— MILAREPA

I STUMBLED ONTO my spiritual path over thirty years ago and was quickly introduced to the promise of spiritual practice. The power of spirituality entered my world when I was a stressed-out undergraduate pursuing a double-degree program in science and music. One day, about mid-term into my second semester, I was struck with a series of fainting spells. I was a fit young man, but one morning I got out of bed and fell smack onto the ground. A teenager like any other, I still believed I was immortal so I brushed it off.

The next day as I got up after class, I was hit with another attack and had to grab the desk to steady myself. As these episodes increased, I finally went to the health center. I was diagnosed with acute hypertension. The doctor told me to alter my diet, increase my exercise, and start a regimen of medications. He also told me to relax.

I changed my diet and exercised more, but resisted the written prescription for medication and the oral prescription to relax. Relaxing meant I wasn't getting enough done. I knew, however, that high blood pressure could be lethal, so I looked into alternative treatments.

I remembered an article about the health benefits of Transcendental Meditation (TM) and the studies that showed it was effective in reducing hypertension. It so happened that there were posters around campus advertising a lecture on TM.

I went to the lecture, which was well attended and professionally delivered. The information was provocative, and the health benefits of TM were professed, but what struck me was the person giving the talk. He was knowledgeable, and that was important to me, but it was his kindness that touched me. What he said made sense, and his mere presence was magnetizing. Something inside me said, "I want to be like him."

I signed up for my first meditation instruction, but I had doubts. In 1975 there was not a lot of spirituality on campus. The TM people were among the first pioneers, and like most pioneers, they had lots of arrows in their backs. Because Westerners were shooting at them from all directions, TM turned to science and began using studies to prove the power of meditation. These studies on the physiological benefits of TM provided a shield against the attacks, and the data seduced me into taking a look.

After sleeping on it—and waking up to another fainting episode— I decided to give it a try.

❧ Breakthrough

On a crisp autumn morning in Bloomington, Indiana, I arrived at the TM center. I was invited into a small shrine room where an instructor greeted me. The instructor, a well-groomed man, explained that he was going to introduce me to my mantra, a sacred sound thousands of years old that apparently had already been selected for me.

We sat on meditation cushions facing the shrine. He began the recitation of my mantra out loud and gestured for me to join him. I did so, and together we chanted this sacred sound. I could feel my mind settling as I focused on the rhythm of our chanting.

We began a decrescendo into complete silence. I was now reciting the mantra mentally, but gradually the mantra itself dropped away. For the next timeless bit of time I rested in deep meditative absorption. My chattering mind stopped, every thought evaporated, and I don't even recall breathing. All the winds that normally rage across the surface of my mind dissolved into space, and the waves of thought stirred up by those winds settled into a mirror-like tranquility. It was a state of indescribable peace, a dimension of being so sublime that words fail me even three decades later.

These are all thoughts and images that I have retrofitted onto the experience, for at that time there were no thoughts or images at all. There was just the ineffable wonder of the experience itself. After soaking in this silent bliss, the instructor brought me up by whispering and then saying the mantra, returning me to the world. I was dumbfounded.

I left the center and roamed around for hours, basking in the glow of that miraculous morning. Everything was alive, shimmering in a soft luminosity. The sunlight danced through the radiant trees, and the flickering golden leaves fluttered as the wind passed through them—and through me. I felt completely transparent, open to a new world that spoke to me in its secret language. It was the first time in my life that I had stopped my mind without falling asleep, and it felt like I had returned to some mysterious home.

I went to sleep still shining, trying not to figure it out. The next morning, the light from the experience was still on, but it was fading, and over the next few days it gradually dissolved into the mist of daily activity. My scientific mind began to analyze what had happened and what I could do to recapture that magical state. I began my daily TM practice and had glimpses of that sacred space, but I could not reproduce it. It was, indeed, pure beginner's luck. But I knew in my bones that I wanted more, and I was going to do whatever it took to get more. My spiritual life was born.

The initial spark of the power of the spiritual path had been ignited, and it would propel me for the rest of my life. But little did I know what this path had in store for me.

❦ The Light Side

After practicing TM for a few months, my hypertension disappeared. Diet and exercise surely played a role but so did my new practice of meditation. The spiritual path is truly the path of great bliss. In my many years of walking this path, I have stumbled upon moments of spiritual intoxication so radiant, so exalted, and so complete that my life still trembles from the force of such transport. Nothing compares. And nothing can describe the power of such transformation.

But the traditions are replete with testimonials that try. Paul Brunton writes, "Finally it happens. . . . [My] sense of awareness has been drawn out of the narrow confines of the separate personality; it has turned into something sublimely all-embracing. . . . With it arrives an amazing new sense of absolute freedom. . . . I find myself outside the rim of world consciousness. The planet which has so far harboured me, disappears. I am in the midst of an ocean of blazing light."[1] R. M. Bucke relates, "Now came a period of rapture so intense that the universe stood still, as if amazed at the unutterable majesty of the spectacle. Only one in all the infinite universe! The All-loving, the Perfect One. . . . In that same wonderful moment of what might be called supernal bliss, came illumination."[2] The Tibetan sage Marpa: "I was overwhelmed with joy. The hairs of my body stood on end, and I was moved to tears. . . . My body was intoxicated with undefiled bliss. . . . There dawned an experience beyond words."[3]

These experiences nourish the spiritual traveler. They provide glimpses of a dimension we yearn to realize and spark the inspiration that propels us along the path. They usher a sense of meaning and purpose to life and touch the deep mystery that saturates this world. Sometimes these experiences are extraordinary, the radiant proclamations of union with the divine. Often they are silent and ordinary, the whispers of wisdom that accompany daily life.

❦ The Dark Side

But enlightenment is not tax free. The light of bliss shines frequently upon the path, but shadows are also found. These shadows can seduce us into their protective circle or induce us to flee their darkness. The path that has brought me such peace has also brought me untold pain.

After I finished graduate school and received my doctorate in dental surgery, I took a few months off before starting work. I had been meditating for a number of years by then and was studying the world's contemplative traditions. Even though TM is one of the best ways to enter the path of meditation—something I still believe—at the time I didn't know what to do next. What was I supposed to do with my grand first experience; how could I develop it? So I started looking for a path to answer these questions. I began a survey of world religions and came upon Buddhism. More than any other tradition, this one helped me understand my experience.

In an effort to explore the Buddhist path, I decided to do a month-long group meditation retreat in the forests of Vermont. It was a stretch. Outside of a few weekends of meditation, I had never tried to practice for so long.

Filled with anxiety, I walked up the road to the meditation center, not knowing if I could make it through the retreat. To meditate for twelve hours a day, thirty days in a row, was really intimidating. Because I felt like I was entering a spiritual boot camp, I was already putting undue pressure on myself. Failing was not an option.

I was greeted warmly and given instructions on the program. We would start meditating at 6:00 A.M. and finish at 10:00 P.M. We would even eat our meals in meditation. The only time off would be during the work period and a half-hour after each meal.

Being an overachiever, I was determined to do this program right. I showed up for each session, followed the rules, and did my best to be a good meditator. I found the days grueling. The first thing to fall apart was my body. My knees throbbed, my back ached, and my ankles tortured me. I was assigned a seat in the front row, and even though the instructions were not to tough it out physically (we could do whatever we needed to stay reasonably comfortable), I was damned if I was going to let others see me squirm. A few people even said to me that they noticed I never moved. I was getting a reputation as a "good meditator" simply because of my posture, and I had to uphold that. This attitude, however, made me the worst meditator. I developed a competitive attitude and a ridiculous sense of pride.

Not only did my body hurt, but my mind was going crazy. Thoughts flew through my mind with a frequency and velocity I could hardly bear. The memory of my blissful TM experience was lifetimes away, and after seven days I began to doubt that I could complete the retreat. What made it worse was that it seemed I was the only one going through this anguish. We were in silence, so I wasn't able to share my heartache with others or determine how they were doing. My only sense of comfort came when I plopped into bed at the end of these grinding days and could finally indulge my discursive mind.

The meditation instruction was to label the thoughts that arose in my mind as "thinking," and that was hard work. But night time was my time. I left the rigors of the day behind to feast on my delicious thoughts. It was almost a mutiny against the instruction. I looked forward to my evening banquets where no one but my thoughts was invited, and where I could escape the discipline of these interminable days.

After the first week my body started to soften and the pain became workable. My determination not to move in meditation made it unnecessarily difficult, but I thought I could make it to the end of the retreat. After twelve days, however, it got surprisingly worse. I began to notice that the momentum of all the labeling, the force of the meditation technique, was starting to extend into my bedtime. For a few nights I was able to keep it out, but as the days passed and the technique built momentum, I could no longer keep meditation from entering my postmeditation world. My only avenue of escape had been cut off.

I was anxious, unable to control my mind. My mind went ballistic as part of me tried to indulge my thoughts and the other part kept labeling whatever arose in my mind as "thinking." I had read that meditation releases the demons buried within you. Maybe it was true.

In the darkness and solitude of one dreadful night, alone with my uncontrollable mind, I was in a state of panic. I had no idea what was happening to me. I thought about waking up my meditation instructor but had no idea how to find him. I lay in a cold sweat all night, making the pledge that when the sun arose, I would leave the retreat. It has been said that religion is for those who are afraid of hell, while spirituality is for those who have been through hell. I had no idea that spirituality could *put* you through hell.

At daybreak I called my wife and, through tears of embarrassment and dejection, told her that I could not complete the program. I packed my bags but as a gesture of courtesy decided to tell my meditation instructor I was leaving. My eyes were red and swollen from crying all night, so before I met him I went to the bathroom to stuff my pockets full of tissue paper. Tears would surely flow when we met.

My meditation instructor was a good one. As we sat across from each other in the interview room, I broke down. He didn't say anything but looked at me with incredible kindness, providing the space for me to express my pain, my fear, and my embarrassment. I had tried so hard to keep it together for the last thirteen days, but I just couldn't anymore. Although I had tried to be a good meditator, he was seeing me for what I truly was—a failure.

I told him there was no way I would go back into that shrine room and that this path was not for me. I poured out the pain of the evening before and the repressed heartache of the past two weeks. After listening with patience, he told me that of course I could leave. But he asked me one thing: "Where do these feelings of panic come from?" I told him that I felt it in my stomach and my head and . . . He interrupted me and asked again, "No, that's not what I mean. Where do these thoughts come from?" I told him that they probably came from my childhood, perhaps from my parents or . . . He stopped me again, and said, "You might want to take a closer look."

At this point the flood of emotion stopped. I asked him, "What do you mean?" He said, "Why don't you find out for yourself? Look, you can leave now if you want, that's not a problem. But you can't get a ride out of here for a few hours, so why don't you have some breakfast?" He had gently pulled me out of myself and started to reach something deeper than my pain. He made a suggestion: "If you feel up for it, I want you to consider something. I want you to consider going in just for the morning session. I know it may not be easy, but you might want to give it a try. If you go in and still want to leave after the session, you have my blessing. Have some breakfast and then decide."

I left the room reflecting on his suggestion and went to get some food. I kept my head down, fearing that others would see I had been crying, and ate alone outside. I didn't know what to do. I was set on leaving, yet the calm confidence of my meditation instructor haunted me. I looked out across the lush forest and decided that if I could get through four sessions a day for the past thirteen days, I could probably do one more.

When the gong started to signal our lineup for entering the shrine room, my heart began to pound. I told myself I would give it a few minutes in the shrine hall, and if I didn't like what was happening, "reputation" or not, I would leave. It took more courage to enter that meditation hall and face my mind than it had with any previous event. I looked up and saw my meditation instructor at the front of the line, opening the door. Catching my eye, he gave me a reassuring smile. I went in, walked to my front row cushion, and sat down. I had nothing left. I had been up all night, had cried myself dry, and sat there utterly spent. I finally just gave up.

Within a few minutes my mind settled. I began to look at the feelings that remained and to ask myself the question my instructor had posed: where is this feeling coming from? I really looked and tried to find its source. I could not. Every time I looked I found nothing. I eventually gave up and just rested in the space that was the "answer." I found myself dropping into that same mysterious atmosphere I had stumbled into years earlier, on that magical morning in Bloomington. My breathing became quiet, every thought evaporated, and I descended into a pool of tranquility.

The morning session lasted three hours and for most of it I sat in deep meditation. My pain was gone, my thoughts and emotions were gone—there was just the silence of being present in sacred space.

❀ Both Sides

I finished that retreat and since then have completed many more, including the traditional Tibetan three-year retreat. In my work as a meditation instructor for the past fifteen years, I have heard countless stories about the struggles of spiritual practice and the ways both young and old students work with their spiritual and psychological pain. In my practice as a doctor of dental surgery and during years of volunteer health care work in developing countries, I have also witnessed, and worked to alleviate, physical pain. This combination of spiritual and material experience has allowed me to explore hardship in intimate detail and to discover that the darkest of times often points to the brightest of lights. And that even pain, or perhaps especially pain, can be deeply spiritual.

Even after all these years of practice, there are times when I am the most unstable of meditators, one day enjoying the fruits of the path and the next day being lost in discouragement and doubt. These experiences have inspired me to reconcile the highs with the lows. Why does a path that bestows such bliss also bowl us over with such pain? Why does it have to hurt so much? Why is it such hard work? It is my purpose in this book to explore these questions. The Tibetan teacher Anam Thubten writes,

> There is no magic wand, so it is very common to lose that initial love that we had with our spiritual practice. Spirituality is not about fixing all of our problems and the earlier we find out about this, the less disappointment we are going to face. We have to let go of all of these fantasies. . . . If we hang on to them, we often run into disappointment and that can sometimes create a huge obstacle to inner awakening. It can completely draw us away from the path.[4]

The key to a good journey on the spiritual path is balance. Look at nature: during the course of twenty-four hours it is light half the time and dark half the time. To reject the night is to reject reality itself.

The path is about learning how to accept and work with darkness and the inevitable hardships of life just as much as it is about learning how to work with joy. The eleventh-century sage Padampa Sangey says, "Approach all that you find repulsive! Anything you are attracted to, Let go of it!"[5]

If we lose our balance we fall off the path, retarding our progress. It is my aspiration to help us work with these two extremes, thereby coming to understand the roller-coaster ride that awaits us along this transcendent but challenging path.

Over the years I have studied dozens of ancient traditions and contemporary methods for spiritual awakening. Twenty years ago I took to heart the Zen warning: "Chase two rabbits, catch none." I made my commitment and took refuge as a Buddhist. Chasing dozens of rabbits had worn me out, and I realized that sooner or later it helps to settle down. I do not believe Buddhism is the only way, but it is a good one. It speaks to me. Its vast doctrine has illuminated my life, and its meditations have transformed me.

❧ The Four Noble Truths

The heart of the Buddha's teaching is contained in the first teaching he gave after his awakening—that of the Four Noble Truths. It is common to every school of Buddhism. The philosopher Alfred North Whitehead once said that all of Western philosophy is but a series of footnotes to Plato. Similarly, all of Buddhism is but a series of footnotes to the Four Noble Truths. They are called "noble" not because they are elitist but because they are so uncompromising and practical. It takes a noble character to look deeply into this world and to accept its uncompromising reality. These truths cut to the root of what the Buddha saw after his enlightenment.

The Four Truths are: 1) the truth of suffering, 2) the truth of the origin of suffering, 3) the truth of the cessation of suffering, and 4) the truth of the path leading to the cessation of suffering. The Buddha summarized them thus: "I teach one thing and one thing only: suffering and the end of suffering." Suffering is not only the overt hardship of things like disease and disaster but also the everyday experiences of dissatisfaction, anxiety, and unhappiness. If we simply open our eyes and acknowledge what we see and feel, we will discover the truth of suffering in its many guises.

Here was a teaching so compelling that one of the world's great religions was born from these very words. Since then countless beings have studied and practiced the words of the Buddha, and they have done so, and will continue to do so, because these words promise that there is a way to end our human suffering—there is a way to be happy.

But what is not overtly taught, and what confuses many followers, is that the path leading to the cessation of suffering necessarily includes suffering. There is irony here in that the path leading to unceasing peace and happiness requires us to fully welcome suffering. It means that hardship is an unavoidable component of waking up. The path does not create suffering, but it presents many opportunities to find liberation in suffering. Zen writer Barry Magid says,

> My old teacher Joko Beck used to say that it took many, many years for students to finally discover what [meditation] practice really meant, and when they did, most of them quit. That's because the end of suffering that we realize we can achieve through practice turns out to be an end of separation from suffering. Suffering ceases to exist when it is no longer something we experience as impinging on our life, as an unnecessary, avoidable intrusion that we finally learn to exclude from our lives once and for all. Instead, what we realize is that suffering is inseparable from life. I like to describe what happens by saying that suffering doesn't disappear from our life, but into our life.[6]

In this book we will explore what could be called the four truths of the path—the four aspects of the fourth Noble Truth. In other words, my struggles along the spiritual path have shown me that "the truth of the path leading to the cessation of suffering" is composed of four parts. These parts are not traditional, but I believe they are widely experienced. Everyone who walks a genuine path will encounter at least the first one and will hopefully be illuminated by the final three. We might think of them as the four "inner" truths of the Fourth Noble Truth. They are: 1) there is hardship along the path, 2) the hardship has an identifiable cause, 3) there is the possibility of the cessation, or lessening, of that hardship, and 4) there is a path that leads to the cessation, or lessening, of hardship. Learning about these truths, our journey in this book, is like meeting a spiritual guide, someone to accompany us along the path and to whisper advice into our ears when things start to hurt. The contemporary spiritual teacher Eckhart Tolle writes,

> Suffering has a noble purpose: the evolution of consciousness and the burning up of ego. The man on the cross is an archetypal image. He is every man and every woman. As long as you resist suffering, it is a slow process because the resistance creates more ego to burn up. When you accept suffering, however, there is an acceleration of that process which is brought about by the fact that you suffer consciously. . . . In the midst of conscious suffering, there is already the transmutation. The fire of suffering becomes the light of consciousness. . . . The truth is that you need to say yes to suffering before you can transcend it.[7]

❧ The Three Turnings

This book explores the obstacles that tend to arise on the spiritual path, starting with more general material and moving into progressively esoteric topics. This mirrors the increase in the subtlety and difficulty of the obstacles that arise along the path itself. When spiritual aspirants first start out on such a path, the bumps and twists are relatively easy to recognize and manage. Toward the end, however, the obstacles become increasingly difficult to detect and handle. As the traditions maintain, the greater the obstacles, the greater the realization. This book reflects that process. It will help long-term practitioners understand their current and past experiences and will help novices understand what they might expect in terms of hardship. Knowing about these hardships may prevent them or help you relate to them properly.

On one level, we are all novices. After all these years of traveling the spiritual path, I am still a beginner. So when we discuss things like "the end of the path," "enlightenment," or "nonduality" and the obstacles that might occur at more advanced stages, I can rely only on my limited experience and on what I have been able to digest from the wisdom of my teachers. In Taoism it is said: "He who knows does not speak; he who speaks does not know." When it comes to topics like enlightenment and the end of the path, this admonition should be brought to mind. This does not mean we should never speak of such things, but that topics that circumambulate absolute truth cannot be put into words and that humility should accompany anyone who ever tries.

After his awakening, the Buddha taught for forty-five years. It is said that he taught eighty-four thousand dharmas, or collections of teachings. This number implies that there is a teaching appropriate for everyone. This ocean of wisdom is classified in a number of different ways, but one of the most useful is the Three Turnings of the Wheel of Dharma. "Dharma" is a Sanskrit word that means "truth, law, or teaching." The Three Turnings were presented as a skillful means, a way to reach his audience depending on their level of intelligence and experience.*

---

* The Three Turnings were an organizational tool the Buddha used to reach his students. They represent the historical unfolding of his entire doctrine and also reflect the personal development of disciples that followed in his footsteps. Scholars are not in agreement about exactly how the Three Turnings unfolded. Some say that the doctrine itself was presented from a Second Turning sutra (*Sutra Unraveling the Thought*), while others assert it first appears in a Third Turning sutra (*Sandhinirmocana*). A sutra is simply a discourse of the Buddha. The fact that the Three Turnings were presented from a Second or Third Turning perspective suggests that

This book reflects the Three Turnings and how they might relate to progressive experiences of difficulty along the path. The actual path and one's experiences are of course never this tidy. Life is a mess, and the spiritual path, while it attempts to work with and eventually clean up this mess, is itself a hodgepodge of experiences. We can have any experience at any stage along the path, but there tend to be types of experiences that arise more frequently as we progress upon it. And there are therefore patterns of hardship that also tend to accompany each turning of the wheel.

By associating patterns of hardship with each of the three turnings, we can detect order in chaos and bring wisdom into our confusion. This awareness of patterns is itself a great help in relating to hardship. But it is important to realize that while a map can be of benefit, we never want to stuff the territory into a map. Experience is always bigger and more mysterious than any map, no matter how sophisticated. But there do seem to be patterns of difficulty that the traditions articulate and that my experience echoes.

The First Turning is where most of us will spend our spiritual lives. If we could somehow fully realize the depth of First Turning teachings, this would be a great accomplishment. Knowing there are two more turnings beyond the First Turning tends to make us want to leap ahead, to get to the real goods. But First Turning doctrine is profound and difficult to realize.

The essence of the First Turning is that of egolessness. It is the painful truth that on an absolute level we don't exist. We appear to exist and that is a relative truth that is acknowledged, but in actual truth there is no such thing as "you." Part 1 deals with themes that

---

many First Turning advocates (who probably do not refer to themselves as such) reject the idea of the Three Turnings altogether.

Scholars tend to agree that the Buddha did not suddenly proclaim that he was now moving from the First Turning to the Second, or from the Second to the Third. He probably did not preface his teachings by saying he was about to speak from one turning or another. It seems likely that the classification into the Three Turnings was devised by later traditions within Buddhism to help articulate the evolution of his doctrine.

prepare us for this shocking spiritual truth. It also explores general spiritual topics that relate to hardship at beginning and intermediate levels but that continue to reverberate throughout one's entire journey.

The essence of the Second Turning is that of emptiness, which we will define in part 2. This part starts with a chapter on death, which is the way emptiness is often experienced on the path. Chapters 14, 15, and 16 deal with the five skandhas, a teaching usually relegated to First Turning doctrine. The skandhas, or "heaps," describe the development of ego. They are placed in part 2 because of the level of difficulty in truly grasping the depth of this teaching. Egolessness (First Turning) is emptiness (Second Turning) on a personal level, and that is what the five skandhas are all about.

The essence of the Third Turning is luminosity, which is defined in part 3. This part begins with two chapters dealing with emotional hardship, and they are placed here because we will explore emotions using a spectrum of teachings based on all three turnings. Emotions are just runaway luminosity, or luminosity that is grasped onto, and if we can relate to them that way, we can transform our emotional poisons into spiritual medicine. This is followed by a chapter on meditative absorption and how this profound experience can become a deadly trap. We think we are finally enlightened when we are actually just stuck in the bliss of light. The last two chapters deal with the subtle problems of luminosity per se and the fruition of the path as the union of emptiness and luminosity, the topics of part 2 and 3.

Even though the Three Turnings did emerge at specific times in the Buddha's life, they never became mutually exclusive. It wasn't that he came to a certain point in his teaching when he suddenly and completely switched gears, never to teach from a lower turning again. We can find Second and Third Turning hints in First Turning teachings and First Turning hints tucked into Second and Third Turning doctrines.

This book is similar in spirit. While the Three Turnings provide a helpful template, we do not want the container to force the content. So within the threefold organization of this book flows a fluid collection of material, adhering to the spirit of the turning in which it is presented but never frozen in its letter. The Three Turnings therefore provide a thread, one that bends this way and that, with which we can weave and better understand the fabric of our spiritual lives and the difficulties that are an inevitable part of it. And while I honor the traditional way of relating to Buddhist doctrine, I also offer interpretations born from my personal experience of that doctrine.

It is easy to feel alone on the spiritual path, to think that our hardships are unique and insurmountable. We therefore tend to exaggerate our pain and retard, or completely arrest, our progress along the path. To share the common obstacles and traps, the sheer humanity of this challenging path, is to realize that we are not alone and that there are others who feel the same pain and struggle to understand it. And there are others who can help. This book is the offering of a personal journey, strengthened with traditional wisdom, for those who long to wake up.

Part I

THE FIRST TURNING

1 ❦

The Power

---

*Advanced experiences [in meditation] include profound
peace, concentration and joy, intense positive emotions of love
and compassion, penetrating insights into the nature of mind,
and a variety of transcendent states . . . [also] evidence
for enhanced creativity, perceptual sensitivity, empathy,
lucid dreaming, self-actualization, a positive sense of self control,
and marital satisfaction. . . . [I]t may foster maturation
as measured by scales of ego, moral and cognitive development,
intelligence, academic achievement . . . and states of consciousness.*
—ROGER WALSH, Paths beyond Ego

IT DOESN'T TAKE LONG to realize that something special happens
on the spiritual path. Whether it is yoga, T'ai chi, meditation, prayer,
or any other spiritual practice, there is untold power on this path.
But there are two kinds of power—relative and absolute—and if we
mix them up, we are headed for confusion and disappointment. We
might enter a spiritual path unconsciously seeking relative power and
become confused when we start to feel powerless, helpless, and lost.
Relative and absolute power are not always in opposition, but they
can be.

Relative or conditional power is the holy grail of the ego: it is tem-
poral, material, conventional, impermanent, and therefore ultimately
unsatisfying. It is power as commonly understood. It is power that is

often bestowed from outside or dependent upon external conditions. When we win the lottery, get that promotion, or feel the thrill of victory, we are tasting the fruits of relative power. Examples are legion, and the quest for relative power is nearly universal.

Absolute or unconditional power is beyond the ego: it is timeless, spiritual, unconventional, permanent, and therefore ultimately satisfying. It is not power as commonly understood. This real power comes from within and is not dependent upon external conditions. When we have lost our wallets or our jobs, or have experienced any other kind of defeat and it does not undo us, we are tasting the fruits of unconditional power. When Jesus said the meek shall inherit the earth, he was referring to absolute power.

Relative power is when you have power over the world; absolute power is when the world no longer has power over you. When we can live with inner peace in the midst of a world boiling with violence and corruption, we have discovered real power; when we can find inner happiness in an environment seething with external conflict, we have tapped into true power. What follows are some aspects of this power, unfolded from the perspective of relative and absolute. It is a brief summary of what many have come to experience as the wonder of the spiritual path, a survey of some of the fruits that are commonly picked. Developing an awareness of these facets of unconditional power will help us negotiate the rest of our journey and the many hurdles that accompany it.

This chapter emphasizes the lofty terrain of the absolute and its unconventional power, which is uncovered along the spiritual path. This terrain may seem idealized and inaccessible to mere mortals like ourselves, but it can give birth to the aspiration that fuels our efforts to attain this dimension of experience and the inspiration to share it. The following are but a few vignettes, not necessarily in order of priority, and certainly not complete. The intent is to provide a glimpse of the view from above.

After this we plunge deep into the harsh realities of the relative, how it is that we struggle along the path in our lives, and how to join heaven and earth, the absolute with the relative. The heart of our journey is to acknowledge and explore the hard work that occurs from below.

✤ The Power of Freedom

The pursuit of freedom is a noble endeavor, and liberty is one of humanity's greatest achievements. To move freely and to live one's own life is a common dream. I have been lucky enough to taste it. After my graduate studies, I entered the work force and reaped the financial rewards. I bought the things I wanted and did most of what I aspired to do. I traveled the world and fulfilled my materialistic desires. As nice as this is, it is still relative freedom. Many who achieve this level of freedom agree: even when we seem to have everything we want, something is still missing.

To see it in its extreme form, we need only to glance at the lives of dictators, or the rich and famous. These powerful people may dictate material reality but have no power over the dictates of their own minds. Howard Hughes could do anything he wanted but became a victim of his freedom and power. Relative freedom is the fruit of the worldly path, but because it depends on external conditions, it is not real freedom. When the conditions fade, so does the freedom. You feel free when you go on vacation, get a raise, or retire, but when you are forced back to work, lose your job, or get sick, your freedom is gone.

Absolute freedom, on the other hand, is the harvest of the spiritual path. It is absolute because it is unconditioned. There is no need to go on vacation, get a raise, or retire. You are free now because your mind is free. It does not matter what happens on the outside when your heart is open on the inside. You could be in jail, but your spirit soars; your home may be a shack, but your being is free. There are more poor and unknown buddhas than there are rich and famous ones. You may not control the world, but you control the way you react to the world—you control your mind.

You are not free because you can do whatever you want, you are free because you no longer want. The spiritual path cuts the chains of desire and liberates you into the fullness of what you already have. When desire is transcended, appreciation for the ordinary is born. You erase consumerism, increase satisfaction, and relax into simplicity. And instead of seeking your own happiness, you now have the power to help others find genuine happiness. That is real power—and freedom.

⚘ The Power of Wealth

Absolute freedom bestows the power of absolute wealth, which transcends any amount of relative wealth. Relative wealth is conditional, the common assets of property and fame, but it is a potential prison, for we easily become possessed by our own possessions. I am consumed with my home, car, art, and electronic gadgetry. I worry about my mortgage, mutual funds, and retirement account. I struggle to improve my property and maintain my possessions. And I always want more.

The lust for material wealth springs from a sense of spiritual poverty. We crave external fulfillment because we feel something is missing. We accumulate things in an effort to feel fulfilled, but material goods are mere substitutes. They never satisfy because our real hunger is not for things.

The spiritual path allows us to discover that even in the midst of material poverty, life can be rich, just as it is. This is why we often find happiness in simple events. We feel rich when we play with our children, or immerse ourselves in ordinary tasks. In these moments nothing is missing, there is no sense of poverty, because our focus brings fulfillment. Distraction steals attention from what is happening and instills the sense that something is missing. Distraction ransacks reality.

By training awareness to be present, which is central to the spiritual path, we cultivate the sense of natural wealth. When we bring attention fully into any situation, we will discover its golden nature. This is the miracle of the spiritual path and real wealth.

⚘ The Power of Happiness

The worldly path brings relative happiness. When desirable conditions come together, you are happy. When the sun is shining, your health is good, and your stomach is full, you are happy. But once again, when the conditions fade, relative happiness melts like the morning frost. So much of life is about getting what we want, getting rid of or avoiding what we don't want, and ignoring everything else. We are consumed by the satisfaction of desire, and because desire is endless, so is our dissatisfaction.

The spiritual path, on the other hand, brings absolute happiness. Here we are not happy because we get what we want, we are happy because we finally stop wanting. In the conventional world, we confuse the satisfaction of want with its temporary transcendence. We think we are happy when we get what we want, and therefore we never stop wanting: get that girl, car, job, or house. But if we take a close look, we will discover that we are actually happy when we stop wanting. A moment of satisfaction is just a moment of release from the pinch of desire. That is why the girl, car, job, or house won't do it. External things won't make us happy because the source and satisfaction of happiness is internal.

The spiritual path goes to the heart of the matter and deals not with substitute satisfactions, which are endless and ultimately futile, but with the essence of satisfaction. Zen master Suzuki Roshi used to say that what is ordinary is to strive after something you think is special, and what is truly special is to abide in the ordinary. Stop the pursuit of happiness and you will ironically find it. This is real happiness.

On an even deeper level, we are happy because we can help others. We can put the wants of others before our own. The great Indian master Shantideva says: "If you want to be miserable, think only of yourself. If you want to be happy, think only of others." We stop wanting for ourselves, and start wanting others to be happy.

❧ The Power of Peace

In this world of violence and stress, peace is a precious commodity. We seek it in peaceful places, natural sanctuaries like Hawaii or Bali. These spots of refuge offer temporary peace, but true peace is not out there. We will find it only in ourselves. You can move to a peaceful location, but if your mind is uneasy, internal conflict will follow you wherever you go. As Jon Kabat-Zinn put it in the title of his book: "Wherever you go, there you are." Peace of place does not compare to peace of mind.

In Buddhism, the central meditation is called *shamatha*, a Sanskrit word that means "tranquility, peace." Other traditions have similar meditations. When we practice shamatha, we are literally practicing peace. "Peace" comes from a root that means "to fasten," and this etymology has rich implications. We nurture peace and stability in the uncontrolled mind by fastening it to something.

Sit in meditation for the first time and you will bear witness to a subtle form of fury as your mind races in uncontrolled movement. Thoughts are like flying bullets. But by sitting in meditation, you are fastening your moving body to the stable earth. You have taken the first step into peace.

The next step is to deepen your peace by fastening your moving mind to your body by focusing (fastening) awareness to your body or breath. You start with physical peace and then invoke mental and spiritual peace upon that pacified ground. As every yoga, T'ai chi, and shamatha practitioner knows, a peaceful body invites and hosts a peaceful mind. We enter a session of yoga stressed out and speedy and leave with a sense of tranquility.

Every meditation cultivates some aspect of peace because meditation works with holding and stabilizing the mind. When the mind is gently fastened, with a mantra, visualization, or other method, its pacification ensues. But when you first try to fasten the mind to the body—or any meditative anchor—it bucks in retaliation. Your body is sitting still, but your mind is wild. The ego thrives on motion, and it is trying to throw off the saddle of meditation. With time the kicking is exhausted, thoughts are stilled, and the mind settles down. The lasso that once seemed so tight relaxes as the discursive mind relaxes. At this point we discover the greatest irony: real freedom and peace do not come from a completely free rein—they come from being fastened to the confines of the present moment. This, as the Buddhist nun Pema Chödrön so famously puts it, is the wisdom of no escape.

We may think freedom is found in the fantasies and memories of the roaming mind, but this freedom is a subtle trap. A moving mind actually traps attention in the realm of mere fantasy and dilutes awareness of the life before us. You live in your head and not in reality.

By finding peace within ourselves, we become the peace we want to see in the world. As we radiate this quality, others will fasten themselves to us, for peace not only pacifies, it also enriches and magnetizes. By representing that which so many seek, others will be drawn into our presence. The great saints and religious figures exude that sense of peace and magnetize those who long for it. And why should they care about magnetizing others? Because then they can help them.

❧ The Power of Mindfulness

We can enter the present moment, which is where spirituality begins, in two opposite ways. One is external, the other internal. If our external environment is "loud" enough, if sensory impact reaches a critical threshold, the stimulation can hurl us into our senses. This approach to nowness is the accidental and relative approach. People caught in natural disasters often give testimony to spiritual-level experiences. Veterans of war sometimes reflect with nostalgia about the horrific, yet magnificent, experience of being in combat. Survivors of hurricanes or earthquakes often give similar accounts of being thrown into reality. We get funneled into the moment, but it is a rugged way to get there. And it doesn't last.

We can reach nowness in a more gentle, predictable, and stable way by approaching it from the other direction. Instead of stumbling into a loud external environment, we live with a quiet interior one. If our internal environment is "silent" enough, if discursive mind drops below a critical threshold, then any stimulation can bring us to our senses. We do not have to be an accidental buddha. We do not have to seek or wait for dramatic events; we discover magic in every event. The mind of someone well trained on the spiritual path is so quiet that every moment is loud enough to bring him or her into the present. At the highest levels, spiritual adepts are permanently tuned into reality because they no longer tune out. They are never distracted. And they got that way because of their training in mindfulness. Mindfulness is the practice of fastening the mind to nowness.

The power of now is the power of mindfulness: having a mind-full-of-nowness. Mindfulness is the common ingredient in every form of meditation—it is what makes meditation. If we are focused and attentive in whatever we do, we transform that activity into meditation. When we bring undivided attention to whatever occurs, we discover a richness in life that is normally diluted by half-hearted attention.

There are two stages of mindfulness. The first is deliberate mindfulness. We have to make an effort to bring the scattered mind into the present; it does not happen on its own. There is a degree of hardship involved at this level because we are working against the current of the discursive mind. But as we progress in this training, mindfulness takes on momentum and starts to occur spontaneously. It becomes easier to place the mind in the moment, and the practice starts to carry us. Instead of being constantly carried away by mindless thought, we find ourselves being carried into the moment by mindful awareness. This is the result of the second stage of effortless mindfulness. We become naturally present.

The world suddenly comes alive when we are fully attentive to it. The world hasn't changed, but our awareness of it has. Studies have shown that long-term meditators literally perceive more of reality. They see more, feel more, taste more, hear more, and smell more because they are thinking less. When we are not preoccupied with thought, we can more readily occupy our senses. Seeing, feeling, tasting, hearing, and smelling more brings us to life—and it also brings us to others. It allows us to see more clearly what others need, to feel their pain, to hear their stories, and to more skillfully remove their suffering.

Mindfulness is also how we contact the sacred. The difference between experiencing the sacred or the profane is in the manner in which we make contact with reality. Profanity is mindless grasping; sacredness is mindful touching. One demonstration of this in my experience has been learning about shrines. In my tradition we have shrines everywhere, and we are taught to relate to them with reverence. When I approached my first shrine, I brought a "do not touch" attitude to it. I walked up to it with hesitation and a touch of trepidation. A shrine is something holy, and I should keep my hands off. I discovered, however, that this attitude is completely backward. What the shrine teaches is, "touch all things as you would touch me." Treat everything with the same reverence and sacred outlook. It is a representation of the sacred and a teaching in how to contact it.

In itself, mindfulness is nothing special. But it makes everything else special.

❦ The Power of Kindness

The greatest power discovered by those who tread the spiritual path is kindness and the ability to benefit others. When we achieve the power of freedom, wealth, happiness, peace, and even mindfulness—what are we supposed to do with it? If we keep it to ourselves, that isn't real power. That's ego. Real power is using these resources to benefit others. When we gain these resources on the path, we don't just hang out glowing in our newfound freedom and peace. We spend the rest of our lives sharing it.

Khandro Rinpoche ("Rinpoche" is an honorific term that means "the jeweled or precious one") often teaches that the criterion for whether your meditation is working is that you act with greater gentleness and kindness. My own teacher, Khenpo Tsultrim Gyamtso Rinpoche, once invited a young man to come up and stand before the audience. In front of several hundred people, Rinpoche did something that masters rarely do. He talked at length about how great a meditator this man was, and how he was walking a genuine spiritual path. Why was Rinpoche praising him so much? Was it because he attained great meditative insights? Was it because he attained enlightened peace, bliss, and happiness? No. It was because he took six months off from work to be with his dying mother.

His Holiness the Seventeenth Karmapa has said, "Kindness is the most important point," and the Dalai Lama always says, "My religion is kindness." When ego dissolves, and the artificial barriers that separate us from others dissolve with it, our hearts are gradually exposed, and the kindness, compassion, and love that are natural expressions of that heart are revealed.

When we endure the pain of the path, why should we do so? Why should we tolerate all the inconvenience, loneliness, and heartache? We endure it to bring benefit to ourselves, certainly. Freedom, wealth, happiness, peace, and mindfulness are wonderful acquisitions. But if obtaining these is our only motivation, it won't bring genuine happiness, or meaning, to our lives. We endure the difficulties to help others. In Tibetan Buddhism the deity of power is Vajrapani. He is a formidable presence, wrathful and uncompromising, with tremendous capability and power. Power to do what? To help others. That is the real power of the path.

This is just a sampling of the richness of the path. Books, articles, and testimonials that proclaim its power are common. The spiritual path works. But these glories come at a price, and it is to these challenges that we now turn.

2 🌿

The Pain

It is sometimes easier to wake up when we're in extreme pain.
—DZIGAR KONGTRÜL, It's Up to You

If you haven't cried deeply a number of times,
your meditation hasn't really begun.
—ACHAAN CHAH

UNDERSTANDING THE POWER of the path provides the inspiration that keeps us going forward; exploring its pain provides the understanding of what holds us back. It doesn't take long to discover the power, nor to feel the pain. Waking up hurts. And if we don't understand why, we will run from the pain and abandon the path. There are countless people who have become spiritual dropouts, or who are lost in detours because they have not understood hardship.

When your arm falls asleep, it prickles and burns as it returns to life. Frozen fingers sting when they thaw; we jolt awake when the alarm clock rings. But physical instances of anesthesia are mild compared to the anesthesia born of ignorance, and so is the level of discomfort upon awakening. The longer something has been asleep, the more painful it is to wake it up. If your fingers are merely cold, it is easy to warm them up. But if your fingers are frozen solid, it hurts like hell when they thaw. According to the traditions, unless one is already a buddha, an "awakened one," one has been snoring from beginningless time, and it can really hurt before we completely wake up. Mingyur Rinpoche writes,

> I'd like to say that everything got better once I was safely settled among the other participants in the three-year retreat. . . . On the contrary, however, my first year in retreat was one of the worst in my life. All the symptoms of anxiety I'd ever experienced—physical tension, tightness in the throat, dizziness, and waves of panic—attacked in full force. In Western terms, I was having a nervous breakdown. In hindsight, I can say that what I was actually going through was what I like to call a "nervous breakthrough."[8]

Every tradition is replete with stories of hardship. Christ suffered in the desert, Buddha struggled under the bodhi tree, Mohammed grappled in his cave, the Jain saint Mahavira wrestled with his asceticism, and the Tibetan yogi Milarepa endured the demands of his guru. We will be hard-pressed to find a sage who slid easily into enlightenment, for great realization brings great obstacles.

We may not practice in caves and deserts, but we sit in meditation and wonder why it hurts. We look into our hearts and wonder why we cry. We enter a path and ponder why life falls apart. Understanding hardship helps us to deal with it, whether it is the anxiety of sitting still for thirty minutes, or the fear of entering a three-year retreat.

Dilgo Khyentse Rinpoche, addressing those who have or will undertake a retreat, gives this advice:

> You will fall sick, experience pain, and encounter many adverse circumstances. At such times do not think, "Although I am practicing the Dharma, I have nothing but trouble. The Dharma cannot be so great. I have followed a teacher and done so much practice, and yet hard times still befall me." Such thoughts are wrong views. You should realize that through the blessing and power of the practice, by

experiencing sickness and other difficulties now, you are purifying and ridding yourself of negative actions . . . By purifying them while you have the chance, you will later go from bliss to bliss. So do not think, "I don't deserve this illness, these obstacles, these negative influences." Experience your difficulties as blessings . . . when you do experience such difficulties, you should be very happy and avoid having adverse thoughts like, "Why are such terrible things happening to me."[9]

As Rinpoche advises, relating to hardship properly depends on the strength of one's view. In general, having a view is knowing exactly where you want to go and how to get there. It is the vision of knowing what you want. For example, if you have the view to become a doctor, your vision guides you through financial burdens, physical and emotional difficulties, and obstacles that get in your way. You know it will be difficult and involve sacrifice, but with a strong view, you forge to the finish line.

Similarly, if you want to become spiritually awakened, it is the power of your view that gets you there. If you are having a hard time getting to the meditation cushion, or engaging in the necessary study, it is because your view is not strong enough or is incomplete. A partial view, in this case, is one that doesn't include hardship. You can strengthen your view and accelerate progress by understanding how you lose your view in the fog of hardship, and therefore lose sight of your path.

The Dzogchen Ponlop Rinpoche provides the proper view for the challenging preliminary practices (ngondro) of Vajrayana Buddhism:

Ngondro is the process of working to loosen our negative karmic seeds, our ingrained habitual tendencies, and to bring them to the surface. Once they are exposed, we can deal with them and transcend them . . . we are creating the causes and conditions for our karmic seeds to ripen. That's what is happening. We shouldn't blame the Vajrayana pre-liminary practices for any of the discomfort we feel or the intensity we go through. That's what we are looking for, it's what makes transcendence possible. Otherwise, if we retreat from those experiences, if we don't take advantage of them and free ourselves from those patterns, it's like starting to pull a splinter out, but stopping halfway when it becomes painful. Instead of completing the job, we try to push it back in. We think "I'll pull it out sometime later." Our aim here is to bring about the ripening of our negative karmic causes and conditions, and, when they are ripened, to transcend or overcome them.[10]

Without the proper view, we do not see clearly, so we project. We project the ideal that spirituality will make us feel good and that heaven or salvation awaits. This is a partial truth, the half-truth that makes us enter the path. Who would enter a path that guaranteed hardship? Knowing there is light at the end of the tunnel keeps us going through it, but understanding the darkness in the tunnel helps us to negotiate it. The full truth is that power comes with pain. Hardship is the neglected and misunderstood second half of the truth, and it completes the view. True spirituality is not about making you feel good. It is about making you feel real.

❦ Reality and Spirituality

In common parlance, the spiritual is set in contrast to the material. The material world is the "real" world of hardship and pain, of fleeting joy and things we can't hold onto. It is solid and often so uncaring. The spiritual path is frequently entered to escape from this reality. We want to flee material hardship and find refuge in the spiritual world of love and light. We long for sanctuary in the *unreal*. As the spiritual psychologist A. H. Almaas puts it, "When we embark on a spiritual path, we unconsciously believe that we are setting out for heaven."[11]

With this motivation, entering the path is like going to a movie—we just want to get away. We are fed up and want out. But as Trungpa Rinpoche taught: there is no way out. The magic is to discover that there is a way in. Authentic spirituality is not about escaping from reality but entering it fully. And this is the source of disappointment and hardship. We want to retreat from our pain, not enter it fully. To discover that the path pulls a wicked u-turn and heads directly back into that which we are attempting to escape is what causes many to drop out. It is the great bait-and-switch.

With the proper view, everyday reality *is* spirituality. The spiritual is discovered in the material. The Gnostic Gospel of Thomas says, "The Kingdom of the Father is spread out upon the earth, and men do not see it."[12] This is one meaning of nonduality—the spiritual and the material are not two. If we are leaving the material for the spiritual, we are leaving out half of reality. And we are going to give ourselves a hard time because the abandoned half will come calling. To complete the path, the material is not rejected, but fully embraced. We will return to these themes in part 3.

There is a thin line between the confusion of escaping and the wisdom of renouncing. Being fed up and wanting out can lead to either one. Renunciation of *samsara*, the Sanskrit word for the confused world of suffering, is to be cultivated. Without renunciation we will never give up hope of finding happiness in samsara and we won't see the need to sacrifice our attachment to it. Without renunciation we are trapped in self-deception.

But samsara is not reality. Samsara is not "out there"; it is a projection of my confusion "in here." It is a state of mind, not a state in reality. The Indian master Nagarjuna says, "There is no samsara apart from your own thoughts." And the Buddhist sage Nyoshul Khen taught: "Conceptual thought is the ocean of samsara." Samsara was not created before I was, nor does it exist independent of me—it is a mirror of my own mind. So true renunciation is not giving up reality but relinquishing our confusion about it.

With escapism, on the other hand, we want out and do not embrace what we wish to escape. Liberation based on renunciation involves going into and through our shadows in order to find the light; liberation based on escapism involves denying, repressing, or projecting our shadows in order to avoid the dark. The difference between renunciation and escapism is that renunciation, in a phrase by the philosopher Ken Wilber, "transcends but includes" samsara; escapism merely attempts to transcend. Since samsara, the unwanted, is not included, it is not fully transcended.

Liberation born of escapism is therefore incomplete and the source of unnecessary hardship. As T. S. Eliot wrote in *The Waste Land*: "Thinking of the key, each confirms a prison."[13] What we are trying to escape from will come back to haunt us, as any psychotherapist will be quick to point out. By denying, repressing, or projecting something we are throwing a boomerang and then wondering what it was that just hit us. These little boomerangs, our rejected neuroses, return to haunt us because they are asking to be healed, to be "wholed." They bonk us on the back of the head because they are asking for our attention, for our love and embrace, and wondering why we threw part of ourselves away. They demand to be included. Buddhist scholar Reginald Ray writes: "What we have to do is become the damned—become that part of our self that has been rejected and cast out. We have to allow ourselves to enter whatever hell our despised experience has been cast into, taking on its full identity and reality, and its full human experience. Only when we are willing to do that is redemption possible."[14]

Because we define the spiritual in opposition to the material, and the material world is that of suffering, we assume that spirituality promises the opposite. We expect the path to be blissful. If it is not, something must be wrong. But things may be very right when pain barges into our lives, and bliss can be a real problem if it is related to improperly. There might be eternal bliss when the path is completed, but even then it is not our normal notion of bliss. Until then, if we sustain this view of expecting constant happiness, we face broken promises and endless disappointment as our projections of what spirituality should be are shattered by the reality of what it actually is.

❧ The Middle Path

When we divorce reality from spirituality, we tend to embrace our pleasures and reject our pains. We take sides with part of the cosmos. The spiritual path is not about either extreme, and samsara and nirvana are both extremes. Samsara with its pain is on one end of the spectrum, and nirvana with its happiness is on the other end. But isn't sustained happiness the point of the path? Isn't nirvana the goal?

Because we are drowning in samsara, the promise of bliss in nirvana beckons us forward. We swim for the promised land. It is not difficult to glimpse nirvana on the path. We have a peak experience, a spiritual and often ecstatic breakthrough, and we want more. But attachment to anything, including nirvana-like experiences, is a sign we are still stuck in samsara. Ringu Tulku Rinpoche says, "Who cares for enlightenment [nirvana]? That's the idea. Because as long as you have some kind of attachment to enlightenment, then you're certainly not enlightened. The point is to see nirvana and samsara as one."[15]

An exclusively blissful realization is not complete. It may be a legitimate experience of peace, or even a glimpse of enlightenment, but if it excludes pain it is partial. Paraphrasing Chögyam Trungpa, his biographer Fabrice Midal writes: "The danger of spirituality, he [Trungpa] explained constantly, is to create a world apart, a holy world without ties to the solid and direct experience of each person. Such a vision of bliss can never truly help people. It is a sort of unattainable ideal."[16]

On one hand, the experience of nirvana is cause for celebration—you have glimpsed the top, and you can use this peek to sustain your view. On the other hand, the experience of nirvana can be cause for concern—you might forget about the bottom. It is easy to get stuck on top and forget that you are only part way there. According to some Buddhist schools, this is the trap of the arhat. An arhat is a "worthy one" who achieves individual liberation. Arhats represent the apex of the First Turning and, according to the early schools, attain the same goal as the Buddha. Arhats are revered, and if we could somehow attain that realization it would be a glorious achievement.

But from the perspective of other schools, "arhat" has a slightly derogatory overtone. From the viewpoint of the Second and Third Turnings, arhats still have further to go. It is never this crisp, of course, and it is hard to imagine someone at that level without compassion for others, but the limitation of the arhat is that he or she is mostly interested in getting out of samsara. Arhats do not want to include samsara, but merely to transcend it.

From this perspective, the example of arhats is used to point out that in order to complete the path, we must descend. We must unite nirvana with samsara and join heaven with earth. We must express our wisdom as compassion and that means dropping back into the muck of samsara. Enlightenment is the nonduality of all extremes, including nirvana and samsara. It is the middle path uniting peace and pain.

The most common representation of the Buddha just after attaining his enlightenment is in the posture known as the "earth-touching posture." He is sitting in meditation with his right hand touching the ground. Buddhist author Miranda Shaw explains this gesture: "For me this portrays the sense that enlightenment is not something that is going to remove you from the world of sense experience, is not going to take you to another sphere, but is going to involve a profound groundedness in reality and on earth—an enlightened participation in life. . . . [His posture represents] a profound impulse to affirm the world and a sense that the goal of the practice is not to escape the world or leave it to go to a better place."[17] The Buddha attained a transcendence of this earth, but rooted himself deeply within it.

3 ✤

Necessary and Unnecessary Hardship

Is hardship necessary? On an absolute level it is not. It is possible to awaken without pain, just as it is possible to have a natural childbirth without going through labor. But realistically, if we want to give birth to enlightenment, we have to deal with labor pains. If our paths are filled only with bliss and light, we are probably tripping in self-deception. We are not interested in getting real, but are caught up in feeling good. Patrul Rinpoche says, "When your belly is full and the sun is shining upon you, you act like a holy person. But when negativities befall you, then you act very ordinary." The Dalai Lama says,

> The Buddha's life exemplifies a very important principle—
> a certain amount of hardship is necessary in one's spiritual
> pursuit. We can also see this principle at work in the lives

of other great religious teachers, such as Jesus Christ or the Muslim prophet Mohammed. Furthermore, I think that the followers of these teachers, if they wish to attain the highest spiritual realizations within their tradition, must themselves undergo a process of hardship, which they endure through dedicated perseverance. There is sometimes the tendency among the followers of the Buddha to imagine, perhaps only in the back of their minds, that "Although the Buddha went through all of those hardships to attain enlightenment, they aren't really necessary for me. Surely, I can attain enlightenment without giving up life's comforts." Perhaps such people imagine that, because they are somehow more fortunate than the Buddha, they can attain the same spiritual state as he did without any particular hardships or renunciation. This is, I think, mistaken. . . . If we ourselves want the attainments described by the Buddha . . . then we too must endure some amount of hardship.[18]

Yet the spiritual path is not masochistic. If we are not in pain, it does not mean something is wrong. That is the other extreme of unnecessary asceticism, even self-flagellation. This is an important point. Our journey in this book is to understand pain, not to search for it. Feeling good or bad is not the point. The point is welcoming both onto the path. Relate skillfully to whatever occurs and liberate everything in the space of equanimity. Saying "yes" to whatever arises is a big part of the spiritual path.

This book will help us remove unnecessary hardship and show us how to understand, anticipate, and even welcome the hardship that is necessary. We cannot avoid labor pains, but we do not have to make a career out of them. Many people do. They bog down in the difficulties of life, lamenting their situation and grasping onto their pain. For many people something bad is better than nothing.

So much spiritual hardship is unnecessary. We sit in meditation and spin ourselves into a tizzy trying to figure out why it is so hard. We do a retreat and beat ourselves up because we can't follow the technique. We look back over years of practice and are frustrated because we are not getting anywhere. We drop the whole damn path because things are getting worse. This hardship is understandable but unnecessary.

Unnecessary hardship is often the result of referring a spiritual experience to a materialistic ego. Instead of accepting an experience on its own terms, we tend to relate whatever happens on the path to the ego in an effort to understand it. For example, you are sitting in meditation when an experience of the dissolution of your ego dawns. This can instill either exhilaration or panic. Instead of relating to the experience directly and then letting it go, you hold on, trying to repeat, get rid of, or figure it out. This relationship to the experience distorts it—and creates unnecessary hardship.

It distorts the experience because spiritual experiences do not fit into conceptual frameworks. They are too big. By trying to put it into words or grasp it conceptually, we are trying to stuff an experience into a container that just cannot hold it. Something always gets left out, squashed, or distorted. It never comes out in thought and speech the way it originally came in through experience.

We also create unnecessary hardship because relating a spiritual experience to a materialistic ego is asking the ego to comment on something it knows nothing about. Spiritual experiences are transpersonal, beyond the ego. Egolessness cannot be understood by the ego. We cannot expect it to make helpful comments on experiences that are designed to transcend it. But try we do, for we initially have no other choice. The best result is paradox, irony, or cosmic joke; the usual result is contradiction, frustration, and confusion. And that creates unnecessary hardship. Traleg Rinpoche says, "A mental breakdown or psychotic episode is not the result of an altered state of consciousness or an experience of seeing and hearing things. It is the result of how these experiences are processed by that person's ego."[19] The ego cannot contain transegoic experiences, and when it attempts to do so, it can burst.

So what should we do? Accept the experience for what it is, on its own terms. Do not try too hard to figure it out. When you sit in meditation and feel like you are about to lose your mind, that's okay. Don't try to find your mind, just ride the experience. When sadness or anger erupts and you want to explode, just be with that. And do not think so much about yourself, which only tends to deflate you into depression or inflate you into pride. In fact, try not to think about it at all. Just feel the experience fully, and then release it fully.

We will discuss the proper relationship to such experiences throughout the book; the point for now is not to refer the spiritual to the material. Let it be. If you need to understand it, then talk to a qualified spiritual friend or teacher. Even then, look into your motivation. Why do you need to share the experience? I have had my allotment of meditation experiences, and when I bring them to my teachers, I am usually looking for confirmation. I want to be told how special I am. In most cases I am instructed to simply continue, or sometimes I am even ignored.

Unnecessary hardship disappears when this inappropriate reference to ego disappears. When spiritual experience is not referred, it becomes a breath of fresh air.

❧ Don't Leak

Inappropriate reference has a deeper application. Not only should we avoid referring the spiritual to the material, we should be careful in referring spiritual experiences at all. In ch'i gong, the ancient Chinese art of subtle energy movement, the practitioner works to heighten and move the energy of ch'i. At the end of a session, it is common to seal the energy that has been aroused, allowing practitioners to retain the fruits of their practice. Without this final seal, the energy dribbles away. Similarly, spiritual practice in general, and powerful experiences in particular, generate their own energy. If we do not consciously seal that energy, which means keeping it to ourselves, not only does it leak, but it can transform into an obstacle.

There is a two-way process in relation to obstacle and opportunity on the path. If we take the obstacles in our lives and bring them into the sanctuary of sanity provided by meditation, we can transform obstacle into opportunity. By reframing an experience, in particular a difficult experience, we can transform a curse into a blessing.

For example, one day you get a call from your doctor that you have cancer. This is devastating news, a major obstacle. If you resist the reality and deny or repress the experience, your cancer will transform your life into a nightmare. But if you reframe the experience and bring it into the context of your spiritual practice, you can transform this obstacle into a major opportunity. The cancer can dramatically realign your life, show you what is really important, and trim away meaningless activities. It can bring you into a deep recognition of impermanence and a new appreciation for the simplicity and sanctity of life.

When my mother was diagnosed with rapidly advancing Alzheimer's, I was stunned. After the initial heartbreak, I began to realize just how precious she was to me. I called her much more frequently, flew back as often as I could, and wrote a series of letters that expressed my deep appreciation for her unconditional kindness and generosity. I tried to take this devastating disease and transform it into an opportunity to open my heart, to share emotions that I usually hold back. Alzheimer's helped me learn about love. On the spiritual path, obstacles are opportunities in disguise.

But this maxim works both ways. In other words, if we take a powerful spiritual experience and move it outside of the context in which it arose, we can transform opportunity into obstacle. This happens all the time. We might have a deep meditative experience, powerful dream, or spiritual insight. If we do not contain the experience but give into the temptation to talk about it, not only does the power leak but the experience can transform into an obstacle.

Tulku Urgyen says that talking about spiritual experiences inappropriately is like being in a dark cave with a candle and then giving it away. Your light is lost, and you are left alone in the dark. Silence often gives birth to spiritual insight, and silence is the way to seal the energy of insight.

❧ Hard Path

The spiritual path may seem hard, but it is only as hard as we are. If we have a crusty ego, a closed mind, and a tough heart, the path will give us a hard time. It will do whatever it takes to soften us up, which sometimes requires beating us up. There are times when the ego requires tough love. If, on the other hand, we have little ego, an open mind, and a soft heart, we will have an easier time.

Twenty years ago I worked with the practice of sensory awareness, a wonderful set of exercises designed to bring us to our senses. During one session, we were doing practices that required laying on a wooden floor. I had a hard time with it. It hurt. I found myself grumbling about everything: how hard the floor was, how long we had to hold the postures, and the heat. No one else seemed to complain. Several weeks later I realized that the floor, and everything else, wasn't hard. I was.

With this discovery, I realized I have a choice. I can become more resistant to life when things get rough, and therefore become hardened, or I could soften. This is the choice we have with any difficult situation. We can tough it out, close down, and get bitter, or we can allow it to open us up, and soften. Some elderly people get more cranky and nasty when faced with aging, others relax and gracefully surrender.

In the conventional world there is a place for the maxim, "when the going gets tough, the tough get going." But there is also a place, especially in the spiritual world, for this balancing maxim: "when the going gets tough, the intelligent surrender." This surrender is not an ignoble defeat. It is noble subjugation. For what is defeated, as spiritual psychologist John Welwood points out, is ego and its strategies: "The nobility of this kind of defeat is portrayed by [the poet] Rilke in four powerful lines describing Jacob's wrestling match with the Angel":

Winning does not tempt that man.
This is how he grows:

By being defeated, decisively,
By constantly greater beings.[20]

Allowing ourselves to be defeated by greater beings, those with compassionate understanding for our ultimate welfare, or by the experiences of life itself, accelerates our path. In other words, one way to overcome resistance to the path and to make it easier is to realize that on the deepest levels we cannot really do the spiritual path. We have to let the path do us.

We have to be defeated. The ego may launch us into the path and accompany us part of the way, but in the end the ego cannot complete it. As Chögyam Trungpa says, "You can't attend your own funeral." We eventually have to surrender to the wisdom that gave birth to the path in the first place and allow ourselves to be processed, even beaten, by its methods.

The Tibetan word for "blessing" is "jinlap," which is sometimes translated as "wave of splendor." We may think that this wave of splendor washes over us like the gentle turquoise surf in Hawaii, but real waves of blessing can crash into our lives like a tidal wave.

When I was going through a difficult time recently, I had a dream. I was walking along a beautiful beach when I suddenly heard a roar coming in from the ocean. Within a few seconds, a massive tsunami crashed into the shore line and what was once solid ground turned into churning froth. Everything before me was swept away, and when the waters receded, the shore was littered with wreckage. The message was obvious. Here was yet another blessing, another splendor wave, crashing into my life and sweeping away any sense of solid ground. I am now more certain than ever that if you are on a genuine path, you will get the shit blessed out of you.

❧ Editing

In order for the path to "do you," do not edit the path or your meditation to suit your needs. Do not pick and choose those aspects that make you feel comfortable or that are always convenient. A real path is not a cafeteria. Once we choose a path, stick to it and honor its methods. Give in and give up. Then it becomes easier. Sakyong Mipham Rinpoche says, "The path won't happen on your terms."[21]

When I taught meditation in the prison system, I faced an interesting challenge. On Mondays, a Christian contemplative came to teach the prisoners. On Tuesdays, a Sufi mystic came, on Thursdays, a Hindu, and on Fridays, I came. On one hand, this was a wonderful offering. The prisoners were exposed to a number of rich traditions and meditations. On the other hand, it was a problem because they were picking and choosing bits from each tradition and creating their own meditations. It was like salad bar meditation. They took what they liked from each tradition and slapped it all together into something that suited their individual, and usually egotistic, needs.

This was a problem because it gave them an escape. I had to remind them of the wisdom of having no escape. For example, if they were doing the shamatha or tranquility meditation I was teaching them and things started to get boring or painful, they would choose something from the Hindu or Sufi technique to get comfortable. This is not to deride any meditation technique but to point out the problem in cutting and pasting between them. Hindu and Sufi meditations bring the same level of hardship and the same level of fruition, as any genuine practice—if one really stays with it and does it properly. By editing as they pleased, they were not paying homage to the power of shamatha or the Hindu or Sufi techniques, and therefore diluted their strength. They were not allowing themselves to be defeated. They were skimming across these meditations and nothing was sinking in.

I told them to pick a meditation for their session and then do it purely. Do not contaminate it by peppering in another technique. It's the "chase two rabbits, catch none" problem. If you are doing shamatha meditation and it starts to feel uncomfortable, do not jump to another technique to ease that discomfort. Stay with the hardship, keep your commitment, and reap the fruits. Let the meditation do you. Mixing different techniques to make meditation easier does not feed our path. It only feeds the ego.

❦ Accept the Challenge

Necessary hardship often comes in the form of challenges, which are important tests for the depth of your practice. If everything is easy and comfortable in your practice or your life, you will never know how stable your realization actually is. You may think you are evolving along the path, but maybe you are just getting cozy. Dzigar Kongtrül says,

> Coupled with open-minded questioning, challenging circumstances can help deepen and clarify the purpose of our path because they expose how far our practice has penetrated to the core of self-clinging. Although these experiences often shock or disturb us, they bring our attention to the immediate experience of clinging and the pain it generates. . . . This is why the great yogis of the past practiced in haunted places such as charnel grounds. Places that provoke the hidden aspects of mind are full of possibilities for liberation.[22]

In the last year of my long retreat, I was doing a practice of looking at myself in a mirror and then criticizing the reflection. I found it contrived and patronizing. But when I left my practice room and was insulted by other retreatants, I realized its profundity. The criticism got to me. After years of retreat, there was still an ego that did not like being hit. I still don't like it, but now I use challenging situations to test the stability of my practice. I see these attacks as necessary hardships that point out where I'm still stuck.

In Tibet, meditators go to terrifying locations like burial fields or frightening caves to reveal the depth of their practice. We don't have to go so far to be tested. The everyday insults—having a car cut us off, a coworker criticize us, a friend ignore us—can reveal the measure of our progress. On an absolute level, it is important to remember that this is a journey without a goal and that we do not need to measure anything. There is no such thing as progress. From this point of view, these incidents then provide the opportunity to practice, and to go further in our journey *without* a goal. But on a relative level, there is a sense of progress, and we can see how we are doing by how we react to difficult situations. We can use the relative to arrive at the absolute.

Challenges also develop fortitude and strength. It is no surprise that the rugged Tibetans, who live at extreme elevations and under harsh climatic conditions, go after their spiritual practice with the same resolve they bring to a blustery life. We will find more realized beings on the windswept Tibetan plateau than we will in balmy Beverly Hills. If we don't have any forces working against us, we get weak. People who don't do resistance exercise, like lifting weights, may lead a seemingly more comfortable life but can develop a host of unnecessary diseases and wither away.

One of the biggest problems with astronauts living in space is loss of bone mass due to zero-gravity. With no gravity to resist, the astronauts become weaker. In the biological big-bubble experiment known as Biosphere 2, the trees eventually had to be attached by cables to the framework above. This is because there was no wind in the Biosphere, and with nothing to resist, the trees grew weak and needed support. Similarly, without something to work against— without situations of some gravity—our body and mind begin to atrophy. We need something to press against in life in order to stay strong and grow.

✤ Fear of Hardship

In today's world we love our comfort and loathe any hint of pain. Comfort is virtually an inalienable right. In my volunteer work as a dentist, I spend several months a year working with poor children in Asia. These kids lead tough lives. Their parents, if they are lucky enough to have them, earn less than a dollar a day. Of the thousands I have treated, it is rare to find an uncooperative child. They endure needles and forceps with silent dignity and greet my work with authentic smiles. While their forbearance is tough, their hearts are soft and open.

In my paid work in America, I see thousands of children growing up expecting and constructing pampered lives. Many of them are terrified of the dentist and cry at the sight of a needle. I don't blame them, nor even their parents, for I have grown up to be the same. It is just part of our culture: we are taught that the good life is a comfortable life.

I am a casualty of comfort and live by my comfort plan, which is something like this: nice home, nice wife, nice car, nice furniture . . . nice job. My comfort plan dictates my future plans: nicer home, nicer wife, nicer car, nicer furniture . . . nicer job. Is there anyone who actually plans a life that includes pain? Has anyone ever said, "Next year, I'm going to take a painful two week vacation." Yet when I plan my annual meditation retreats, I sometimes feel like I am scheduling just such a "vacation"—a vacation from the narcotic of comfort.

When the Tibetan master Milarepa was studying with his teacher Marpa, he was put through unspeakable hardship. Through intense physical and emotional demands, Marpa skillfully brought his protégé to the cusp of enlightenment. But he also brought him to the cusp of despair, even to the point of suicide. Marpa forged in Milarepa a strength and resolve so formidable that he was able to enter years of retreat and cut through any obstacle. He is famous for attaining complete enlightenment because of his endurance. Milarepa's own heart advice to his disciple, Gampopa, given as they were saying a final goodbye, was this:

> "Now look!" Milarepa said, and hoisted the back of his robe, revealing the cheeks of his buttocks, all covered with lumps of hard callus, like the hooves of an animal, due to having sat for so long on stony ground without a cushion. He said, "There is no more profound teaching than this. Now you can imagine the hardships I have endured. My attainment of great realization came from this. It has simply

been due to persistent effort that I have accumulated merit and gained accomplishment. You need such effort, not any other doctrine. This is the essence of my teaching."[23]

What made the great meditators great was their unshakable ability to endure hardship, and their resolve never to give up. When things got uncomfortable, they didn't run and complain. They cut through hardship because they understood the reasons for it. They had the proper view.

Masters from the East say that one reason there are no buddhas yet in the West is because we do not understand hardship and are therefore unwilling to endure it. When we get hot, we clamor to cool off; when we get cold, we scramble to warm up. When we are uncomfortable, we move to get comfortable. If something hurts, we stay away from it. And so we stay away from awakening.

❧ Hardship and Compassion

Closely connected to the problem of comfort is the problem of success. When we have finally made it, and everything comes together—our bank account is full, our love life complete, our fame established—that can be a real problem. There is no tyranny as great as the tyranny of success. As Khyentse Rinpoche taught,

> It is said that good experiences are more difficult to deal with than bad ones, because they are more distracting . . . when things are going well and you feel happy, your mind accepts that situation without difficulty. Like oil spread all over your skin, attachment easily stays invisibly blended into the mind; it becomes part of your thoughts. Once such attachment to favorable circumstances is present, you become almost infatuated with your achievements, your fame, and your wealth. That is something very difficult to get rid of.[24]

Success is problematic because it can insulate us from the suffering of reality. We do not want to feel or be real, and success can even be defined as that which keeps us from the harshness of reality. My life is successful if it is soft and comfortable and a failure if it is full of pain. Hardship is un-American.

This "success" is a barrier to awakening and an obstacle to compassion, for how can we "suffer with" others (the etymology of "com-passion") when we are not comfortable with suffering ourselves? There are many stories of people brought to the path by "failure." Personal tragedy is often the gateway to the first noble truth of suffering, and therefore the entrance to the path that removes it. "Failure" puts us eye-to-eye with the rest of humanity and connects us to the suffering of others because we are feeling it in ourselves. As Thomas Aquinas writes, "No one becomes compassionate unless he suffers."[25]

If we allow it, devastation cuts through the cocoon of the ego and puts us in touch with reality. If we don't, it can make us bitter and even more self-centered. Environmental activist Marc Ian Barasch writes, "I've become suspicious of the unblemished life. Maybe the heart must be broken, like a child's prize honeycomb, for the real sweetness to come out. . . . I know this much: when I acknowledge my own pain, I am much less squeamish about drawing nearer to yours."[26] Hardship connects us to our own hearts and then to others. Material failure can lead directly to spiritual success.

4 ❧

Progress or Regress?

In a dark time, the eye begins to see.
—Theodore Roethke, "In a Dark Time"

Happiness is not good, suffering is good.
If you are happy, the five poisonous emotions rage.
If you suffer, previously accumulated evil deeds are exhausted.
Suffering is the kindness of the Lama.
—Patrul Rinpoche

WHILE OUR JOURNEY is to explore and integrate the shadow side of spirituality, it is not to deny the ever present sun. The spiritual path is drenched in wonder and deep happiness. We need to keep remembering this as we plunge further into this book—do not forget the power as we drop deeper into the pain. The Dzogchen Ponlop Rinpoche speaks of "the extreme path to the middle," and that is our approach. We have been stretched so far in the direction of comfort, expecting and demanding it, that now we need to stretch in the direction of pain. This is one way to end up balanced in the middle.

This urge to cultivate comfort and avoid pain is at the heart of ego development and one reason why it is hard to transform. Sandra Maitri, a teacher in the Ridhwan school of spiritual development, writes,

The beginning of cognition originates with the differentiation between pleasurable and unpleasurable sensations, and memory traces of these impressions gradually register in our developing central nervous system. Through repetition of these impressions, memory begins to form. The fact that our first differentiation is between pleasure and pain means that the Freudian principle of striving for pleasure and avoiding pain is the most fundamental principle underlying the ego structure.[27]

This primordial push to pleasure is important to acknowledge because it explains the knee-jerk response we have to pleasure and pain and the patience that is required to reverse it. The spiritual path, with its open invitation to pain, goes against the grain of the very foundation of our ego-centered being.

This means that the path will give us exactly what we need and not necessarily want we want. We may not want to face our fear, loneliness, and heartache but we need to if we want to grow. It is the adult version of having to eat our vegetables. It may not taste good, but fear, loneliness, and heartache can be good for us. Trungpa Rinpoche's wife relates this story:

At one point during the retreat, a person visiting Rinpoche asked him why he was being so tough on one particular staff member. Rinpoche had been relentlessly breaking this person down, waking him up over and over again during the night, criticizing him, and on and on. This visitor was in a car with Rinpoche and the person Rinpoche had been tormenting, so to speak. The visitor asked, "Why are you being so hard on so and so?" Rinpoche said, loud enough so he could be overheard, "I have to make him feel as bad as I possibly can." . . . Later Rinpoche indicated that this person was really very close to him—he wasn't mad or anything. He was trying to get through the façade and work with what was there.[28]

When I was in a long retreat and enduring a rough period, I had a dream. In the dream I was following Trungpa Rinpoche into a dining room, where a table was set for the two of us. As I approached the table, I noticed my plate was full of my favorite foods: fresh salmon, mangos and raspberries, and a delicious garden salad. I smiled as I sat down, looking forward to a great meal with my spiritual master. But as I took my seat and picked up my fork, the food suddenly turned into brussels sprouts. I hate brussels sprouts. At that moment I woke up, and the message was clear: the retreat was feeding me exactly what I needed and not at all what I wanted. When we enter an authentic path, we have asked for our version of brussels sprouts.

❧ The Two Truths

Confusion and unnecessary hardship arises by not understanding relative and absolute truth. These two truths, which we introduced in chapter 1, are important on the path because they point out the difference between the way things appear and the way things actually are. They reveal the relationship between appearance and reality. The two truths show us that we suffer when appearance is not in harmony with reality, when the relative is not in resonance with the absolute. In other words, we need to understand the two truths because being stuck in relative truth is the source of all our suffering, and discovering absolute truth is the birth of liberation.

Relative truth is the common truth of the way things appear. It is material truth, and it is based on reference, measurement, and comparison. Relative truth is dualistic, conceptual, and limited. It is the truth of the head and its prototype is scientific truth. It is truth in the way we usually think about it, and it leads to conventional knowledge. For example, when we say a tree exists, or that we exist, we are uttering a relative truth. Relative truth is more or less obvious.

Absolute truth is the uncommon truth of the way things really are. It is spiritual truth, and it is not based on reference, measurement, and comparison. Absolute truth is nondualistic, nonconceptual, and unlimited. It is the truth of the heart, and its closest prototype is intuition. This is not intuition as wishy-washy thinking, but intuition as it is really defined: "direct perception of truth . . . independent of any reasoning process; immediate apprehension."[29] Until we enter the spiritual path, we don't tend to think about absolute truth. But when we finally do think about it, absolute truth leads to unconventional wisdom. It is the truth of gnosis, when we know something beyond intellectual knowing. When we say the tree does not actually exist or that we do not really exist, we are uttering an absolute truth. Absolute truth is not so obvious.

The Indian sage Chandrakirti summarizes the two truths as follows:

> There are two ways of seeing everything
> The perfect way and the false way
> So each and every thing that can ever be found
> Holds two natures within.
> And what does perfect seeing see?
> It sees the suchness [the reality] of all things
> And false seeing sees the relative truth.[30]

Relative truth is still called truth because it is true from the perspective of confused beings. Things do appear to be a certain way. But appearances can be deceiving. A mirage in a desert is pretty convincing but with further examination is exposed as the illusion that it actually is. Similarly, our sense of self, the idea that we really exist, is pretty convincing, but when examined is exposed as the illusion that it actually is. Absolute truth does not deny appearances, but it does challenge the status of that appearance. Summarizing the Tibetan master Mipham: when things as they are and things as they appear are not in accord, that is relative truth. When things as they are and things as they appear are in accord, that is absolute truth.[31] The two truths are a big deal because bringing appearance in harmony with reality is the fruit of the entire path.

Even though it is important to distinguish between the two truths, it is also important not to reify them or to somehow think that relative is bad and absolute is good. There are three stages of inquiry into the nature or truth of things. At the first stage of "no analysis," we simply have the world as it is before we look into it. At this level the relative and absolute are not even differentiated. At the second stage of "slight analysis," we have what we are talking about in this section, we articulate the two truths and discover their power. At the third stage of "thorough analysis," we discover the inseparability of the two truths. Relative and absolute are unified, and their nonduality is proclaimed. So while it is important to learn about the two truths, it is just as important not to get hung up on them. Their distinction is not the final word.*

The problem with not knowing the two truths is that until we learn about absolute truth, we have no choice but to apply relative truth to absolute experiences. In an effort to understand spiritual experience, as we have seen, we cram absolute territory into relative maps, and something always gets left out. We can sense the errors in juxtaposing relative and absolute when we encounter irony, paradox, or contradiction. Something just doesn't fit. Irony, paradox, or contradiction is just the way nonduality (the absolute) appears from the lens of duality (the relative).

Let's look at some of the problems that occur when relative and absolute are not coordinated. From the relative perspective, the goal is to become somebody, to achieve fame and fortune, and to become self-fulfilled. From the absolute perspective, the goal is to become nobody, to erase the sense of self, and to become self-transcended. From the absolute perspective, there isn't even a goal. The *Course in Miracles* speaks about a "journey without distance," and Chögyam Trungpa wrote a book called *Journey without Goal.* From a relative perspective, we strive for success and avoid failure. From an absolute perspective, we welcome "failure" and shy from success. In a Buddhist chant it says, "Grant your blessings so that I have no desire for honor or gain."

---

* "No analysis" is related to the First Turning, while "slight and thorough analysis" were taught in the Second Turning.

Psychiatrist Jack Engler famously said, "You have to be somebody before you can be nobody." Ayya Khema wrote a book called *Being Nobody, Going Nowhere*. Buddhist scholar Judith Simmer-Brown speaks about "the wisdom of devastation." Trungpa Rinpoche says "the question is the answer" and "the more you give up hope for fruition, the closer it will be." The final stage in Mahamudra meditation (the highest form of meditation in the Kagyu tradition of Buddhism) is "nonmeditation." The examples of clashing relative and absolute are legion. It is not that these statements directly juxtapose relative and absolute, it is that they are absolute-level statements that we try to understand within relative frameworks. That's the clash.

What are we supposed to do with those statements? In order to be happy, do we strengthen the ego or transcend it? Do we stop asking questions, or do we question more? Do we give up trying, or try harder? These are not theoretical questions. Anyone who walks the path will have to wrestle with the issues of relative and absolute truth.

❧ Koans

Zen koans, the quirky spiritual riddles that frustrate the conceptual mind, elevate the clash of relative and absolute into a fine art. For example, what is the sound of one hand clapping? What was your original face before you were born? Paradox, that which is "beyond" (para) "thinking" (dokein), is the heart of a koan, which is all about transcending logic and conceptuality—going beyond thinking. Koans force the student to take an intuitive leap into another level of comprehension, where paradox is resolved in nonduality, the nonconceptual absolute. They are designed to short-circuit the relative mind and to give birth to absolute-level insight. Sanskrit and Tibetan scholar Francesca Fremantle writes,

> Entering the awakened state of mind, even for a moment, is always preceded by an experience, however fleeting, of extreme contrast and conflict. Even on the highest and most subtle levels of attainment, negative and positive con-

tinue together side by side until we make the leap beyond them both. Deliberately inducing paradoxical situations or being confronted by paradoxical statements that the rational mind is unable to reconcile can sometimes shock a person who is ready for it into a breakthrough. Great teachers have been known to precipitate an awakening in their students by a sudden outburst of anger or some other totally unexpected action.[32]

With a koan, at least we know what we are getting into. We know we are being set up. But the spiritual path, right from the outset, is peppered with koan-like statements and situations that are not set up as formal koans. We do not always know what we are getting into, and we often don't understand what is going on. Your teacher may say one thing, but do something else. Your meditation is supposed to calm your mind, but your mind goes crazy. Spirituality was going to get your life together, but it's falling apart. You went into retreat to get enlightened, but now you are more confused than ever. With a koan, we know we are not supposed to get it initially; with the spiritual path—which is one big koan—we often just don't get it. So experientially, the result of unwittingly juxtaposing relative and absolute is confusion.

✤ Working with the Two Truths

The best way to work with the two truths is to first realize that there are two truths, and then remember the three levels of analysis. On their own terms, they are easy to handle: relative is relative, and absolute is absolute. To understand and honor their respective domains is the way to reconcile them. The problem is when they are unconsciously juxtaposed, which is epidemic when we first enter the path. This is because the spiritual path is soaked in the absolute, and we are still firmly planted in the relative.

One way to detect the problem is to be aware that irony, paradox, and contradiction are often symptoms of their juxtaposition. Once we detect the juxtaposition, we can tease apart the two truths, integrate them properly, and remove a lot of confusion.

Let's take the example, "you have to be somebody before you can be nobody." From the relative perspective, having a healthy functioning ego, being "somebody," is a good thing. It allows us to operate in the world and communicate with others. The ego develops for a reason. But growth does continue beyond the ego. If it doesn't, the ego becomes a form of arrested development. To evolve we need to become egoless, to become "nobody," which is the domain of the absolute. Without a healthy ego, however, we will not evolve properly beyond it.

Unraveling the two truths is not a panacea for every paradox or contradiction, but it is an effective tool for dealing with confusion on the path. For our purposes, the two truths help us understand that something seen from the perspective of relative truth as regress can, from the higher perspective of absolute truth, actually be a sign of real progress.

❧ Hardship as Progress

In the material world, pain is an indication that something is wrong. A toothache or backache suggests trouble. Our normal response is to remove the pain by seeing a doctor or taking a pill. In the relative world, pain is a sign of regress.

In the spiritual world, with the perspective of absolute truth, pain is approached differently. Pain and its cousins chaos, hardship, anxiety, insecurity, and fear can all be markers of progress. As the great Indian master Padmasambhava says, "Adverse conditions are a practitioner's true wealth."[33] This is one of the painful ironies of the path.

Ken Wilber writes,

> Discovery begins at the moment you consciously become
> dissatisfied with life. Contrary to most professional opinion,
> this gnawing dissatisfaction with life is not a sign of "mental
> illness," nor an indication of poor social adjustment, nor a

character disorder. For concealed within this basic unhappiness with life and existence is the embryo of a growing intelligence, a special intelligence usually buried under the immense weight of social sham. A person who is beginning to sense the suffering of life is, at the same time, beginning to awaken to deeper realities, truer realities [the absolute]. For suffering smashes to pieces the complacency of our normal fictions about reality, and forces us to become alive in a special sense—to see carefully, to feel deeply, to touch ourselves and our worlds in ways we have heretofore avoided. It has been said, and truly I think, that suffering is the first grace. In a special sense, suffering is almost a time of rejoicing, for it marks the birth of creative insight. . . . The emergence of suffering is not so much good as it is a good sign, an indication that one is starting to realize that life lived outside unity consciousness [the absolute] is ultimately painful, distressing and sorrowful. . . . .We suffer, then, not because we are sick, but because intelligent insight is emerging. The correct understanding of suffering, however, is necessary in order that the birth of insight is not aborted. We must correctly interpret suffering in order to enter into it, live it, and finally live beyond it.[34]

Dzigar Kongtrül Rinpoche echoes this key point: "The important thing is to appreciate our underlying sadness. It is a hint of a deeper intelligence that is normally obscured by the distractions of daily life. In solitude, this natural faculty of our mind comes out of an almost dormant state. Looking out at the natural beauty around us, we realize how much there is to appreciate beyond the narrow focus of ego—and how meaningless is our madly driven lives."[35]

When we finally acknowledge it, feeling "off" is a good sign. The Sanskrit word for suffering is "duhka," and it refers to an axle which is off-center with respect to its wheel, or to a bone that has slipped out of its socket. Feeling "off" is a sign we are outside the "axle" of the absolute, an indication we are still living in duality. The drive to resolve that healthy dissonance, the bumpy ride, is what spurs us onto the path. Zen teacher Frank Ostaseski says, "We don't really serve a person by taking them away from their suffering. We serve them by helping them come into contact with it."[36]

In the spiritual world, therefore, we relate to pain differently. Material pain draws our attention to something we want to isolate and exclude; spiritual pain usually draws our attention to something we need to embrace and include. But until we discover this, we bring our established material protocol into the spiritual world and retard our progress. Patrul Rinpoche offers this uncompromising spiritual advice:

> Praise is not good, blame is good.
> If praised, then pride and arrogance increase.
> If blamed, then one's own faults are exposed.
> Defamation is the gift of the Gods.
> High position is not good, a low position is good.
> If you are high, pride and jealousy arise.
> If you are low, openness and dedication increase.
> A low position is the seat of superior ones.
> Wealth is not good, poverty is good.
> If you are wealthy, there is the great suffering of collect-
>   ing and protecting.
> If you are poor, austerity and the holy Dharma are
>   accomplished.
> The body [life] of a beggar is the goal of the religious
>   person.
> Being given to is not good, being stolen from is good.
> If one is given to, then the lord of karmic debit increases.
> If one is stolen from, then the debts of future lives are
>   paid back.
> Contentment is the crown jewels [common wealth] of
>   the Noble Ones.
> Friends are not good, enemies are good.
> Friends hinder the path of liberation.

Enemies are the objects of patience.
The practice of equal taste is the crucial juncture.[37]

There are times when the spiritual path can be frightful, a real
nightmare. But nightmares have one powerful purpose—they rouse
us from our complacency and slumber. James Pagel, sleep researcher
and professor at the University of Colorado Medical School says,
"The classic nightmare places the dreamer in a situation where there
is no way out but [to] awake."[38] His comment also applies to spiritual
awakening. The Armenian mystic Gurdjieff, the Buddha, and many
other awakened masters referred to mankind as being asleep. It is
therefore a nightmarish blessing to finally discover there is no way
out but full awakening.

If something is painful enough, it will wake us up and keep us from
falling back asleep. One day we will wake up, just as we now wake up
from our nightly dreams, and wonder how we could have been so
fooled. And we will have our nightmares to thank.

Spiritual practitioners should be grateful for problems because
right *there* is where the practice is. That's where the alarm clock is
ringing. The Tibetan master Khenpo Karthar writes,

> Usually when we feel we are starting to experience a string
> of disasters, it is actually a cleaning process of some kind.
> For example, if you have some very dirty clothes and you
> just let them sit somewhere, they seem somewhat dirty but
> not quite as dirty as they are. Once you start to wash them,
> more and more dirt starts coming out—it seems like end-
> less amounts of dirt. But eventually you do get to the end
> of the dirt, and the clothes are clean. In the same way,
> people often say that the practice of dharma [the spiritual
> path] seems to be extremely troublesome, bringing up
> more problems than it solves. In fact, it is solving problems
> by their rising up. Also, if you have a big fire, you are going
> to get a lot of smoke. When you find that you are doing
> this practice [or any practice] and it seems to be bringing

up obstacles, you must become even stronger in it. It is a sign that something is happening, so it is very good.[39]

Tenga Rinpoche agrees: "When you want to clean something, first you have to stir up the dirt that is in it. By practicing [deep meditation], negative results which would have been experienced in a future life, will occur now."[40]

Pain along the path is not always a marker of progress or a good sign. It is just not that tidy. Pain *can* be such a sign. It would be naive to say that we should blindly embrace every hardship that arises. Until we get to the point where everything that happens is perceived as empty (part 2), and everything becomes our meditation (part 3), there are pains and obstacles that need to be removed if they distract or arrest our meditation. This is the criteria, at the level of the First Turning, for what to accept and what to reject. Accept that which enhances your spiritual practice and reject that which does not. Our mission, as we progress through the Three Turnings, is to expand our embrace and attain the view that everything is spiritual, that everything—the good, the bad, and the ugly—can be embraced and brought onto the path.

❧ Order out of Chaos

Chaos theory offers a number of universal principles that can help us understand hardship as progress. In chaos theory an evolving system breaks down at one level of organization and then reorganizes itself at a higher level. For example, when we turn on the faucet, we can adjust the flow to a low level where the stream is smooth and steady. But if we increase the flow, the stream falls apart and splatters. If we keep increasing the flow, the stream will reorganize at a higher volume and become steady again. In many illnesses, people, especially children, temporarily break down until their immune system develops the appropriate response. When their immune system reorganizes at a higher level, they become immune to future exposures to that illness.

This phenomenon occurs throughout nature and applies to human beings on the spiritual path. We can be flowing along at a steady stream in life and suddenly be hit with all manner of turbulence. A life that was once together completely falls apart. We feel lost, disorganized, and swept away in chaos. If we understand what might be happening, we can better adapt to the upsetting new flow of energy or information, and instead of resisting the flow and trying to get our old selves back together, we can surrender to the chaos and discover ways to reorganize our life at a higher level. Zen teacher Joan Halifax writes, "Catastrophe is the essence of the spiritual path, a series of breakdowns . . . the circumstance that liberates strength, wisdom, and kindness from within the suffocating embrace of fear."[41]

In other words, with the right view we can find higher order in the midst of chaos. If we understand the chaos, we can evolve; if we do not, we just fall apart. Nobel laureate Ilya Prigogine coined the term "dissipative structure" to describe instances of chaos (disequilibrium), and subsequent higher self-organization (new equilibrium). "Dissipative structure" is a paradoxical term that points to the essence of chaos theory. *Dissipation* implies chaos and falling apart; *structure* implies order and a holding together. On the spiritual path the implication is this: we fall apart in order to get it back together at a higher level. This is what Trungpa Rinpoche meant when he said that chaos should be regarded as extremely good news.

But we can only uncover the good news if we remain open to the bad news. In other words, when things are falling apart, we often evolve the best if we go with the flow and surrender. This is necessary chaos and hardship. Necessary defeat. If we resist and try to sustain the lower level of order, we may be fighting with the opportunities that the universe is presenting and retard our path. This is unnecessary hardship born from the resistance itself. John Welwood says, "We have to be willing to come apart at the seams, to be dismantled, to let our old ego structures fall apart before we can begin to embody sparks of the essential perfection at the core of our nature."[42] Anam Thubten writes,

Sometimes it seems that the world becomes even more challenging when we are on the path because the spiritual path wakes us up. . . . We have to be careful what we wish for because sometimes if we pray for liberation right now, then the world can be very wrathful and very challenging. When the world presents difficulties and obstacles to us it means that now, fortunately, we have the opportunity to pass through all of our reactions, all of our habits. . . . Therefore, if we are determined to discover awakening at any cost, then we must also expect and be prepared for the fact that we may run into challenges and difficulties. . . . As spiritual seekers we don't have to invite challenges but we do have to celebrate challenges when they visit us . . . we must know how to surrender to them and accept them. We even have to be jubilant in a crisis and think, "Oh, this is such an extraordinary, golden opportunity to practice how to accept what I don't like."[43]

Once again we have a choice. Life inevitably presents situations where things crumble, where we are challenged and stretched. How we relate to that turbulence is critical, for chaos can lead to a breakdown, or a breakthrough. These are called "bifurcation points" in chaos theory, and they offer a choice of orders. We can choose to surrender to the chaos and progress to a higher order, or we can choose to fight the chaos and remain stuck at our existing level of order, or even regress into a lower level. Bifurcation points are milestones in a system's evolution. Do we choose stability, ease, comfort, and to remain stuck; or do we choose instability, disease, discomfort, and to evolve? Trungpa Rinpoche says, "The way to work with that is, in making that choice, not to go according to your sense of comfort."[44] Chaos and bifurcation points are golden gates of opportunity. It is up to us whether we accept the challenging invitation and elect to pass through those gates.

One month after my marriage ended, my beloved mother died,

and I was struck with incredibly painful kidney stones. My life was in shambles. I was heartbroken, hurting, and on the verge of depression. As I went home to an empty house night after night in the dead of winter, I realized I had a choice. I could let this painful situation bury me in depression, or I could use it as an opportunity to work with pain.

Even with this view it was hard, but I realized it was up to me. No one was going to save me. When pangs of loneliness and desolation swept over me, I allowed myself to surrender to the loneliness, and instead of resisting the feelings, or running to some form of "distraction therapy," I turned to face the heartache and pain directly. When else would I have such a golden opportunity to work with these feelings so intensely? When else could I learn how to remove the sting of loneliness and transform it into simple aloneness?

There were times when it was too intense, and I just couldn't do it. Sometimes I had to call a friend for help or turn on the TV. I realized that grinding it out, even for the purpose of evolution, was too aggressive. I allowed myself to breakdown and grieve, but I did not stay down. I tried to return to the emotional chaos with an open heart and transformed my relationship to a slew of negative feelings. I made the choice that I would work with the chaos and let it teach me.

As I explored these bitter emotions I began to befriend them. The chaos slowly evolved into a higher order where these feelings no longer took me down. My emotional immune system learned how to properly respond. It's not that I became immune to the difficult feelings. I still felt them. I was affected by sadness and loneliness, but I was no longer infected. I felt the pain, but it did not hurt as much.

The idea is to choose evolution but to do so with kindness. For those on the spiritual path, this becomes the natural selection. Establish a relationship to chaos and hardship, and let it order us into a higher level. A friend who was going through a difficult time concluded a long conversation in a statement tinged with wisdom and humor: "Just another fucking learning experience." She had endured lots of chaos in her life, and her good cheer allowed her to learn from it. The path to find order in chaos, to select progress and not regress, is always the middle path: do not resist the chaos and do not indulge it.

5 ❦

Suffering or Pain?

Those things that hurt, instruct.
—Ben Franklin

Some of the world's greatest meditators have cried a lot.
—Sakyong Mipham

A COMMON COMPLAINT early on the path is that things seem to be getting worse. I felt this way after my first grand experiences in meditation. Meditation was supposed to calm me down, but at times my mind was crazier than ever. Instead of having fewer thoughts, it felt like meditation was increasing them. It was only after talking with experienced practitioners that I realized this is normal—and a good sign.

❦ The Pain of Seeing

Things were not getting worse, I was just seeing for the first time how bad they really are. I was slowing down enough to cut through the speed that glossed over my life and was discovering the first noble truth: that beneath all the busyness was a lot of pain. I was seeing things I had not seen before and did not want to see. Pema Chödrön says, "After we've been meditating for a while, it's common to feel that we are regressing rather than waking up. 'Until I started meditating, I was quite settled; now it feels like I'm always restless'. 'I never used to feel anger; now it comes up all the time'. We might complain that meditation is ruining our life, but in fact such experiences are a sign that we're starting to see more clearly."[45] We are coming alive, but it is coming at a price.

Studies have shown that meditators literally perceive more. Using a tachistoscope, a fancy kind of strobe light, scientists tested people ranging from nonmeditators to seasoned practitioners. They found that meditators were able to detect the gaps between flashes of light at higher frequencies than nonmeditators. As a gross example, we don't notice that light bulbs flash on and off as the current alternates back and forth, we see a continuous stream of light. But a meditator might be able to detect these tiny gaps.[46]

This sensitivity lends itself to irritability and can be baffling both to the meditator and to those around him or her. Family and friends may comment on the seemingly negative results of practice: "You weren't so touchy before." "You seem more unstable, less sure of yourself." This leads only to further confusion and even a doubting of our meditation.

Part of the problem is that we project an image of a spiritual person as always being calm and cool, impervious to the events around him or her. But spirituality is raw and rugged. When you finally strip off the ego and expose your heart, you may find yourself vulnerable and fragile. In the Shambhala tradition, the ego is referred to as a cocoon. Meditation punctures the cocoon and allows fresh air and brilliant light to flood in. This ventilation is delightful, but like a new born baby's experience of its new environment, it can also feel like an assault.

❧ Reduce or Elevate

The following sections show us how to relate to pain and suffering, or any level of hardship, and what we need to understand before exploring the gritty practicalities. They also portend some of the more difficult material we will turn to later in our journey.

A number of traditions assert that reality, just the way it is, is always already perfect. In Tibetan Buddhism, this is the teaching of Dzogchen, which means "great perfection." The Dzogchen teachings are considered the highest, and they contradict most of what we have been taught about human nature and reality. Instead of original sin, Dzogchen proclaims that we are originally good; instead of behavior based on competition and survival of the fittest, Dzogchen teaches love and compassion as basic human traits. The Great Perfection proclaims that reality is sacred and pure. For most of us this is not our normal view.

Because of the influence of science and its description of a materialistic reality, most of us live in a world that we believe to be governed by reductionism, in its many guises. Reductionism has two central meanings. The first is the view that phenomena can be explained by analyzing the simplest physical mechanisms or components that make up those phenomena. The second is the sense of reducing something to a lower status, diminishing the importance of something. We will engage both of these definitions and point out the wisdom of the former and the confusion of the latter.

The prevailing view of science is that everything derives from matter and can therefore be reduced back to it. In its strong version, everything—consciousness, mind, love, joy, sadness—can be reduced to (that is, can be explained by) subtle forms of matter. In this extreme version, spirituality reduces to psychology, which reduces to biology, which reduces to chemistry, which reduces to physics—which reduces to matter.

There is nothing inherently wrong in reducing reality to its components. Even Buddhism subscribes to reductionism as it dissects the ego and its world. Reductionism allows us to examine the parts that make up things, and in the spiritual world, it helps us discover the parts that generate the illusion of unity and solidity. This is not just an academic affair. We suffer because we take things to be solid and unitary, in other words truly existent, and reductionism attacks this false sense of reality. We will have much more to say about this in part 2. As valuable as this is, this first meaning of reductionism is only one way to view reality. Used properly, it is a powerful tool; used improperly, and taken absolutely, reductionism transforms into a serious trap.

The problem with reductionism on the path is this: what are we reducing reality to? On the spiritual path, we use reductionism to reduce relative reality to its constituent parts. This is a healthy analysis. We will use this form of spiritual reductionism when we reduce the ego to the five skandhas later. On the worldly path, reductionism also reduces reality to its constituent parts, but then these parts are asserted to be material. Things are not merely reduced into parts, but into matter, which then reigns supreme. This is the problem.

The spiritual path, on the other hand, especially in the Second and Third Turnings, asserts that reality is not made of matter, but of "mind." It is beyond the scope of this book to explain just what this mind is, but it is more than the traditional Western view of mind. It is more like heart-mind-spirit. This heart-mind-spirit is beyond the distinction between mind and matter, and therefore inclusive of, but not limited to, either. It is the union of luminosity and emptiness, the "irreducible" description of reality that we will return to in part 3.

All these terms point to that which cannot be pointed to, the ineffable matrix of reality from which everything arises. The religious scholar Huston Smith speaks of it as the "Infinite," and delivers the point: "Thus everything derives, ultimately, from the Infinite. And since 'derives' cannot in this last case involve separation—the Infinite is like a celestial void: nothing escapes from it—everything abides in the Infinite's luster."[47] That luster is what is lost if we remain stuck in the degradation of reductionism—the first meaning of reductionism infected with the second.

Instead of reducing everything to matter, spirituality "elevates" everything into this ineffable heart-mind-spirit. What is elevated is our view of things, our recognition of everything as Infinite and sacred. So instead of a flat and lifeless world, one that is profane and degraded, the spiritual path lifts us into a vibrant and sentient world, one that is sacred and good. Buddhist writer Stephen Levine paraphrased this when he said that we are not physical beings with spiritual experiences; we are spiritual beings with physical experiences.

Since everything derives from heart-mind-spirit (the Infinite), as Huston Smith points out, nothing can be separated from it.* The articulation of reductionism and "elevationism" is not designed to further separate our world into good and bad, sacred and profane. It is meant to unite them. It is meant to join Heaven and Earth by reminding us that heaven saturates the earth, that sacred goodness permeates everything, that the relative is soaked in the absolute. The point is their nonduality, which is lost in gross reductionism. In order to see the world in this proper way, we have to elevate our gaze, which is what the path is all about.

In many ways, the transformation from a material to a spiritual world, from reductionism as degradation to elevationism, is the heart of spirituality. Infusing spirit into matter lifts everything up, it en-lightens the world. But this lifting is difficult. Seeing the world through the Dzogchen lens, as perfectly pure and sacred, is not easy.

This is because, whether we know it or not, we are all members of the culture of scientific materialism. We were born into this culture and raised to share in its worldview. Our scientists are the high priests of the age, and we look to them for answers about reality. As the Dalai Lama says, "Science is the religion of the secular world." The reality it describes is made of lifeless matter, where mind is merely a bubble, an epiphenomenon, arising out of the complex interplay of that matter.

The transformation from a world made of matter to one made of heart-mind-spirit is monumental, which is why attaining enlightenment is so monumental. For you see, we have it completely backwards. Mind cannot be reduced to matter; matter needs to be elevated to mind—to be *recognized* as being of the same sacred nature as mind.

---

* "Mahamudra" in Tibetan Buddhism is translated as "the Great Seal" and refers to how all of manifest reality is "sealed," or "stamped," with the imprint of the Infinite. Nothing can escape being perfectly pure and sacred since everything is an emanation of perfect purity. Everything bears the "seal" of the Infinite.

Spirituality accomplishes this elevation, liberating things back to their pure source. Huston Smith writes,

> The mistake of reductionism—spirit reduced to metamorphosed matter (Darwinism), truth reduced to ideology (Marxism), psyche reduced to sex (Freud: there is no way "to sweeten the sour apple")—lies in its attempt to explain the greater in terms of the less, with the not surprising consequence that the greater is thereby lessened. It is this, at root, that sets us against the modern outlook and turns us back toward tradition where the drift is always the reverse: to explain the lesser by means of the more, a mode of explanation that tends to augment rather than deplete, for in both cases explanation produces a kind of rub-off. . . . [Reductionism] closes the door on the domain to which magic pertains, it again makes the higher depend on the lower [when it is actually the lower that depends on the higher].[48]

❧ Lifting Meditations

A central Buddhist practice that is designed to accomplish this elevation is called deity yoga, which involves visualizing yourself, and all beings, as deities. It also involves hearing all sound as sacred mantra and viewing everything as luminous and perfectly pure. From a materialistic perspective, this is utter fantasy. But this fantastical view is the way the enlightened ones actually perceive things, and through deity yoga, we are invited to join them in this pure perception. The entire world is lifted up.

In Shambhala Buddhism, there is the practice of raising "wind horse." This is a joyfully uplifting practice where we mount our basic goodness and rouse a wind of delight that elevates us from a material into a sacred spiritual world. The weight of materialism gets us down and makes us feel flat. It fills our world with unnecessary burden and hardship, and it also makes us forget. We forget our basic goodness, the heart-mind-spirit that is who we really are. We forget that we are not our bodies, nor any form that we can identify with. Identifying with form reduces us, as Levine's statement asserts. Wind horse lifts us up and helps us remember our goodness and that of the world.

Reductionism and elevationism are not merely philosophical issues. If someone came up to us and told us that we were full of shit, we would probably nod in agreement. We are so used to taking ourselves and others down that we readily agree when someone points out our materialistic and samsaric nature. We flip each other off, call each other names, and don't think twice about reducing each other to the lowest form of matter. This is emotional reductionism.

If, however, someone came up to us and told us that we are full of purity, goodness, and love, we would probably reject that compliment and tell them that *they* are full of shit. But purity, goodness, and love is who we really are. This is why we are exhorted to see ourselves and others as deities. Deity yoga and raising wind horse lift us into our innate purity. This is emotional elevationism, the recognition of our pure true nature.

Dzogchen presents the scenery of the absolute, the fruition of the path. From the relative perspective, the world is full of suffering and situations demand remediation. But in their absolute essence, before we start to mess with things, those situations are perfectly pure.

❧ The Relationship of Pain to Suffering

Reductionism and elevationism are at the heart of understanding suffering and pain and provides the view that helps us relate to any unwanted situation. The problem is not with reality and anything that arises within it. The problem is how we relate to reality. "There is nothing either good or bad," as Hamlet said, "but thinking makes it so."

What is an inappropriate relationship? Wanting to run away or to alter the painful situation. In other words, not establishing a relationship at all. Our usual response to pain includes anything but a relationship. We can't relate to it. It hurts, so get rid of it. This is an inappropriate relationship—and the heart of suffering. Suffering is the result of an inappropriate relationship to pain.

There is a big difference between suffering and pain. Pain is unavoidable; suffering is completely avoidable. Even buddhas feel what we would call pain, they just relate to it in a very different way. Instead of trying to get rid of it, they feel it completely and relate to it directly. In so doing they ironically prevent suffering. Psychiatrist and author M. Scott Peck says, "Wise people learn not to dread but actually to welcome problems and actually to welcome the pain of problems. Most of us are not so wise."[49]

We, on the other hand, do not feel our pain completely and just want to get rid of it. In so doing we create suffering. The Buddha discovered that in order to avoid suffering, we have to enter and relate to our pain. The pain may not disappear, but the suffering will. It is the difference between necessary and unnecessary hardship: necessary hardship is just pain; unnecessary hardship is suffering.

Trungpa Rinpoche says,

> We could say that the real world is that in which we experience pleasure and pain, good and bad. But if we are completely in touch with these dualistic feelings, that *absolute experience of duality is itself the experience of non-duality.* [Italics added.] Then there is no problem at all, because duality is seen from a perfectly open and clear point of view in which there is no conflict; there is a tremendous encompassing vision of oneness. Conflict arises because duality [pain] is not seen as it is at all. It is seen only in a biased way, a very clumsy way. In fact, we do not perceive anything properly. . . . So when we talk about the dualistic world as confusion [painful], that confusion is not the complete dualistic world, but only half-hearted, and this causes tremendous dissatisfaction and uncertainty.[50]

When I have a headache, instead of running to the medicine cabinet, I explore the pain and enter it. What is this pain made of, what happens if I surrender to it? I may not get rid of my headache, but I certainly change its character. It is no longer so imposing or unwanted—it is no longer so painful. Then if I need to, I take an aspirin. Proper relationship, not masochism, is what is important.

This approach applies to psychological and spiritual pain. When my heart was broken over the end of my marriage, instead of fleeing into distraction therapy—watching TV, drinking, keeping busy— I stayed with my broken heart. I made friends with my pain. The heartache didn't go away, but its edge softened. Stephen Levine writes, "One day we will realize how much of our life is a compulsive attempt to escape discomfort. We are motivated more by an aversion to the unpleasant than by a will toward truth. . . . We are constantly attempting to escape our life, to avoid rather than enter our pain, and we wonder why it is so difficult to be fully alive."[51] The great psychologist Carl Jung summarized it by saying, "Neurosis is always a substitute for legitimate suffering."[52]

In order to establish a proper relationship to pain, many traditions incorporate painful situations as part of spiritual training. On my first trip to Tibet, I traveled to a remote monastery high in the Himalayas. Because I was providing care for the monks, I was allowed to stay inside the monastery, which is usually forbidden. On my first morning I woke up before dawn to the sounds of young monks outside my room. I stepped outside to see the exposed courtyard lined with monks reciting and memorizing sacred texts in the biting cold. The monks were bobbing back and forth furiously, trying to stay warm. I was struck with this level of discipline, it seemed nearly abusive to me, so I asked one of the discipline masters pacing behind the monks about this degree of hardship. He replied, "Tough on the outside, soft on the inside."

The discipline forged a resolve in these monks that would serve them as they grew into even more demanding spiritual practices. The rigors of the path are always held in the context of tough love. It is rough on the ego, but loving to the spirit.

6 🌿

Always Practicing

In the garden of gentle sanity, may you be bombarded
by coconuts of wakefulness. —CHÖGYAM TRUNGPA

Even having encountered the Dharma, you will still find it
extremely difficult to continue and succeed in your practice—
inner and outer obstacles will pour down like rain.
—LAMA ZOPA, Transforming Problems into Happiness

THERE ARE SPIRITUAL PATHS and worldly paths, the road less traveled and the road well traveled, and we are always on one or the other. Until we discover the spiritual path, most of us are firmly rooted in the worldly path. For most Westerners there isn't even a worldly path per se, there's just life. There is nothing to compare and contrast it to, so we do not see that we are on the worldly path. We entered this path when we were born and have been following it most of our lives.

Traditions may disagree about the end of the spiritual path and what enlightenment is, but the end of the worldly path is clear: the fruits are all about form, or matter, as much of it, and in as many shapes, as we can get. Fancy house, car, boat, bike, stereo, furniture . . . It's about finding happiness in things or thoughts—in *form*. We want happiness to take a particular form. So if things do not do it for us, perhaps ideas, politics, religious beliefs, or even the thought of enlightenment itself will.

To illuminate the worldly path is to make the unconscious conscious and that is the seed of liberation. Waking up is largely about waking up to the unconscious drives that dictate our lives. By flushing our unconscious processes up to the surface, we finally have a choice: we can elect to stay on the worldly path or we can choose to jump off. Before that it is choiceless. There is just life the way most of the world lives it. As Socrates once put it, "The difference between you and me is that I know that I do not know." For the majority of the Western world, we do not see that we do not see.

At the highest levels of the path, there is nothing to jump away from. The Third Turning works more with transformation than renunciation. In other words, at the level of the Third Turning, we transform the worldly into the spiritual by relating to the worldly properly. Therefore we don't get rid of anything. But we are still on the First Turning, where renunciation and the challenge of what to accept and what to reject are central tenets. In this context, an understanding of spiritual and worldly paths helps us accept the former, and reject, or at least soften, the latter.

❦ Familiarity

The word for "meditation" in Tibetan is "gom," which means "to become familiar with." One implication of "gom" is that, whether we know it or not, we are always meditating. The mind is always becoming familiar with whatever is in front of it. It is like a sponge, constantly absorbing the medium into which it is placed. We are always becoming increasingly familiar with the worldly or the spiritual; we are becoming more or less involved with matter.

Put an apple in front of you, and you will become familiar with it, you are meditating on it. Put a grenade in front of you, and you will become familiar with that. Whatever is placed in awareness becomes an object of meditation. That we are always practicing, even if we do not know it, is the heart of "worldly" meditation. We are becoming more familiar (and subsequently entrapped) with the forms of this world without knowing it. Ignorance, therefore, is at the heart of the worldly path.

The worldly path is based on unconscious processes driving our "conscious" lives. If enlightenment is about waking up, this is what it means to be asleep—doing something without knowing it, or without knowing why we are doing it. This is why it is so hard to wake up. We are masters of material things because we have been walking the worldly path from the day we were born, or for those who believe in reincarnation, we have been meditating on matter from beginningless time. We are also virtuosos in the perverted arts that accompany the worldly path and that are generated from it. We are masters of selfishness, anger, passion, greed, competition, jealousy, and the countless other vices that characterize our relationships to material objects. These rotten fruits of materialism come so easily to us because we have been practicing them forever.

Buddhism speaks of five paths leading to enlightenment, which are actually five stages along one extended path. The first of these paths is the Path of Accumulation, and it refers to the accumulation of merit and wisdom. Merit is meritorious action, virtue, or good karma, the accumulation of good deeds, and wisdom refers to seeing things as they are, which we will define in part 2 as seeing emptiness.* The idea of a "path of accumulation" could also be applied to the worldly path, and our bloated bodies, stuffed closets, packed bookshelves, and fat bank accounts are evidence that we are well along on the worldly path of accumulation. The worldly path of accumulation

---

* Karma is one of the most complex topics in Eastern thought. Only a fully enlightened Buddha can understand karma. Karma means "action" and refers to the laws of cause and effect—that actions have consequences. Only an action (mental, verbal, or physical) free from passion, aggression, and ignorance is without karmic effect. Only at enlightenment, when everything is related to with equanimity, is no further karma produced. Karma is not determinism. Karma provides the situation but does not determine our response to the situation. Proper relationship, our response to the situation (the central theme of this book) is the point—and either creates or does not create further karma.

also applies on a more subtle level. We have accumulated so many bad habits, there is so much momentum behind seeing the world materialistically, that turning the tide brings real hardship.

Even if we consider ourselves spiritual persons and have been meditating for decades, we can still be firmly on the worldly path. True renunciation of materialism is rare. We may have lived our entire life in a monastery, but if we still put ourselves first and only think about benefiting others when it is convenient, we are still walking the worldly path.

If our meditation still has to fit into our routine, and our spirituality has to be more-or-less convenient, we are embracing spirituality with material arms, and our meditation is another form of self-improvement. This is what Trungpa Rinpoche famously referred to as "spiritual materialism." It arises whenever we take a spiritual teaching or practice designed to transcend the ego and subvert it into strengthening the ego. It happens all the time. It is not a question of *if* we will be infected with spiritual materialism, but rather when. Spiritual materialism is one of the most pervasive and subtle stains and one of the last to be removed.

❧ Renunciation

Renunciation of the worldly path does not mean we have to run away to an ashram. We can spend our life in an ashram and be more attached to things than someone in the material world. One master told me before I entered my long retreat, "Just because your body is in retreat doesn't mean your mind is." True renunciation, genuine retreat, is an inner transformation. If our attitude is spiritual, then Times Square becomes our ashram.

There are two stages in being truly spiritual: aspiring and entering. Most of us spend our lives at the level of aspiration. There is nothing wrong with this, indeed it is a noble stage. We do the best we can with the obligations of life. But to completely renounce the worldly path and fully enter the spiritual path is as rare as a daytime star. The word for renunciation in Tibetan is "nye" (definite) "jung" (to arise)—definite arising away from materialism. Lama Yeshe says this:

> What the development of true renunciation implies is that we no longer rely on sensory pleasures for our ultimate happiness; we see the futility of expecting deep satisfaction from such limited, transitory phenomena. It is important to understand this point clearly. Renunciation is *not* the same as giving up pleasure or denying ourselves happiness. It means giving up our unreal expectations about ordinary pleasures. These expectations themselves are what turn pleasure into pain. . . . Simply stated, renunciation is the feeling of being so completely fed up with our recurring problems that we are finally ready to turn away from our attachments to this and that and begin searching for another way to make our life satisfying and meaningful. . . . To develop renunciation means to realize how our ordinary reliance on pleasure is preventing us from tasting [a] higher, more complete happiness.[53]

Chögyam Trungpa says that if we ever gave up hope for samsara, liberation would be close at hand. The reason why it is important to understand the difference between aspiring and entering, or "partially arising" and "definite arising," is so that we do not kid ourselves. It can also inspire us to generate the resolve necessary to make the transition from aspiring to entering and strengthen our renunciation.

The transition from aspiring to entering does not have to be a dramatic proclamation or a radical move. The path is marked with humility, and an authentic entrance is often silent and gradual. We should realize how fortunate we are to even hear about the spiritual path but also acknowledge that it can take a long time to fully enter it. We should honor those who have found that courage and aspire to emulate them. Mother Teresa was once approached by a person who introduced herself by saying, "I am a Christian . . ." This humble saint looked her in the eye and said, "Already?"

❧ Habitual Patterns

By understanding the worldly path we can respect the extent of its influence and the hardship of renouncing it. We feel the full force of worldly materialism only when, having discovered that this herd we have lived our life in is stampeding toward a cliff, we try to turn around and head in the opposite direction. As long as we go with the flow, we do not feel its enormous impact.

The difficulty of stepping off the worldly path is the result of facing the law of momentum, or karma. Simply knowing that we cannot jump from one path to the other without wrestling with these forces helps us handle the difficult switch. Every time we try to make the jump and fully enter the spiritual path, the momentum of the worldly path knocks us backward.

The influence of materialism is formidable, but it pales in comparison to the power of the momentum within us—the force of our views about reality. Internal momentum is more powerful because it is more insidious. It is like gravity. Gravity is the most omnipresent of cosmological forces, but we rarely take notice. We forget how it keeps us from flying into space and influences every step we take. Internal momentum has this same degree of influence and controls our life at the level of habitual patterns.

Habit creates enormous hardship on the path and paying homage to its power helps us relate to it more skillfully. Like gravity, "force of habit" unconsciously controls our every step and keeps us glued to the worldly path. Just when we think we have broken away from the sphere of materialistic influence, habit yanks us back. We hear an inspirational master and make the resolve to integrate his or her insights, but the inspiration fades. We come out of retreat fired up to change our life, but soon find ourselves stuck in the same old ruts. This has happened to me countless times.

The force of gravity depends on the mass of an object. The greater the mass, the more forceful the gravity. Jupiter has a lot more influence than Pluto. Every time I repeat a selfish or materialistic act, I am slapping more weight onto the path of materialism and making it harder to get off. Habit means that when we do something once, it becomes easier to do it again. We are more familiar with it, "goming" to it. This is the essence of any form of training, where the force of habit is consciously directed toward a goal. We learn to play the piano by creating good finger habits. Direct your fingers thousands of times into the same patterns and they become habitual. It becomes natural at a certain point, and you become a virtuoso, but it did not come naturally, it took work.

Habit is a personal application of a universal law: the laws of force and momentum. Cheat on your spouse once, and it is easier to do it again. Steal something once, and it gets easier to steal again. These tenets are almost platitudes because they are so obvious, but they are obvious the way gravity is obvious. It is so obvious it is nearly unconscious. And that is what makes it so deadly.

To summarize: we started life with only the worldly path. Unless we were born into a very spiritual family, we had no choice. We then traveled the worldly path unconsciously, not even knowing we were on it, until we discovered that this path is a dead end. Looking for an alternative, we consciously enter the spiritual path. By becoming increasingly familiar with this new path, we transfer our allegiance from the material to the spiritual. At a certain point, our refuge in the spiritual path is complete, and everything is brought onto that path. We have finally renounced the worldly path.

7 🌱

Repetition

Again! —Khenpo Tsultrim Gyamtso Rinpoche

At some point, we need to stop and realize that the [path] is not custom-made to please us. It is supposed to go beyond our trips. If it becomes too comfortable, it isn't working. —Sakyong Mipham

Spiritual training involves scrubbing out deeply ingrained habits, which takes time and reiteration. It is like trying to flatten a scroll that has been coiled up for thousands of years. One pass with our hands across the surface won't do it. We have to press it out again and again. The other way to flatten it would be the "extreme path to the middle," where we try rolling it up in the opposite direction. Sounds good on paper but it doesn't feel so good on our psyches as they are twisted from one extreme to another.

Accomplishment in any discipline involves repetition. If we want to build muscles, we don't lift ten thousand pounds at one time, we lift a few pounds thousands of times. Just as repetition is the source of necessary hardship for a piano student aspiring to be a concert pianist, it remains so for spiritual students aspiring to wake up. We hear the same teachings continuously, we practice the same mantras ceaselessly, we return to the meditation cushion, and then to our breath, incessantly. In the Tibetan tradition, one does one hundred thousand prostrations, one hundred thousand mantra recitations, one hundred thousand mandala offerings, one million guru yoga recitations—and that's just for starters. These may seem like outrageous numbers, but they are nothing compared to the numbers we have already accumulated in our practice of materialism.

I have had selfish thoughts millions of times, bragged about myself, criticized others, gossiped, cheated, lied, and practiced self-centered actions millions upon millions of times. I have been mindless billions of times. I have forgotten the truth countless times. The numbers are astronomical, and so is the sphere of their influence.

Now when my teacher tells me I have to recite one million mantras that cultivate compassion, I know why. He is not torturing me, even though it sometimes feels that way. He is simply using the universal laws of reality, the same ones that I have unconsciously used to get me so stuck, to now consciously get me unstuck. When I visit my teacher Khenpo Rinpoche, he listens patiently as I relate my litany of problems. Then he might compose a spontaneous verse and tell me to recite it one thousand times or to read an entire book ten times. He is legendary in his use of repetition, and he uses it because he understands the laws of cause and effect.

On the spiritual path we replace unconscious habits of confusion with conscious habits of wisdom. Instead of my unconscious practice of sloth, impatience, greed, anger, or any of the selfish habits that come so easily to me, I consciously practice discipline, patience, kindness, love, and any of the selfless habits that are still foreign to me. I am working to become familiar with good habits.

The spiritual path is hard because we are stopping old habits that come so easily and replacing them with difficult new ones. For example, mindlessness is natural to us. It is easy to space out and be distracted. Try to look at an object without wavering for a few seconds and you will see your talents for distraction. This is a bad habit, formulated over countless repetitions, and is a central unconscious practice on the worldly path. It is no longer even a practice, but a constant performance. We have accomplished mindlessness.

On the spiritual path we want to replace this bad habit with a good one. Even though mindfulness is a natural expression of the awakened mind, it has been buried under eons of mindlessness, so we have to work to dig it out. The initial stage of mindfulness practice is called deliberate mindfulness because it takes effort to bring our wandering minds back. It is difficult only because it is unfamiliar.

One sign of progress on the path is that deliberate mindfulness evolves into spontaneous mindfulness. With enough practice, it becomes effortless. We have formed a good habit, even if we did not have a good time doing it.

The path is full of magic, but it is also full of mechanics. The skill of a concert pianist is magical, but this skill is the result of causes that are painfully mechanical. Similarly, the skill of effortless mindfulness is magical, but its causes are equally mechanical. There is nothing glamorous about the hard work of repetition. Understanding the mechanics of spirituality dispels illusions about the ease of its accomplishment.

Science speaks about phase transformations, or punctuated equilibrium. A common example is the manner in which water comes to a boil. Put a pot of water on the stove, turn on the heat, and wait. Depending on the intensity of the heat and the temperature and volume of water, it will boil slowly or quickly, but either way there is a period where nothing seems to be happening. All this energy is going into the water with no obvious result. The phase transformation from water into steam takes time.

Similarly, when we engage in spiritual practice, we have placed ourselves on the stove and turned on the heat. If our practice is half-hearted, then it takes time for that low temperature to transform us. If we practice wholeheartedly, the higher temperature brings us more rapidly to a boil. But either way there is a period where nothing seems to be happening. All this energy is going into our practice but nothing is cooking.

As long-term practitioners reflect over years of practice, they discover they are starting to get warm. The changes come slowly because the water that is being heated is so cold, and the heat of our practice is usually tepid. But sooner or later we come to a boil. After years of practice we "suddenly" transform from an uptight, aloof person to an open, loving one. The phase transformation occurs, and we have suddenly gone from a confused sentient being to an awakened one.

❧ Emptying the Warehouse

Buddhism refers to this phase transformation as the gradual path to sudden enlightenment (the accumulation of merit transforms into wisdom), which is discussed as the transformation of the ground consciousness, or *alaya*. "Alaya" means "range," as in the mountain range Himalaya. The alaya is also called the storehouse consciousness. It is the unconscious warehouse, or range, where all our habits, or karmic seeds, are stored. As a confused being, this warehouse is stuffed with negative habits, and the alaya is constantly sending up its stock of negativity that directly influences the way we perceive the world and every action we take upon it.

If we look at our experience, we see how these ripening seeds affect everything we do. For example, we usually react to situations in self-referential terms: how does this person affect me, what can I get out of this situation? We are heavily predisposed to think and act in terms of me and mine, and this predisposition is the direct result of the storehouse consciousness. It "forces" us to react in self-serving ways. I am the center of my universe, and everything orbits around me. The alaya is the ego's center of gravity, where all the heavy weight of our accumulated habitual patterns exert their influence.

On the path we empty out this collection of negative habits and restock it with positive ones. Since the warehouse is jammed with negative seeds, it takes time to clean it out, and it also takes time to restock it with positive seeds. During this unloading and loading, nothing seems to be happening. I know many meditators who hit the ten- and twenty-year stretch of spiritual practice and get discouraged. Perhaps the heat of their practice is too low, or their warehouse is really full, but they get tired of the whole spiritual trip because they don't see the results.

But if their practice is genuine, something is definitely taking place. One of the signs that the warehouse is being restocked with wisdom is that our reactions start to shift, from "What's in it for me?" to "How can I help?" The warehouse stops sending up selfish tendencies and starts to deliver selfless impulses. We are starting to get warm.

Lasting spiritual changes arise from simply being present, again and again. "Religion" means to "link" (ligio) "back" (re). "Linking back" on the spiritual path takes place every time we return to our breath, our body, our mantra, or the present moment. With each return we are taking a small step toward enlightenment because being fully present is a fundamental expression of enlightenment. It may seem like nothing and that we are getting nowhere, but each step brings us closer.

The word for "mindfulness" in Tibetan is *drenpa*, which means "to remember." The essence of spiritual practice is remembrance, which implies that one of our biggest problems is that we forget, a forgetfulness that expresses itself in the many forms of mindlessness. We forget to come back to the present moment, or that we already are a buddha, so a central practice is constant recollection, which is why repetition is imperative.

❧ No Quick Fix

A common source of hardship stems from unrealistic expectation and impatience. Sogyal Rinpoche says that expectation is premeditated disappointment. We live in a world based on speed and expect quick results. We have fast food restaurants, high speed internet, instant coffee, federal express, microwave ovens, and countless conveniences driven by speed. We praise people by saying they are "quick" and insult others by referring to them as "slow."

When we enter the spiritual path, many people expect to become enlightened quickly or at least attain glorious states of meditation. Having expectations is natural in anything we do, but on the path it is a source of unnecessary hardship. Traleg Kyabgon says, "People are always saying 'Meditation is so hard'. This is because they have certain expectations about what the meditative state should be, and they try to fabricate a state that corresponds to those expectations.

When this fails, they get infuriated and frustrated with their practice because it is so often full of struggle."[54]

As we have seen, the spiritual path is a journey without a goal. On an absolute level, there is no purpose to meditation. We just do it—without expectations. The Dalai Lama writes,

> When you start practicing, you should not expect too much . . . you may feel that inner development is an automatic thing for which you press a button and everything changes. It is not so. Inner development is not easy and will take time. External progress, the latest space missions and so forth, have not reached their present level within a short period of time but over centuries, each generation making greater developments based on those of the previous generation. However, inner development is even more difficult since internal improvement cannot be transferred from generation to generation.[55]

The best approach to spiritual practice is patience and open-minded curiosity. As medical scientist and psychologist Joan Borysenko says, "Make no appointments, have no disappointments." In this way we unframe our experience. We drop our expectations and accept everything with equanimity. This is the beginner's mind approach that is most conducive for spiritual growth. My teacher Khenpo Rinpoche always teaches his students to be open . . . spacious . . . and relaxed.

Patience is also critical. The place where I did my long retreat is called "Sopa Choling," which means "dharma place of patience." Sopa also translates as "forbearance" and implies the endurance necessary to wake up. The Dalai Lama continues:

> I have met Westerners who at the beginning were very enthusiastic about their practice, but after a few years have completely forgotten it, and there are no traces of what they had practiced at one time. This is because at the beginning they expected too much. Shantideva's *Engaging*

in the Bodhisattva Deeds emphasizes the importance of the practice of patience—tolerance. This tolerance is an attitude not only toward your enemy, but also an attitude of sacrifice, of determination, so that you do not fall into the laziness of discouragement. You should practice patience, or tolerance, with great resolve. This is important.

Inner development comes step by step. You may think, "Today my inner calmness, my mental peace, is very small," but still, if you compare, if you look back five, ten, or fifteen years back, and think, "What was my way of thinking then? How much inner peace did I have then and what is it today?"—comparing it with what it was then, you can realize that there is some progress, there is some value. This is how you should compare—not with today's feeling and yesterday's feeling, or last week or last month, even not last year, but five years ago. Then you can realize what improvement has occurred internally. *Progress comes by maintaining constant effort in daily practice.* (ibid., emphasis added)

Better not to measure our practice, but if we are going to measure it, then extend the yardstick back far enough for a more accurate reading.

❧ Honor the Relative

There are teachers who proclaim that the only thing necessary to wake up is to "just do it." They tell us that we are already enlightened, we just do not recognize it. I have studied with such teachers, and their "quick-fix" approach is seductive. But after hearing the same message repeatedly, I became discouraged. I couldn't do it. It sounds true, it feels true, but no matter how many times I heard these teachings, I could not bring them into my experience. Others also felt the exhilaration and promise of sudden enlightenment, but no one was getting enlightened.

These teachers deliver an accurate message, but they do so from an exclusively absolute perspective. This is where lofty views, like Dzogchen, are problematic if taken out of context. Even Buddhism asserts that the only difference between a buddha and a confused being is that buddhas know they are buddhas while sentient beings do not. While these proclamations are absolutely true, they are not relatively complete. They are speaking half of the truth and can generate hardship for their followers by not acknowledging the other half.

It is true that we already are a buddha, that everything is perfectly pure, and enlightenment exists here and now. But we cannot realize this truth without a path and without practice. Throughout history a handful of supremely gifted individuals were able to achieve sudden enlightenment, but these were people who admitted they traveled the path in previous lives. They were completely ripe. If these absolute proclamations are not balanced with relative realities, they can lead one astray.

It is easy, and almost lazy, to proclaim the glories of the absolute; it is hard, but more realistic, to acknowledge the labors of the relative. The best approach is to balance the two. Maintain the absolute view that shows us where we are going, but acknowledge the relative work involved in getting there.

We have to honor the laws of spiritual reality. The momentum, or karma, of the worldly path must be acknowledged and exhausted. We cannot stop a freight train on a dime, and we cannot accelerate a freight train instantly. The momentum of the spiritual path must be cultivated and sustained—slowly but surely.

The "absolute-only" gurus proclaim the notion of "no path" and that any path leads one off track. At the highest levels *of the path* this is the proper view. When we have struggled through the necessary hardships of the relative path and exhausted our bad habits, then we can relax into the absolute. Only then can we make the shattering discovery that the path was unnecessary. But we have to endure this painful joke in order to appreciate its punch line. Otherwise we just won't get it.

We have been stressing the importance of proper view, and here we see the problem with having only the absolute view. The resolution lies in the middle. The absolute without the relative is lame—we are not going to get where we want to go. The relative without the absolute is blind—we have no idea of where to go. As the Indian master Padmasambhava says, "Your view should be as vast as the sky, but your conduct should be as fine as barley flour."

John Welwood talks about spiritual bypassing, "using spiritual ideas or practices to avoid or prematurely transcend relative human needs, feelings, personal issues, and developmental tasks."[56] This bypassing manifests in what Welwood calls "advaita-speak," where "advaita" is the Sanskrit word for "nonduality," a state ascribed to God, Brahman, or the Absolute alone. This superior state cannot be reached by reason or relativity. It is above the fray of humanity.

But if nonduality does not honor duality, it becomes sterile and disconnected. It becomes "a one-sided transcendentalism that uses nondual terms and ideas to bypass the challenging work of personal transformation. Advaita-speak can be very tricky, for it uses absolute truth to disparage relative truth, emptiness to devalue form, and oneness to belittle individuality" (ibid.). In other words, it engenders escapism.

❧ Bipolar

When we discover the spiritual path and the exhilaration of its potential, it is common to enter a challenging bipolar phase, one that can last a lifetime. We have placed one foot on a new path heading in one direction, yet our other foot remains firmly on the old path. The promise of awakening lures us forward, yet the comfort of staying asleep pulls us back. Half of us wants to plop back into the safety of our cocoon, and we feel nostalgia for our cozy habits; the other half wants to leap into the freedom that awaits us, and we feel the excitement of exploring a new world.

Two things need to happen to get beyond this. First, we have to cultivate renunciation toward the old path and stop adding momentum to bad habits. This occurs with honest assessment of the futility of the worldly path. Trungpa Rinpoche was blunt: "Nostalgia for samsara is full of shit." Secondly, we have to add more momentum to the new path. Spend less time on the material; add more time to the spiritual. Until enough new momentum is created, we will be thrown back by old habitual patterns. To get the ball rolling in the new direction, we have to give it a long sustained push. Then it takes on a life of its own and starts to carry us along. This is why, as the Dalai Lama stated, constant effort in daily practice is critical. By understanding the bipolar phase, and the extraordinary power of habit, we can stop giving ourselves such a hard time.

8 🍃

Put It in Perspective

Any feedback that assaults our ego is a blessing in disguise. If we're willing to see the world as our teacher, we appreciate the honesty. We are not afraid to be blamed, cut down, shredded, or destroyed or to have our feelings hurt. Decent people do not subject themselves to this kind of abuse, but in this case we appreciate it—not because we're masochistic, but because of the greater vision we hold inside.
—DZIGAR KONGTRÜL, It's Up to You

It is precisely because the practice is working and our karma is ripening so quickly that we find ourselves sailing in a very choppy sea.
—REGINALD RAY, Secret of the Vajra World

A GREAT DEAL of confusion along the path is born from misunderstanding its stages and the larger context in which it always takes place. By losing sight of where the path fits into the larger scheme of things, we set ourselves up for unnecessary trouble when we are eventually forced to relate to this larger context. If we have the view that shows us where we are headed, outlines the stages of our travel, and provides the proper motivation for traveling, then the hardships that greet us along the path can be held within the proper perspective. This, again, is the strength of framing our journey within the Three Turnings.

We can avoid lots of trouble by simply having a good map. We may have some notion of where to go on the path, but without a clear map describing our destination, where we are in relation to it, and how to get to it, it is easy to spin off into endless detours. Imagine a foreigner landing in Seattle who is trying to find his way to Yankee Stadium without a map. First he has to get to the state of New York. If he is unwilling to ask for directions, it could take years of driving around just to get to the east coast. Then he has to get to New York City, and once there he still has to find the stadium. He can do it on his own, but a good map accelerates the journey.

The fiercely independent Western mind is as much a hindrance as a help when it comes to maps. We like to find our own way, and that stubborn resolve creates unnecessary delays. The trail has already been blazed and mapped, why waste time hacking it out on our own? Before I stumbled upon a map I could relate to, I spent years lost in dead-ends.

There are many reliable maps, but the one I am most familiar with is that drawn by the Buddha. I have studied others, and respect many, but have found that the Buddha's map most accurately describes the territory I have already traveled and most reliably predicts the terrain I am about to enter.

A simple way to summarize the Buddha's map is to view the journey as an inverted pyramid, or the letter "V." We begin at the bottom, where the path is initially all about me. We start with ourselves. At this level our path is necessarily narrow and "selfish." We engage in spiritual practice in an effort to clean up our act, so we isolate ourselves and go to work inside. The primary concern is individual liberation, and the meditator's world is as wide as his or her meditation cushion. The idea is that we cannot bring peace to the world until we discover it in ourselves. This level is called the "Hinayana," the "lesser" or "narrow" vehicle.

At a certain point, when we have attained some stability, we get off our seat and start to engage the world. We begin the ascent up the "V." It is time to expand our view to include others. Our sense of what meditation is also expands, and the path becomes wider and more inclusive. As we ascend, our sense of personal self becomes smaller as our sense of identifying with others becomes larger. Our identity grows to embrace others. This is the "Mahayana," the "greater" or "wider" vehicle.

At the top of the "V" our sense of self is gone; we have reached the summit of egolessness. Our identity now includes everything. Our sense of meditation also expands to include everything: our entire world becomes a meditation, and we never leave it. There are no sessions or breaks. Sleep, dream, sex, death—everything becomes meditation. At this level there is no more need for retreat, for our life has become a retreat. Everything we do now is for the benefit of others, for at this stage there is no self to benefit. We are selfless, radiant like the sun, and completely expansive in our ability to benefit others with our light. This is the "Vajrayana," the "indestructible" or "diamond" vehicle.

❧ Top Down

This thumbnail sketch helps us to understand hardship and prevent it because it creates a larger perspective that situates our spiritual practice, and can therefore accelerate it. It is like having a global positioning system in our pocket—we know where we are and where we need to go. It also gives us a view from the top and helps us understand our place in relation to it. Instead of wandering with no view of where we are going, we can look down from the top with a clear perspective. It may be a theoretical glimpse given to us by those who have been up there, but it helps us map our way. So much hardship is born of poor eyesight. We cannot see where we are going, so we confine our vision and create our pain.

The three yanas are related to the Three Turnings: the Hinayana is virtually synonymous with the First Turning; the Second and Third Turnings are included in the Mahayana; and Vajrayana, often considered a subset of the Mahayana (its view is the same, only the methods for realizing the view differ), is outside of the Three Turnings.

Without this farsighted perspective, normal hardships can become insurmountable. After a few years on the path, we may not want to study and practice any more, it is just not worth the effort. But a proper perspective immediately changes our motivation to travel the path and our willingness to endure its challenges. We are no longer doing it for ourselves. Even at the earliest stages, where the motivation is for personal liberation, we now discover that this personal liberation is ultimately for the benefit of others. With this fresh perspective, we are now willing to endure hardship because it is no longer just our trip. We are going to clean up our act, to endure the difficulties, because now we are doing it for others.

It is like a parent going to work for their family. There are days we just don't want to go, but we do it for them. Inserting this perspective into any hardship instantly transforms it because so much hardship is created by implosive focus on "me." I suffer because of my nearsightedness. But if I can use my pain as a trigger to think bigger, I immediately remove or reduce the level of hardship. Injecting this view forces me out of myself and provides instant relief. I have jumped to the top and reestablished the proper view. Being self-centered is the source of much unnecessary hardship, so remove that hardship by becoming other-centered.

In practical terms, when we begin a study or practice session, set the aspiration that we will endure the rigors for the benefit of others, and at the end of the session, dedicate what we have done to others. It is a powerful irony, but doing spiritual work to benefit others is the most effective way to benefit ourselves. It is the best and perhaps only way to accelerate our progress on the path.

At the level of the Vajrayana, this principle is so important that the Vajrayana simply does not work without compassion. Trungpa Rinpoche says that having the Vajrayana without compassion is like having a modern house with every conceivable electrical gadget but no hookup. So if your practice is not working, perhaps you forgot to plug it in.

❧ No Interruption

The "top down" perspective of the three yanas also expands our sense of what constitutes spiritual practice. When we start the path and are still at the "bottom," the point of practice is to attain peace of mind. This attitude is initially healthy, but if we remain within that narrow view, then we limit ourselves and our path. We have sessions of peace in meditation, but then there is the rest of the world to deal with. Meditation is put in contrast, and perhaps even opposition, to daily life. The spiritual is set against the background of the material.

If we sustain this view, then life will interrupt our meditation. At this point we need to look up, our view is too narrow. We need to expand our practice to include the rest of our life, and the top-down model helps instill this perspective. When we are still at the "bottom," we should realize what we are doing in meditation and why, then we should take the insights from our practice and expand them into the world. We need to bring more of the world onto our path. At some point, the spiritual path is no longer held within the context of the material world, and is therefore no longer set in contrast and opposition to it.

When we reach the top and become a buddha, nothing can interrupt our meditation. But while we are still at the bottom, our meditation is always being interrupted. Every thought that pops into our mind interferes with our practice. But at the level of the Vajrayana, thought *becomes* meditation. Obstacle has been transformed into opportunity. The barking dog, annoying boss, and uncontrollable child that once cut into our spiritual life now becomes an integral part of it.

People often complain that if only they didn't have to work or raise children, or if they weren't sick, then they could really get down to spiritual practice. To get to the point where work, children, and illness are actually aids is to hold the highest view. Even though this fruition may be years away, cultivating this view transforms the way we relate to interruptions now. Take the theoretical fruition of the path and put it into immediate application. Import the view from the summit to help us see our way to it. We may not be able to relate to our annoying boss as part of our practice, but holding the view that he really is can help us stretch our mind to include him.

This view reverses our relationship to unwelcome situations.

Advanced meditators actually place themselves in difficult situations as a way to enhance their path. Instead of removing ourselves from distractions and interruptions, we place ourselves in the middle of them. We test the fortitude of our meditation in the marketplace.

This is another instance of "aspiring and entering." We may not be able to immediately apply these lofty views, but we make the aspiration. We can believe in it and do our best to implement it. If we persist in our aspiration, then one day we can enter. We "fake it till we can make it." Rhetoric becomes reality, and we find ourselves living at the levels that our aspirations paved for us.

⚘ Death as an Advisor

Several years ago I went to a dinner party with a friend. There was a rich woman there who, during the course of the evening, presented a parade of petty complaints. She griped about the weather, her maid, the economy, and an endless list of similar "hardships." She made a major career out of minor inconvenience. Despite her wealth, or perhaps because of it, she was miserable. Her life was filled with a level of self-imposed hardship that most people from the developing world would long to suffer from. At some point in the evening my friend turned to me and whispered, "This lady needs a bigger problem." The lady had no sense of perspective. Her vision was so narrow that she had no choice but to magnify the items that occupied her small world.

It is easy to see in others what we are blind to in ourselves. Many spiritual practitioners suffer from similar levels of self-imposed "hardship," where the smallest irritations inflate into the biggest problems. If the problem is loss of vision and perspective, then the solution is to reestablish that perspective. When we are having a hard time on the path because our back is hurting, or we cannot afford to go on retreat, or it's just too difficult, think about a bigger problem. To make it easy, contemplate the biggest problem and watch our petty "hardships" disappear. Think about death.

The benefits of "top-down" perspective apply not only to the end of the path but to the end of this life. We are going to die. If we can look down from that perspective, we will energize our path and erase our overblown problems. The Buddha says, "Of all footprints, it is the footprint of the elephant that is the deepest and most supreme. Of all contemplations, it is contemplation of impermanence that is the deepest and most supreme." Our problems with the economy and the weather will evaporate with one phone call that informs us that we have cancer.

Because it is so hard to accept the noble truth of death, I work with reminders throughout the day. I read an obituary in the morning paper, and touch into the lives of those destroyed by crime, natural disaster, or tragedy. I attend every funeral of friends and relatives and visit nursing homes to remind me of the harsh reality of old age and death. We do not have to look far to be reminded of the truth of impermanence—we just have to open our eyes.

My meditation table is lined with photographs of loved ones who have died, which helps me remember that one day I too will be just a photograph. I place my sacred texts on these photos. My liturgies literally rest on portraits of death. I have written the word "DEATH" on sticky notes and placed them inside drawers or cabinets. They continue to startle me because I forget I put them there, just like I forget about my impending death. These reminders are not pleasant, but they keep my life in perspective.

Have you ever wondered what transformed the prince Siddhartha into the Buddha? What is it that made the Buddha the Buddha? For his first twenty-nine years he lived the dream life. Sequestered safely in his palace, he indulged every sensory pleasure and epitomized the ideal of material success. But at age twenty-nine, over the course of several trips outside the palace walls, he was stunned to discover the reality of old age, sickness, and death. He was given a dramatic tour to the "top." With this new view of impermanence, he could no longer return to his comfort-infected life and fled the palace in search of truth.

For the next six years the prince submitted himself to the hardship of spiritual practice, which he endured because of the strength of his view. Because his vision was so big, any form of hardship became small. Of the twelve historic deeds of the Buddha, his reflections on impermanence were the sixth—the pivotal deed. It turned him from looking outside to looking inside and switched him from the worldly to the spiritual path. Death turned him into a *nangpa*, an "insider," which is the Tibetan word for "Buddhist." The Indian master Atisha says that if you don't contemplate death in the morning, the morning is wasted; if you don't contemplate death in the afternoon, the afternoon is wasted; and if you don't contemplate death in the evening, the evening is wasted.

Remember that there is no tyranny as great as the tyranny of success, and the greatest success story is that we are healthy and alive. But health is just the slowest way to die. This success breeds the most insidious of tyrannies: the illusion of immortality. We read about death in the paper, hear it on the news, and see it all around us. We are swimming in an ocean of death and still do not acknowledge it.

If we felt the cold breath of death on the back of our neck, we would practice the way Milarepa did and attain his enlightenment:

> Fearing death, I went to the mountains.
> Over and over again I meditated on death's unpredictable
>   coming,
> And took the stronghold of the deathless unchanging
>   nature.
> Now I am completely beyond all fear of dying![57]

In the Hindu epic Mahabharata, the sage Yudhisthira is asked, "Of all things in life, what is the most amazing?" Yudhisthira answers, "That a man, seeing others die all around him, never thinks he will die." Over 250,000 people will die today. In the course of reading this one paragraph, 50 more will be dead. We look at death as if we are looking through the wrong end of a set of binoculars—it is a lot closer than we think. Death is but one breath away—breathe out, don't breathe in, and we are dead.

I belabor these teachings because alone the uncompromising

perspective of death, without recourse to any other remedy, can remove more hardship than anything else. I have heard masters say that when we finally acknowledge impermanence and develop true renunciation, 50 percent of the path to enlightenment is complete. Trungpa Rinpoche says that until we contemplate death, spiritual practice is dilettantish. Hardship melts in the lens of death, and what remains is seen in an entirely different light.

❧ Painful Peers

In the early stages of the path, if our friends and family do not understand what we are doing, we can expect some challenges. We might be accused of neglecting our responsibilities, having joined a cult, or being self-indulgent with our time in retreat. Do not let yourself be swayed by the forces of the world that are designed to make you move. Hold your seat, keep your perspective, and look upon those comments with compassion.

Our culture is well suited to help us attain the developmental norm, but ill prepared to help us grow beyond it. As a child, Western society grabs us by the back of the collar and lifts us into its collective consciousness. This accelerates our evolution up to a point. The worldly path is well paved, easy to travel, and full of temporary benefits. But if we want to grow beyond the status quo and switch to a spiritual path, then the power of our culture will be just as effective in retarding our evolution. Society grabs us by the collar again and holds us back. If we want to grow beyond it, we are often on our own.

From a spiritual perspective, the collective consciousness is actually the collective unconsciousness. This world is asleep, and waking up from this massive slumber party is a solitary and difficult venture. In some depictions of the Buddha's life, he is seen walking out of the palace where he had spent his first twenty-nine years, tiptoeing between sleeping men and women, some of them half-naked and drooling. He walked out of that orgy of narcolepsy, the sleep of samsara, alone—and the only one awake.

Eastern cultures can be more conducive to spiritual growth. The

Dalai Lama has said that in the East, even if one is not a practitioner, the culture pulls one toward the dharma, but that in the West, even if one is a practitioner, the culture pulls one away. This does not mean we should pack up and move to India. I have been to India many times, and it presents its own set of spiritual challenges. What it does mean is that we should be aware of what we are up against in the West and the incredible power of our culture to seduce us into its materialistic fold.

Joseph Campbell reported that during the Nazi rallies in Germany, Jews would be forced to attend in order to swell the ranks. Many of these Jews would later admit being swept away by Hitler's collective hysteria and found themselves needing to resist the urge to join their "peers" in crying out "Heil Hitler!"

Peer pressure often forces difficult choices for spiritual practitioners. Do we want people in our life that will lift us up, or drag us down? Well-intentioned friends and family present obstacles as they express their concern, or even outrage, at our unusual path. They just do not get it, and they can keep us from getting it because of their field of influence. The contemporary Sufi Jamal Rahman says that we should choose friends, the sight of whom reminds us of God.

Peer pressure is a powerful factor in the loss of spiritual insight. We make progress along the path only to relapse when we hang out with friends that don't share it, for directly or indirectly, consciously or unconsciously, they pull us back. The temptation to revert to familiar and comfortable habits is overwhelming. It is always easier to revert to established ways of being than it is to move into uncharted territory. This type of recidivism is especially evident after coming out of retreat. We can attain profound states of realization in retreat, but they are often fragile, disappearing within weeks—especially if we hang out with the wrong crowd.

Just like an ex-convict relapses into criminal behavior when he meets his criminal buddies, so too are we prone to being pulled back into habitual preretreat patterns when we reenter society and associate with old friends. Acknowledging the influence of an ego-based culture and the people in our life still embedded within it is not easy. If our friends are holding us back, we may need to cut those anchors; if our society is retarding our growth, we need to switch our allegiance.

I feel this tug every time I come out of retreat. When I am sequestered safely in my retreat cabin, I sometimes feel like I am indestructible. My insights seem so sturdy, and my resolve to lead a new life based on kindness and compassion seems unwavering. But when I come out of the sanctuary of retreat, I slowly succumb to the temptations of the world. My small and petty mind gradually returns. This has happened so often, and so predictably, that instead of beating myself up about it, I now recognize when I get swept away and try to remove those situations—and people—that keep pulling me away. I also realize the importance of everyday practice, my short daily retreats, in helping me stay out of the prison of samsara.

These painful minideaths, letting go of situations and people that pull us back, can be softened by putting them in the proper perspective. We let go to grow. The Buddha left his palace, even his loving wife and child, to find truth in retreat. But after finding the truth he returned to the world and brought the truth with him. His wife and son became his students. His perspective was so vast that he could reenter any nefarious environment and transform it. Instead of being pulled down into the confused fold, he was able to pull the fold up. Absolute power, remember, is when the world no longer has power over you, and this power is cultivated with the right perspective. When we change our attitude and view, we can change everything.

This is where pockets of spiritual culture, communities of like-minded practitioners, can help. It is like having a touch of India in the midst of Manhattan. Genuine spiritual communities are sane asylums, sanctuaries for growth beyond the ego. We can take refuge in them and let their vision lift us up.

Part II

THE SECOND TURNING

One hammer blow after another is usually needed
to destroy the sense of duality.
— RAMESH S. BALSEKAR, A Net of Jewels

WITH THE GROUND of the First Turning beneath our feet we can now progress into the more refined Second Turning and some of the challenges that accompany it. The central message of the Second Turning is that there is no ground beneath our feet. The Second Turning is about discovering that nothing is solid, lasting, and independent. Things do appear, but there is no essence to that appearance. In blunt terms: nothing truly exists; the world is like a dream.

With the First Turning we take reality apart and dissolve our sense of unity and solidity. But we still believe that the parts are real. It is too shocking and unbelievable to proclaim that nothing exists, so the First Turning warms us up to this truth by showing us that things are not as solid as we might think. Once we have broken reality into pieces, it becomes easier to melt those pieces into emptiness.

Emptiness is the heart of the Second Turning, and it is a shocking doctrine. The key to the Second Turning is its proper delivery. If the timing is perfect, it will stun you, shatter the ego, and give birth to profound insight. If it is taught too early, it won't be understood; if it's taught too late, it has no impact. But when properly timed and taught, the effect of this teaching is devastating. For the ego, it is death.

Emptiness may be deadly to the ego, but it brings life to the spirit. From the ashes of selflessness is born the warmth of compassion. So while the Second Turning has a cutting edge, that edge is designed to expose a tender beating heart.

9 🍃

The Pain of Letting Go

When the barriers come down, we don't know what to do.
We need a bit more warning about what it feels like when the walls
start tumbling down. We need to be told that fear and trembling
accompany growing up and that letting go takes courage.
—PEMA CHÖDRÖN, The Places That Scare You

What we are letting go of often seems to be "us," who and what
we think we are, and it does often feel as if we are falling apart,
disintegrating, dying, or even going crazy. . . . it is important
to realize that this is ultimately not a negative or destructive process.
For, in letting go of all our identity fixations, we become able
to touch the utter freedom that lies within us.
—REGINALD RAY, Touching Enlightenment

A LOT OF unnecessary hardship stems from our inability to let go. We are attached to the things of our life, to our possessions, our bodies, opinions, and thoughts. The samsaric mind is made of Velcro—it sticks to everything. These attachments keep us from progressing and actually constitute the Buddha's second Noble Truth. In other words, the truth of the origin of suffering can be reduced to one word: attachment. And the fourth Noble Truth, that of the path leading to the cessation of suffering, can be funneled into two words: let go.

Attachment is therefore a major obstacle, and it is a form of desire. Desire comes in two primary forms, active and passive. Active desire is easily recognized: it is wanting something we do not have. Passive, or frozen, desire is not so easily recognized: it is sustained desire for something we already have. Passive desire is attachment and is often detected only when something is taken away from us. When we are forced to let go, then attachment is recognized because it is felt. It hurts. But in order to be free, we must let go of everything that keeps us pinned to the ground. Every thread of attachment must be cut, and that spiritual cut is deep and painful. It is the necessary blade of the Second Turning. And it is a form of death.

Buddhism describes the process of death and dying in precise detail. What happens during death is just a concentrated version of what happens along the path, and by becoming familiar with this process, we can apply its teachings on the path. Physical death can occur quickly, spiritual (ego) death takes more time, but the process is similar, and understanding it helps us relate to hardship—and why we need to "die." Strictly speaking, the vast literature on Tibetan thanatology (the study of death) is not specifically associated with any of the Three Turnings, but a big part of the spirit of the Second Turning is about dying, in the broadest sense of that term, and the Third Turning is about becoming "born again," coming back fully into life after the ego's death. Goethe talks about the spiritual long-ing to die and be reborn in his poem "The Holy Longing":

> Tell a wise person, or else keep silent,
> because the massman will mock it right away.
> I praise what is truly alive,
> what longs to be burned to death.
>
> In the calm water of the love-nights,
> where you were begotten, where you have begotten,
> a strange feeling comes over you
> when you see the silent candle burning.

Now you are no longer caught
in the obsession with darkness,
and a desire for higher love-making
sweeps you upward.

Distance does not make you falter,
now, arriving in magic, flying,
and, finally, insane for the light,
you are the butterfly and you are gone.

And so long as you haven't experienced
this: to die and so to grow,
you are only a troubled guest
on the dark earth.[58]

According to Buddhism, the moment of death is a grand opportunity for enlightenment. If we approach death with the right understanding, it can be transformed into the most liberating opportunity. We will attain complete awakening. If we don't, death remains one of the most dreaded and painful events of life. But before we reach this holy grail, we often have to go through holy hell. We have to let go of everything—the ego has to die.

Spiritual liberation, during life or at the moment of death, demands dying to everything we have, and everything we think we are. This process is called "the painful *bardo* of dying." "Bardo" means "gap, in between, or interval" and refers to the gap between two states, in this case the state of life and the state of death. The painful bardo of dying is painful because it hurts to let go. And letting go is just a euphemism for dying. The poet Kabir writes,

What we call salvation belongs to the time before death.
If you don't break your ropes while you are alive
Do you think ghosts will do it for you afterward? . . .
What is found now is found then.[59]

During the painful bardo of dying at the end of this life, we will go through a process of forceful release. It is forceful because it is choiceless. We have to let go whether we like it or not. The Tibetans describe eight stages of letting go, progressing from gross to subtle. In the first five stages we let go of every aspect of our body. We lose our sense of sight, sound, smell, taste, and touch, going from the most distant to the most intimate sense (sight is the farthest sense, touch is the nearest). We have already let go of our possessions, friends and family. Now we are letting go of our body. We are losing everything.

At the end of stage five, our body is gone. Our breath stops, and from a clinical stance we are dead. But this is only the end of the "outer dissolution." We have lost our body, now we are about to lose our mind. The final three stages of the "inner dissolution" strip away every aspect of our mental world. From gross to subtle, we die to every form of thought and emotion. By the end of the inner dissolution, we have been forced to let go of everything we thought we had, and everything we thought we were. This process is described in great detail, well beyond our scope, but it points to one brutal truth: dying hurts because it forces us to let go of everything we can even think of.

But when we finally do let go completely, liberation dawns. In eight painful stages, the ego has been ripped to shreds. We have become nothing, and at that instant enlightenment shines forth. This is one fruit of the Second Turning.

For most of us the precious opportunity at the moment of death flashes by unrecognized. Because we have not practiced dying while still alive—because we have not cut our attachments—we do not recognize the enlightenment of death. We pass out into deep unconsciousness. Then we wake up into a dreamlike after-death state where the first thing we do is grasp. We find ourselves floating in a disembodied state and panic at the lack of ground. To reestablish ground we again attach ourselves to the objects of perception, and therefore begin our bondage into suffering. This postdeath bardo is called the "karmic bardo of becoming." We become something again.

As we headed into death/enlightenment, we were forced to release all attachment, and as we head away from enlightenment and into our next rebirth, our fear drives us to reattach to new mental and physical forms. Fear ignites the process of rebirth altogether, which takes place not only in the postdeath bardos but in life itself. We grasp in life like we grasp during death, attaching ourselves to subtle and gross forms.

Enlightenment demands letting go till it kills us, giving up and giving in till the ego dies. When there is nothing left to give, only then will we finally get. But who wants to die? Who is willing to pay this price? The death of the ego is the fine print in any genuine spiritual contract, and we gloss over it when we sign onto the path. Then we wonder why it hurts. We first ask for it, then complain when we receive it.

Spiritual masters, on the other hand, glide through the bardo of dying and gracefully settle into the enlightened state at the end of the inner dissolution. It is not painful. They are not attached to anything, so the bardo of dying—the bardo of letting go—is easy. They have already "died" and face the bardo of letting go without fear. When the Gyalwang Karmapa, an enlightened being, was dying, he said to one disciple, "Nothing happens."

❧ Offerings

The necessity of letting go is one reason why offering is stressed in spiritual practice. In Buddhism, offerings are a central ritual. Every shrine has a row of offerings, we enter and leave a shrine room by offering a bow, we offer incense to open the shrine, we offer tea to the protector principle, we offer the merit of our meditation and study, we offer music, mudras (sacred gestures), tormas (offering cakes), and mandalas (symbols of the universe). The Buddha discovered that giving is one of the best ways to practice letting go.

Generosity is the first of the six paramitas, the six transcendent actions of a bodhisattva, or buddha-in-training. In one sutra it is said that "generosity is the virtue that produces peace." By making offerings to shrines and deities, we are being taught how to give. The shrines and deities couldn't care less, they do not need our offerings. But we do. When we can give without reservation and offer that which means the most to us without pain or regret, then we have mastered the practice of offering and we will live—and die—with ease.

At more advanced stages, offering takes on the form of sacrifice, which means to "make holy," to make whole. This is a wonderful etymology for it implies that the only way to become whole is to give. The way to feel full is to empty; the way to live is to "die." We can feel this when we give to others wholeheartedly, for it is then that we feel the most complete. It is heart-warming, and paradoxically fulfilling, to give.

If the giving generates hardship, then offering takes on the painful connotation of sacrifice. But by knowing that our sacrifice is needed to make us whole, that we are actually going through a form of the painful bardo of dying now, we are better equipped to handle the hardship. By viewing our pain as an offering, we can reverse our attitude to the necessary sacrifices along the path to wholeness.

When I was in the third year of my retreat, I finally understood the power of offering. After practicing for five months in the privacy of our rooms, we came together for several months of group practice. I dreaded these events, preferring the solitude of my room. In this particular group practice, we had to create an elaborate shrine lined with hundreds of offerings that needed to be replaced daily. It was a major pain. We had to prepare all these offerings in our spare time, get up early to set them out, and stay late to take them down.

In addition to the extensive material offerings, the practice included the offering of endless music, mantras, and mudras. I got so bored and irritated with all these offerings that I started to count how many times we had to give every day but stopped after I reached one thousand. I clearly wasn't getting the spirit of giving.

One day, about half way through the two-month event, I was in the leader's position guiding the practice for the day. I had the bird's-eye seat and was looking at this ornate display of offering. Hundreds of lights, candles, offering bowls, and tormas were spread out before me. It had been raining gently all day, and as I listened to the steady stream of water and surveyed the offerings in front of me, I finally got it.

The rain of blessings is constantly falling, but in order to receive these blessings, we have to open up and create the proper container to hold this magic. In order to do that, we have to completely let go, and the offerings were "forcing" us to do so. It's as if the circuit has to be complete in order for the blessings to enter, and the only way that can happen is to give. By offering, the flow can be established, and the blessings can finally enter. Blessings don't flow into us. They flow through us.

At that moment I realized how "constipated" I had been. The blessings couldn't enter me because I wasn't allowing them to flow through me. To open the circuit and let the magic circulate, I had to give, and that is exactly what these endless offerings were trying to show me. It was the perfect paradox. The only way to hold the blessings was to allow them to flow through me, and my offerings initiated the flow.

My relationship to offering was completely transformed, and my resistance was replaced with delight. Instead of rushing through the creation of my countless tormas, I slowed down and made them with joy. I have since tried to view every day, and even my life, as an offering. Not in any self-aggrandizing way, or like I have anything special to offer, but I can offer who I am and allow others to receive or reject my gifts. I offer without expecting anything in return and for the delight of touching into the spirit of that rainy day.

🌱 Final Exam

The painful bardo of dying is like a spiritual final exam. If we travel the path properly and let go of our attachments, if we die before we die, then we will pass this rugged test and death will lead to enlightenment. But if we cannot die before we die, then we will fail this final exam with regret. We will grasp frantically as everything we know and love dissolves. Instead of diving into the waters of enlightenment, we will drown. Psychiatrist R. D. Laing famously said that the mystic swims in the same ocean where the psychotic drowns. We may not be psychotic, but we will go down as one if we don't prepare for the deep waters of death.

Death, of course, is not a designed test, and this is not meant to be a fire and brimstone preaching. But death is a condensation of the path, and by understanding its process and the liberation that can result, we understand what needs to be done while we are still alive and what awaits us if we don't. The spiritual path is death in slow motion. When literal death finally comes we are either prepared or we are not.

One way or the other it is going to hurt. That is why it is called the painful bardo of dying. It either hurts now, when we can control it to some degree and let go on our terms, or it hurts later when we have no control and have to deal with death's nonnegotiable terms.

Like the uncompromising truth of the laws of nature, this is a noble truth because it describes reality. It is like gravity. We cannot argue with it, bargain with it, or deny it. The hardships of death and the spiritual path are just the hardships of truth, and the level of hardship for both is directly proportional to the level of our attachment and our resistance to this noble truth.

This is why the death of a loved one or the loss of a cherished object is so painful. This is why getting the news that we have a terminal disease is so shocking. These events expose our level of attachment. Death, or its harbingers, is a litmus test for how deeply we believe in the existence of things and points to the necessity for understanding the emptiness of those things.

☘ Meditation as Dying

For a meditator, the process of dying sounds familiar. As sensory stimulation is progressively removed, the dying person is increasingly forced to relate to his or her mind. The physical world is disappearing, and sensory distraction evaporates. The inner world comes alive as the outer world dies. By the end of the outer dissolution, the outer world is gone. Mind has become reality. The dying person is forced to relate to his or her mind simply because there is nothing else to relate to. We are being forced to become a nangpa, an "insider."

This is exactly what happens in meditation. In classical sitting meditation, the body is held dead still, environmental input is reduced, and mental states become more vivid. The inner world gets louder as the outer world gets quieter. It's like what happens when we go to sleep. Turn off the lights, turn down the senses, and watch your mind turn on. The only difference is that with meditation we want to wake up. This is why people complain that meditation seems to create more thoughts when in fact the meditator is simply more aware of them.

Meditation is about establishing a proper relationship to our mind, and that relationship is emphatically introduced by curtailing physical activity. We are "forcing" ourselves to relate to our mind. In advanced stages of formless meditation, we can even progress through a simulation of the inner dissolution. We have already disidentified with the outer world and the physical body (just like with the outer dissolution); we now learn how to disidentify with even the inner world.

The Indian sage Ramana Maharshi fashioned his entire teaching around the question, "Who am I?" If we truly ask ourselves this question, the answers will lead us directly to enlightenment. When the Buddha did this from a First Turning perspective, his answer was the five skandhas, which we will explore later in the book. But let's keep it simple and reduce the Buddha's answer to the following.

If I try to answer this question, I may initially think that I am my body. It is the most obvious form of "me." But then I realize that I speak in terms of "my" body. If it is "mine," it can't be me. "My" and "mine" are things I possess. "Me" must be something more refined.

So then I look within to more subtle forms of "me," and conclude that I must be my thoughts and emotions. But then again I realize that if it is "my" thoughts and "my" emotions, it can't be me. These forms may be more refined than the body, but thoughts and emotions are still something "I" possess. "I" am more refined than even these relatively formless thoughts and emotions.

With meditation I can gradually descend into formless awareness—who I really am. I die to all gross and subtle forms and drop into the state of egolessness-emptiness.

Through these progressive stages of disidentification I reach the punch line. I discover that by dying to everything, something still remains. This something is not a thing nor a form, but the formless awareness that lies "beneath" all things, the empty essence of all form. And because it lies beneath all existence, this formless awareness cannot die. It is immortal, eternal, and it is who I really am. But we are getting ahead of ourselves, for these are the issues of part 3.

This view allows us to endure the necessary deaths along the path because now we know where we are going. We know that on the other side of death, and at the end of the path, is deathless, formless awareness. But "you" won't be there to enjoy it, because egolessness means the death of the ego. Even with the proper view, this death still hurts, but now we can better endure it. It gives us something to look forward to and allows us to transcend fear.

From this perspective, death is a forced meditation, a crash course in disidentification and letting go. This is why meditation is a rehearsal for death. By meditating and dying now, we learn how to let go and relate to our mind on our terms. Now we have the choice and can practice a gradual spiritual death. But when we physically die, "meditation" becomes choiceless. We are forced to let go in a bang. We are forced to relate to our mind and to disidentify with all form on reality's terms.

❧ The Heightening of Samsara

In the painful bardo of dying, the outer dissolution consists of the elements dissolving into each other. Earth dissolves into water, which dissolves into fire, which dissolves into wind, which eventually dissolves into space. These "elements" are associated with certain qualities and are both literal and metaphorical.

It is taught that just before one element dissolves into the next, it is heightened. When earth is about to dissolve into water, earth is exaggerated. We feel heavy, as if a ton of bricks was sitting on our chest. When water dissolves into fire, we feel like we are being swept away by a flood. When fire dissolves into wind, we feel hot, and when wind dissolves into space, we feel like we are being blown away, and then finally blown out.

In the same fashion, just before samsara itself is about to die, it spikes. Samsara becomes heightened, and everything seems to get worse. Perhaps there are more emotional upheavals than before and more chaos. In my experience, the pimple gets juicy right before it pops.

Khenpo Karthar says that for a person who is nearing enlightenment, it is like the word getting out that someone with a lot of debt is leaving town. All the lenders come calling. The creditors are our karmic debts, and they do need to be settled before we make our final exit from samsara. Karma spikes just before it is exhausted. With this understanding, that spike won't hurt as much.

10 🌿

Fear Is the Fare

I understood this thing called self [ego]: it is man's defense against
seeing absolute nothingness. . . . Somehow I knew that with the birth
of fear, self would spring alive with all its weaponry, for it was now
obvious that fear—the mother of all inventions—was the core around
which the self was built and upon which its life so depended
that self and fear were here, all but indistinguishable.
—BERNADETTE ROBERTS, The Experience of No-Self

The time has come to recognize that negative circumstances
can be transformed into spiritual power and attainment. . . .
Utilize adversities and obstacles as the path!
—PADMASAMBHAVA

THE BARDO TEACHINGS provide guidelines for how to approach hardship on the path, and they also help us work with fear. By relating to fear properly, we can accelerate our journey and discover that fear is not a sign of regress but one of progress. Without this understanding, fear becomes a big "STOP" sign, or a "Do Not Enter" sign. With understanding, fear is transformed into a welcome mat to growth.

What is fear and why does it have such power? How does it control our lives? Ignorance is the common ingredient behind fear. We are afraid of the unknown. We are anxious about a job interview because we don't know how it will go. We are nervous about a blind date or a speaking engagement, an operation or a big trip, retirement or a job loss because we do not know what will happen. We are phobic of gays, lesbians, Muslims, or Rastafarians because we do not know them. Whether it is the butterflies in the belly of a child giving a piano recital, or the panic of someone on his or her death bed, we are afraid of the many faces of darkness.

The level of fear is directly proportional to the level of ignorance. If we are not sure about our blind date, that level of ignorance gives birth to mere anxiety. If we are clueless about death, that level of ignorance gives birth to abject terror. The more we know, the less we fear. If ignorance is correlative with fear, then knowledge is correlative with fearlessness. Learn about gays and lesbians and you will not fear them, learn about death and you will not fear it. Learn about fear itself and become fearless.

Becoming fear*less* is a slight misnomer. We do not attain fearlessness by getting rid of fear but by going through and beyond it. "Fear" is linked to roots that mean "go through" and "fare": fear is the fare that must be paid if we want to grow.

To grow beyond the ego, we must die to it. We are afraid of this death, as we are of any, because we do not know what happens after egoic death. But we can learn. The crucifixion and resurrection of Christ is symbolic of this kind of death and represents transpersonal evolution—evolution that transcends the persona (ego). Jesus crucified his ego before he resurrected into a deathless transpersonal state. A. H. Almaas writes,

> Transformation . . . means letting go of part of one's identity, and this surrendering can be experienced as a dissolution, a disintegration, a fragmentation, or a sense that you are falling apart. This juncture can be very painful or frightening because the old sense of your identity is crumbling and falling away and you don't know what—if anything— will take its place. What you've held on to has felt real to you, and now you're letting it go and heading into what

feels like unknown and uncharted territory. It feels like jumping into an abyss and it can be terrifying.[60]

As we progress along the path and start to touch into egolessness, the emptiness-death of the self, the weaponry of the ego springs up in ultimate self-defense. A principal weapon is fear. When the realization that we don't really exist begins to dawn, the ego scrambles its defenses to keep us from this realization. Fear is therefore the mood of the self-contraction and is why the contraction occurs in the first place. In its active form, fear manifests as panic when the self evaporates; in its passive form, fear diverts us from the path through laziness and distraction. In either case, fear is fiercely effective in keeping us from growing up.

When Freud was a young doctor he traveled to France to witness a demonstration of hypnosis. What he witnessed changed the course of Western psychology. A subject was placed under hypnosis and then told that upon receiving a certain signal, he would pick up an umbrella and open it over his head. Sure enough, when the signal was received, he found his umbrella and opened it over his head. Freud was impressed. But what stunned him and helped formulate his work on the power of the unconscious was what happened next. When the subject was asked why he did what he did, he came up with the most rational explanations for his irrational behavior, when in fact he had no idea why he was performing this act.

In the same fashion, we have given ourselves the hypnotic suggestion to avoid fear at all costs. It's as if the ego is constantly whispering to our subconscious mind to do whatever it takes to avoid the painful truth of our nonexistence. Like the hypnotized man, we spend our lives opening umbrellas, doing all kinds of irrational things without any deep understanding of why we are doing them. We mostly follow the herd, a herd that is heading toward a cliff, and just do what others do. But deep inside we are clueless about the springs of most of our actions.

"Buddha," the awakened one, can be translated here as the dehyp-

notized one. Waking up along the path is waking up to the unconscious seeds that drive every action and acknowledging the fear that
moves us. It is waking up to the truth, which from the ego's perspective is not pleasant.

❦ Fear and Growth

We can avoid all kinds of difficulty by realizing that growth beyond
the ego means to transcend but include the ego. This transcendence
may feel like death, but it is merely growing pain. Egoic death means
that we have to die to this arrested level of development.

When we grow from five feet tall to five feet one inch, we do not
"kill" five feet. We transcend but include five feet. When we grow to
age twenty, we do not "kill" age nineteen, we transcend but include
it. Similarly, when we grow from ego to buddha, we do not kill the
ego, we transcend but include the ego. Because the ego is included,
we always have access to it, just as we always have access to five feet.
We may stoop to that view in order to see eye-to-eye and communicate with others who remain at five feet, but we no longer live at
that level. We have outgrown it. The view is so much better that
dropping back down to five feet does not make sense. Buddhas stoop
to our level in order to talk to us, the same way we stoop to communicate with a two-year-old, but living like a two-year-old is silly
for an adult. After bending down and meeting us eye-to-eye, spiritual
masters gradually stand back up and take us with them, lifting us into
their transcendent view.

Without this perspective, transcendence does not look inclusive to
the ego's eye. It looks exclusive. It looks like death. But with the view
of "transcend but include," we can transform fear into fearlessness.
Instead of the darkness that surrounds death, we are now equipped
with the view that sheds light on the other side. Now we know that
the view is even better on the other side of the ego. It is a much
higher view.

So instead of that STOP sign that once popped up with fear, fear is now a sign that says "come this way for growth." Not only can fear be a good sign, it is also one of the clearest indicators of where we need to go to wake up.

Fear for our biological survival may have evolved to ignite a "fight or flight" response to life-threatening situations, but this knee-jerk response should be left in the material domain. By habitually transposing this material response to frightening spiritual situations, we short-circuit the opportunity for growth. We confuse genuine life-threatening situations with ego-threatening opportunities, and therefore run away from, or fight, that which we should run into and embrace. In order to grow, we should walk directly into what we fear instead of away from it.

If you are wondering where you should go on your path, look into those areas that scare you and you will find your next step. Do the opposite of what you normally do, of what the ego wants to do. That darkness is actually a spiritual beacon directing you forward, like a lighthouse pointing the way to a safe spiritual harbor.

It may not be safe to your ego, but the darkness is pointing toward a refuge for your spirit. It does so because darkness is the cover for ignorance, and enlightenment demands its illumination. Every dark corner of your world must be brought into light, ignorance must be transformed into wisdom. We have to walk into the dark and flip the switch.

❧ Ignorance

Ignorance is the final and most notorious obstacle to awakening. This is not merely academic ignorance, not knowing about something intellectually. Our concern is with ignorance so deep and subtle that we do not even know that we do not know. We think we are awake, but we are sleepwalking. To even begin to relate to this ignorance properly, we first have to find it, and the only way to do that is to walk into the shadows of our life—the darkness and fear that are the minions of ignorance.

The Buddha taught about *klesha*, which is the Sanskrit word for emotional upheaval, or poison. There are three root poisons in Buddhism, going from gross to subtle: aggression, passion, and ignorance. Students will often talk about having a "klesha attack," which is being in the midst of an uncontrollable emotion. I can always identify when I am having a klesha attack of passion or aggression, but I have never been able to say, "I'm having an ignorance attack." This is an irony because I am constantly under the attack of ignorance.

If I see the world as being separate from me, that is evidence that I am under attack. If I see your suffering as separate from mine, I am under attack. Ignorance may be insidious, but it is not passive. It is the most active force in samsara. With the fury of a nuclear warhead, it is constantly ripping reality into self and other, leaving endless suffering in its wake. The irony is that we just can't see it. It is too close.

During the night of the Buddha's enlightenment, he discovered twelve links (*nidanas*) that chain us to samsaric existence. The first of these links is ignorance, which is depicted by a blind grandmother. Ignorance, by definition, does not see.

Because ignorance is so slippery, we cannot face it head on. So we have to understand that fear is the active expression of this "passive" force. For a spiritual practitioner, therefore, fear is a gift. It will always tell us where we need to go to unearth the next layer of ignorance. Buddhas have no fear because they have no ignorance, but they only got to be fearless by working directly with their fear and exposing its underlying cause. They transformed darkness into light by plunging fearlessly into the dark.

Like everyone else, I tend to run from my fear. But when I have summoned the courage to plunge into it, to use fear as an invitation, the rewards have far surpassed the "toll." When I first thought about entering my long retreat, I felt a rush of exhilaration that was rapidly replaced with wrenching fear. It took me eight years to gather the courage and prepare, but I followed the black light of fear. I used it as my trustworthy guide, and it led to real growth. It is a lot easier to "follow your bliss" than it is to "follow your fear," but fear keeps us directly on the path while bliss can easily divert us.

Spiritual traditions are often called warrior traditions. Trungpa Rinpoche taught about the "sacred path of the warrior," and Don Juan spoke volumes on spiritual warriorship. In Tibetan, meditators are called "brave ones." The inner meaning of jihad, or holy war, refers to engaging the real enemy of ignorance. This is greater jihad, the warfare in oneself against evil and temptation. (Lesser jihad is the defense of Islam against aggression.) It takes courage to face our mind and the fear that harbors ignorance.

I continue to use this unusual rule, "follow your fear," but I do so in moderation. The point isn't spiritual thrill-seeking. If we jump recklessly into any fearful situation, our motivation may be twisted, and we may be ill prepared to handle the consequences. The path is always the middle path, and Joseph Campbell's advice to "follow your bliss" is well taken. Having the courage to follow our bliss is also difficult, and we will return to this challenge in part 3. But if we only follow our bliss, we can get blissed out, and if we only follow our fear, we just get freaked out. Our journey works with the extreme path to the middle, which suggests that we pay more attention to fear as an invitation for growth.

❧ Fear of the Light

The *Tibetan Book of the Dead,* which is a principal source of the bardo teachings, shows us how to work not only with death but with any difficult situation. This text is a book on life disguised as a treatise about death. It is as if the authors realized that its teachings are too intense for the living, so they softened the impact by directing the message toward the dead. Death is so intense that it is easier to see how these teachings can be applied then—to those who really need such uncompromising guidance. But repeated readings of the *Tibetan Book of the Dead* exposes its skillful design. It is the consummate guidebook for how to live.

The book describes that in the afterlife a brilliant light will come to us. The instruction is to stay with the bright light, do not look away. This is difficult, for not only is the light intense, but softer and more seductive lights appear at the same time. There is a strong temptation to drift toward the softer lights. According to the *Tibetan Book of the Dead*, staying with the bright light is the key to liberation. If we stray into the softer lights, we stray off the path.

The book then goes on to describe the consequences in the after-death state of staying with the bright light or being seduced into the softer lights. These teachings apply to life in the following way. The bright light represents any challenge to growth. It symbolizes unfamiliar territory, blazing with potential, but intimidating in intensity. The light is an invitation laced with hazard. It also represents hard truths we do not want to look at, the uncompromising face of reality.

The soft lights, on the other hand, represent the comfortable and habitual, that which is easy and predictable. They seduce us with the sense of safety and familiarity. We drift into the soft lights whenever we soften situations by telling white lies, beat around the bush, or say what people want to hear. The bright light symbolizes where we need to go; the soft lights symbolize where we want to go.

The path is designed to push us past our comfort zone and stretch us beyond the soft lights, so it constantly presents challenging bright light situations. If we accept the challenge, the light leads to magic. Trungpa Rinpoche says,

> The point at which we can either extend ourselves further and go towards an unfamiliar brilliance, or return to a more soothing and familiar dimness is the threshold of magic. It is very personal. We feel pushed, hassled, and exposed through our practice. All kinds of irritations and all kinds of boundaries begin to come up, and we would like to stay within our territory, within those boundaries. We don't really want to step beyond them. . . . we fear that we might destroy ourselves if we go beyond the territory of survival. Such boundaries or thresholds always come up, and we really do not want to push anymore. But some kind of push is necessary. We might say, "Well, we have given our income and our possessions to the church. We have

committed ourselves. We have signed our names on the dotted line. We pay our dues. We subscribe to your magazine. We do everything." But there is still something left behind. We are still missing the point. Those commitments are very easy to make. At this point, it is a question of giving up our arms and our legs. Even that might be easy to do. We can give up our hair, we can give up our beard, we can take off our clothes. But we have no idea, none whatsoever, how to give up our heart and brain. Once we give up our heart and brain, the magic begins.[61]

When we cross from the worldly to the spiritual path, we cross the first threshold. We have discovered the inadequacy of the soft lights in our life and taken our first step into the bright light. This is just the first threshold. The spiritual path presents many thresholds because it presents opportunities to grow. Rinpoche continues,

We find ourselves on a threshold, and at that point, we can, in fact, push ourselves one step further. That threshold occurs when we think we have gone too far in extending ourselves to the world. There is some kind of warning, and at the same time a faint invitation takes place. Quite possibly, we chicken out at that point because it requires so much effort and energy to go further. We feel we have put in enough effort and energy already, and we don't want to go beyond that. So-called sensible people wouldn't take such a risk: "Oh no! We have gone far enough; we mustn't go too far. Let's step back."[62]

The metaphor of bright light is not to be taken too literally, for it is often darkness that presents the brightest of lights. Not knowing what will happen if we cross a threshold, or facing the unfamiliar, are all bright light encounters. It is the sense of the unknown and the intimidating, tinged with invitation and opportunity, that constitutes a bright light encounter. Bright lights simultaneously point out the way to go and suggest the hardship in getting there. They are both illuminating and blinding.

Stated in exaggerated terms to emphasize the point, the bright and soft lights of the *Tibetan Book of the Dead* deliver this message: the worldly path is relatively easy along the way but full of hardship at the end; the spiritual path is full of hardship along the way, but easy at the end. A complete worldly path is full of comfort and familiarity, the known and predictable, the soft and simple. Although it has its painful moments, it is the easy life. Until the end. Then the dream of material life transforms into the nightmare it really is. Everything material falls apart, we lose all that we know and love, and with great suffering we are forced to die.

A complete spiritual path, on the other hand, is full of discomfort and unfamiliarity, the unknown and unpredictable, the rugged and difficult. Although it has its blissful moments, it is the hard life. Until the end. Then the nightmare of spiritual life transforms into the dream that it really is. Everything spiritual comes together, we gain everything we know and love, and with great peace we are liberated into eternal life. In Gustav Mahler's monumental *Resurrection* symphony, the finale sings wrenchingly of this spiritual transformation:

> O Pain, piercer of all things,
> From thee have I been wrested!
> O Death, thou master of all things,
> Now art thou mastered!
> With wings which I have won for myself,
> In love's fierce striving,
> I shall soar upwards
> To the light to which no eye has penetrated!
> I shall die in order to live![63]

This view transforms our relationship to hardship and the necessary deaths on the path. The path is supposed to be hard now so that it will be easier later. Abraham a Sancta Clara, a Christian mystic, summarized the point of these last two chapters when he said: "He who dies before he dies, does not die when he dies."[64]

11 🌱

Spiritual Detox

I felt that [Trungpa Rinpoche's] approach, how he worked
with himself and with others in retreat, was the spiritual equivalent
of the tough [dressage] training that I went through in Vienna.
He was creating an uncomfortable space for himself and other people,
an almost ruthless space where you constantly felt groundless—
you have the ground pulled out from under you. . . .
This process is very, very uncomfortable.
—DIANA J. MUKPO, Dragon Thunder

THROUGHOUT THIS BOOK we have discussed a number of metaphors for the spiritual path: it's a path of waking up, thawing out, dehypnosis, or coming out of anesthesia. They all imply a process of reversal and suggest levels of discomfort we are familiar with. Perhaps the most potent metaphor, one that is more literal than metaphorical, is that the path is one of detoxification. Unless we are a recovering substance abuser, we may not be familiar with the process of detoxification, which is why we struggle to understand the difficulties of the path. But we are going through detox on the path and knowing so can help us accept that painful process.

With conventional addiction it is relatively easy to see how we are addicted, and therefore to understand the process of detoxification. If we are a drug addict or an alcoholic, sooner or later, through our own honest admission or the pointing out of others, we can come to the painful conclusion that we are hooked. There is some level of contrast. We have nonaddicted people or our own condition before we became an addict to compare our present condition against.

Perception is always generated with such contrasts. For example, we see these black letters because they are set against the white background of this page. Discovering and admitting conventional addiction is difficult, but at least there are accepted standards, or backgrounds, against which this perception can be made.

Our addiction to materialism is more guileful. We can call this level of addiction "ground addiction," for this term implies several things. First of all, it is the baseline addiction upon which all conventional addictions are but secondary and exaggerated manifestations. We are all ground addicts by virtue of being born in the realm of desire, which we will discuss below. Secondly, we are all addicted to the sense of existence. We think things are real, and nothing is more real than the ground upon which we stand. So "ground addiction" also refers to our addiction for existence itself, how desperately we want things to be real. It is a deep and subtle addiction with which we are afflicted. "Ground addiction" therefore carries a double meaning, and both types of ground addiction are difficult to detect, and even more difficult to detoxify. We will discuss the first meaning in this chapter and the second meaning in the next.

Because of the wily nature of these addictions, these two chapters are more difficult than previous ones. We are entering real Second Turning territory. They describe hardship that occurs more intensely in advanced stages of the path, but which we can feel even at the outset. They cut to the root of problems we did not even know we had. Both meanings of "ground addiction" point to the primordial ignorance upon which we live our lives, and which causes endless suffering. This is the ignorance we introduced in the last chapter: not knowing the nature of reality. As we will see, it is not seeing emptiness, the heart of the Second Turning.

❧ Ground Addiction I

Let's explore our first definition of ground addiction. According to Buddhist cosmology, there are three realms of samsaric existence: the realm of desire, the realm of form, and the formless realm. We live in the realm of desire. Describing these realms for the inhabitants that live within them is describing the very medium in which they live. It is like pointing out to a fish that it lives in the realm of water. In other words, beings in each realm are so deeply immersed in their respective waters that they do not know they are in them. They are too close to see, and there is no contrast. So for us the realm of desire is not seen as such, our world is just the regular world. We don't see that we don't see, which is the definition of primordial ignorance. We are blind to our addiction to this realm.

This is why pointing out this level of addiction is so difficult—we have nothing to compare it to. With conventional addiction, as we have seen, there is a contrast with nonaddiction. There are accepted standards of normalcy—there are addicts and nonaddicts. Ground addiction means everybody is an addict but nobody knows it. In any realm, the inhabitants bootstrap their definition of normal. They have no choice. I look at you to help me define what a normal human being is, and you look back at me. In this unspoken way, we boot-strap our definition of normal: we lift each other up. This is codependency at the deepest unconscious levels. But we are not lifting each other up, we are dragging each other down. Because we do not have anybody to compare our pathology to, we unwittingly cure it by consensus. I'm not okay; you're not okay—and that's okay.

Whether we know it or not, and many of us do not, we have been trained to see the world the way we do. As well intentioned as our parents and teachers may have been, we have been brought up by addicts, taught by addicts, and live in a world of addicts.

If we take a frog and place it in room temperature water, then slowly raise the temperature of the water, we can boil the frog alive, and it will never know it. The frog never notices the contrast. Before it is aware of anything, it is in very hot water. Similarly, if we are gradually exposed to a noxious environment, raised in it from birth, we will never know that we are being poisoned.

Our ground addiction is exposed when we encounter those rare beings who really are okay. These are the spiritual masters whose bodies still inhabit the realm of desire, but whose minds have transcended it. They are detoxified. They are the enlightened ones who plunge back into the realm of desire to rescue those still drowning within it. It could be through their written or spoken words, or most powerfully through their very presence, but there is something different about those who have transcended the realm of desire. They do not move, speak, or think the way we do. For the first time we have something to compare our pathology to, a new standard of being, and a diagnosis can now be made. Perception has finally been generated through contrast: he's okay, I'm not okay—and that's not okay. And so the path begins.

Living in the realm of desire means that desire is what moves us. I move to eat because I desire to feel full; I move to scratch my back because I desire to get rid of the itch; I move to pee, to work, to make love . . . The list is endless because movements are endless. It is so obvious we do not see it: we move because we want. Even aggression is a form of desire, for it is the urge to move something away. We are submerged in an ocean of desire and express it in every movement.

The realm of desire is a euphemism, for it is more accurate to say we live in the realm of addiction. We can glimpse this truth by witnessing the exaggerated manifestations of endless conventional addiction. Millions are addicted to drugs, alcohol, food, gambling, money, cigarettes, sex, work, exercise, television, entertainment, stimulation, and countless other things. We see in others what we are blind to in ourselves.

Virtually everything we do is habit forming. Once we realize we live in the realm of addiction, it is not surprising that conventional addiction is epidemic. It's a "natural" expression of being in this realm. What is surprising, and very difficult to see, is that we, the seemingly nonaddicted, have our own (ground) addictions. This is what detoxified spiritual masters see when they look across the realm of addiction, and this is what we can discover for ourselves as we travel along the spiritual path.

We are substance abusers, and the principal substance in the realm of desire is movement. As we have seen, desire is what moves us, without it we would never get out of bed. Movement is the direct expression of desire and virtually synonymous with it, but we abuse it constantly, for any self-serving action is substance abuse at this primordial level, and almost everything we do is for ourselves. We are addicted to movement. We are not human beings, we are human doings.

The painful truth of our addiction to movement is exposed on the spiritual path. Any form of detox involves removal of the addicting substance. When we admit ourselves to a drug rehab unit, the principal treatment is to keep us away from the addicting drug. To recover from gambling, we must stop gambling. To recover from alcohol, we must stop drinking. If movement abuse is the expression of our ground addiction, the first thing to do is stop moving. Stop doing and start being.

❧ Withdrawal from Ground Addiction I

A central ingredient in most forms of spiritual practice is therefore stillness. Prayer, contemplation, and meditation all nurture it. Many moving meditations like yoga, tai ch'i, and ch'i gong work with slow motion. We do not associate spirituality with rapid movement, but rather with silence, serenity, and stability. As Sylvia Boorstein playfully puts it, "Don't just do something, sit there."

Earlier we discussed the practice of shamatha, the meditation of peace, or "fastening." The idea is to stop moving our body and to use that anchor to slow down and still the moving mind. Through meditation we discover that all our colorful thoughts and juicy emotions are just mind in motion. On an absolute level that's it, and when we get it, this discovery is liberating.

It takes time to really see that thought and emotion are mere movements of mind. They are, after all, the fabric of who we think

we are, and everything we do is an expression of thought and emotion. We take them so seriously. But take a close look, test this against
your own experience, and see for yourself. If we can gain this recognition, we are on our way to freedom for instead of being sucked
into the contents of our mind and acting out everything that arises
within it, we will watch those contents melt like snowflakes falling
on a hot rock.

According to the Bon tradition, the indigenous shamanistic tradition in Tibet, we have about eighty thousand thoughts a day, which
means that the mind moves eighty thousand times a day. We can feel
the velocity of this movement within the first minutes of sitting meditation. This discovery then leads to the next: the voluntary and involuntary physical movements that constitute our life are just the natural
extensions of the voluntary and involuntary movements of our mind.
We move physically because we move mentally, and the speed of our
lives is a natural expression of the speed of our mind. As it says in the
Pali Canon, "The mind leads all things." Our fundamental addiction
to movement, therefore, is habituation to the movement of mind.
We are addicted to thought.

That is the ground addiction. Thought provides mental ground,
and we are hooked on it. Upon that ground of movement sprout the
countless secondary movements that constitute our physical lives.
What we watch on the meditation cushion is what makes up our life
when we are off the cushion: the movements of our mind generate
the movements of our life.

When we sit in meditation, our addiction to movement is exposed.
Stillness provides the contrast that allows us to see the volume of
thought that fills the normal discursive mind and to diagnose our
addiction to that movement. Stillness is like a white canvas upon which
we paint, and then observe, the moving portrait of our mind. With
this new background, we see things we have never seen before.

By beginning sitting meditation, we have admitted ourselves into
rehab, and the principal treatment is to remove the substance we
abuse. All movement is curtailed, which is why extended sitting meditation gets so uncomfortable. When the substance of the realm of

desire is removed, our painful addiction to that substance is revealed. We realize just how much we want to move. When we first sit in meditation, twenty minutes seems like eternity. We start to fidget, suddenly needing to make that phone call or return an e-mail. We want to jump out of our skin and do something. We are feeling the pain of detoxification.

A lot of hardship arises from our addiction to thought and movement, and meditation withdraws us from this ground addiction. By physically withdrawing from a world teeming with movement, we are able to begin the process of material withdrawal. We are withdrawing from materialism. Then by withdrawing from a mind teeming with movement, we progress into more subtle forms of withdrawal. We are withdrawing from our addiction to thought. By understanding the necessity of this detox, we are able to endure the fires of purification and to greet the discomfort of extended meditation with equanimity.

Meditation withdraws us from the narcotic of distraction, and we suffer in direct proportion to our level of addiction to it. If we are an entertainment junkie, someone always on the go and constantly injecting distraction into our life, then sitting still is extremely difficult. We feel like we are going to lose our mind. But what we are really losing is the illusion of ground provided by a moving mind.

When I taught meditation in the federal prison system, I would hear about inmates at the supermax unit near Cañon City, Colorado. These are people in twenty-four-hour lockdown who go out of their cells only for brief periods of exercise and hygiene. Even though they have television and other forms of distraction, word got around of how much they suffered from being unable to move. In my experience in extended retreat, I endured similar but voluntary levels of lockdown. I spent eighteen hours a day in a meditation box, an open-ended wooden frame that I came to call "ego's coffin." This meditation box was in my tiny room, and the building itself was surrounded by a large fence.

Within this tight physical container, I practiced meditations designed to further restrict the movements of my mind. I was physically and mentally confined, and the pain of withdrawal was intense. It is grueling to do nothing at such a level. This retreat exposed my addiction to movement and unleashed its fury. I desperately wanted to get out of myself, out of my meditation box, my tiny room, and the compound. During the few breaks I had, I would jog around the compound like a dog on a short leash. It was one way to feed my addiction to movement.

It was only under these extremely confining conditions that I was finally able to detect my submersion in the realm of desire. I was able to do so because I had entered a new "realm" where I was unable to express it. Every avenue to express my desire was cut off, and I understood the wisdom of no escape. I finally had the necessary contrast to see. The great meditation master Jamgon Kongtrul Lodro Thaye says, "The entryway into the initial mind practice is surely renunciation, without which there is no way. If authentic renunciation arises, compulsive activities will be few; if activities are few, the significance of non-action will be near. When non-action is realized, it is the true nature. There is no other buddha outside of that."[65]

❧ Substance Use

It is important to remember that thinking is not bad, nor is movement inherently problematic. The movement of thought, and its subsequent expression in physical action, is just the substance of the realm of desire. It is what this world is made of. What is bad is substance abuse. When we become attached to thought and addicted to movement, that is substance abuse.

To understand this abuse we must realize that there are two forms of thought, two ways to either use thought or be used by it. The first might be called "cursive" thought, thought that is "on course." This is the proper use of thought. The second is "discursive" thought. *Dis*cursive thought is thought that has gone "off course," and this is thought abuse. It is unrecognized thinking that seduces us into endless distraction and fantasy, and it is highly habit forming. It is habit forming the way watching TV and being entertained is habit forming.

Discursive thought, in other words, is like a narcotic that sedates us from the hardship of facing reality. It involves gross and subtle levels of daydreaming that we buy into in an effort to soften the demands of life. My daydreams are better than reality, so I check out of reality thousands of times a day to take flight in the realm of fantasy. I am an entertainment junkie, and the nearest theater is right here in my discursive mind.

When I was in my retreat, I would long for the precious moments just before going to sleep. My days were full of disciplined meditations, allowing no time for discursive thought. At the end of these tough days, I would lean back in my meditation box and indulge my discursive mind. As I related in the introduction, it was such a relief to finally let go into my samsaric mind. My absolute lust for entertainment was never so obvious, and my virtuosity as an escape artist was never so clear. I now see how micromovies and daydreams pop up like spam in my mind and buffer me from the boredom of life. This was my discovery of substance abuse—the seductive power of discursive thought.

Cursive thought, on the other hand, is thought that is "on course." It is the proper use of the inner substance of the realm of desire. In meditation, cursive thought is thought that is immediately recognized, and therefore self-liberated. It does not carry us off to the movies. A thought pops into our mind, we see it, and it instantly evaporates.

It is difficult to say what takes place in the mind of an awakened one, but cursive thought is a good candidate. Buddhas still think, they just don't think the way we do. Thoughts arise and immediately dissolve, like writing in water. Meditation masters do not entertain their thoughts by feeding them with attention, hence these thoughts are kept "on course" for self-liberation.

On the path, cursive thought is the essence of contemplation, where we take a spiritual thought and reflect upon it. In daily life, cursive thought is directed and concentrated thought used to accomplish things. It is the proper use of thought for creative ends, and we could not function in the world without it. Spanking every thought is not the issue. The issue is to discover the difference between cursive and discursive thought and to cultivate the former while curtailing the latter.

It is also important to realize that stillness, or nonthought, is not inherently good. Spacing out in nonthought is not helpful. Because so much of early meditation is about discovering stillness, and because stillness is discovered in contrast to movement, we tend to place stillness in opposition to movement and believe that stillness is good and movement is bad. But without movement stillness could never be discovered. Stillness needs movement. They provide respective backgrounds for each other, and we should have a preference for neither.

We create unnecessary hardship when we struggle to achieve stillness and wrestle to eliminate movement. When we label "thinking" in meditation, we are not saying "bad"; we are just recognizing that the mind has moved. Movement is just the play of the mind. The problem is unrecognized movement.

In the practice of meditation, we start by cultivating stillness, and it is easy to get hooked on it. Because we are so frenetic, the experience of stillness is seductive. Once we have tasted it, we think stillness is it, and we want more. But stillness is just part of it. To progress along the path we must reenter the frantic world and find stillness in movement.

In other words, we must destroy the notion that to be spiritual is to be still and realize that complete spirituality is embodied in both stillness and movement. To limit spirituality to stillness, the popular image of the silent holy man, is a common mistake. It is also the source of unnecessary hardship because our images of what it means to be spiritual are once again shattered by the reality of what it actually is.

If the proper use of thought is the discovery and use of cursive thought, then the proper use of physical movement is compassionate activity. Inner substance abuse is selfish discursive thought; outer substance abuse is selfish discursive ("off-course") activity. We suffer because we want and move for ourselves. Spiritual practice transforms this selfish passion into selfless compassion: we stop wanting for ourselves and start wanting for others. "Compassion," recall, means to "suffer with" others, to want for others, and it is this motivation that seeds proper physical movement. Compassion generates proper substance use in the realm of desire.

This is the fruition of detoxification. The realm of passion is transformed into the realm of compassion. Spiritual practice purifies our greatest selfish vice into our greatest selfless virtue. Instead of thinking about ourselves, we think about others; instead of moving for ourselves, we move for others. We can transform the realm of passion into the realm of compassion on the spot by simply asking ourselves before we speak or act, "What is my motivation?" "Why am I moving?" If we are moved to speak and act for our own welfare, we are expressing our ground addiction to the realm of passion. If we are moved to speak and act for the welfare of others, we are expressing our freedom in the realm of compassion. Catch our motivation and liberate our action. That is the way to detoxify.

12 ❧

Ground Addiction II

The magic cannot begin unless we are willing to step over the threshold.
We might get a mild shock, or a violent shock in the process, but that
is absolutely necessary. Otherwise there is no magic.
— CHÖGYAM TRUNGPA, Journey without Goal

THE SECOND MEANING of "ground addiction" is even more subtle than the first. When we are being swept along with the rest of the world in endless thought and action, it is hard to break away and discover our addiction to thought and our craving for movement. It is even more difficult to discover our addiction to ground itself.

We take ground, the sense of material reality, for granted. The earth and the objects upon it are so obviously real that they literally provide the framework upon which we live our lives. To challenge the status of this reality borders on psychosis. But to believe that things are real, and that the ground beneath our feet actually exists, is to manifest a form of madness that becomes the basis of samsaric existence.

From the enlightened perspective, it is insane to believe that things truly exist. To realize this nonexistence is to realize emptiness, which is where we are headed. Eckhart Tolle says, "One can go so far as to say that on this planet 'normal' equals insane. What is it that lies at the root of this insanity? Complete identification with thought and emotion, that is to say, ego [complete identification with subtle and gross things (existence), the progeny of ego] . . . Recognize the ego for what it is: a collective dysfunction, the insanity of the human mind."[66]

We are insanely addicted to existence, to physical reality, to the facade that things are solid, lasting, and independent, and the higher reaches of the path involve the difficult journey of detoxification from this view. There is no greater hardship than the withdrawal from this crazy addiction to ground.

This addiction is epidemic, and because everybody believes in physical reality, the force of this collective madness is overwhelming. We are born into it, brought up within it, and firmly locked into the view that things exist. It is utterly axiomatic, a given, the unquestioned status quo.

Trying to detoxify this view is therefore doubly difficult. We have to break away from our own person addiction and then the gravity of social consensus. We might blast off on the path only to have the gravity of society pull us back down to the ground. By understanding this insidious addiction, we can better relate to the rigors of detoxification that must be faced along the later stages of the path.

❧ The Bane of Existence

We begin by asking: why do we suffer? We suffer because we want, because we are selfish, driven by attachment, and infected with ego. These are accurate but secondary reasons. The primary reason we suffer, and the ground from which all these secondary reasons spring forth, is because we believe in the existence of things. We think that the book we are holding is real, that the chair upon which we sit exists, that our body, mind, and world are solid, lasting, and independent. Existence is as blatantly obvious as the ground beneath our feet.

But this is all an illusion. It is the lie of appearance, and we suffer because we believe in it. It is a biting irony: thinking that things are real and solid is the greatest illusion, a completely contrived relative truth. Discovering that things are unreal and illusory is the greatest reality, an uncontrived absolute truth. Flipping from the former to the latter—from the lie of appearance to the truth of reality—is the goal of the path.

The purpose of the path is to relieve suffering. In order to do that, the path points out the illusory nature of reality and removes our belief in existence. This is where defining the spiritual in opposition to the material is appropriate. Materialism is *mis*taking things to exist; spirituality is discovering things to be empty of existence.

It is precisely because we are so attached to existence that we suffer when its illusory nature is pointed out. The level of our addiction to existence is exposed when existence—when a person or possession— is taken away from us. It hurts when someone close to us dies or when something we own is destroyed or stolen. When the substance of an addict is removed, addiction to that substance is revealed, and the hardship of withdrawal ensues. Grief is therefore a form of withdrawal.

Our attachment to people and things is so complete we do not even see it as attachment. This is desire so totally frozen that it forms the matrix of our reality. But when we are forced to detach, we get a glimpse of the level of our addiction to existence by the level of our pain. The degree of our hardship is directly proportional to the degree of our addiction. If we are not attached, we will not suffer when something or someone is taken from us. If we are really attached, it will really hurt.

This does not mean we should not feel pain when we lose someone or something we love. Spirituality is not about apathy. What it does mean is that we should understand why it hurts so much and how to work with it. We can learn how to do this from those who have realized the illusory nature of reality. The masters realize that the world is dreamlike and that objects are fleeting mirages dancing upon a dreamscape. This manifests as a deep awareness of impermanence. When someone dies or an object is destroyed, this is recognized as simply the play of illusion. Buddhas are not addicted to existence and do not suffer from withdrawal when the illusory nature of things is inevitably pointed out. They feel the pain of loss, but they do not transform that pain into suffering.

Imagine that we are driving after a rainstorm and see a brilliant rainbow. We stop to admire the vision, and as we gaze in wonder, it doesn't even cross our mind to try to grab the rainbow. We don't think about taking it home, pushing it away, or trying to buy it. We just appreciate the play of light and space, and the fleeting nature of the appearance makes it that much more precious. This is a momentary phenomenon, soon to dissolve back into space. We can't freeze it or possess it, so the only thing to do is delight in the appearance, then watch it disappear.

This is the way enlightened beings relate to everything. Their world is made of rainbows, where everything briefly appears, then gradually or suddenly disappears. Imagine how our relationship to the world would change if we realized it is all made of rainbows. You are sitting on a rainbow. You are holding a rainbow book in your hands. You go to sleep on a rainbow bed and cover yourself with a rainbow blanket. You eat and drink rainbows, put rainbow clothes on a rainbow body, and make love to a rainbow mate. When your rainbow house disappears, it's no big deal, that's just what rainbows do.

When a rainbow body dies, it is recognized as an inevitable evaporation. We do not think about grabbing or pushing away rainbows that are shaped like people or things because we realize it is all a mirage. It does not even cross our mind to accumulate or destroy things—because there are no things out there.

This rainbow view does not detract from our delight in things, it enhances it. Realizing that there are no things out there ironically makes us appreciate things more. Part of the reason rainbows are so precious is because they are so fleeting. Realizing that they have no future makes us appreciate their presence. We do not take rainbows for granted.

This rainbow view brings things to life by showing us their imminent death. After a near-fatal heart attack, the psychologist Abraham Maslow said, "The confrontation with death—and reprieve from it—makes everything look so precious, so sacred, so beautiful, that

I feel more strongly than ever the impulse to love it, to embrace it, and to let myself be overwhelmed by it. My river never looked so beautiful."[67] For example, when we are visiting a person or place for the very last time, the experience is empowered by the sense of its impermanence.

A few months ago my mother died. I spent the last weekend of her life at her side. At the end of the weekend, as I was about to leave for the airport, I knew I would never see her again. I realized how precious these last moments were, and as I held her hand and whispered my final goodbyes, everything in the room became sacred. A soft light bathed her body, and the hospital room was glowing. In this atmosphere of death, everything became magically alive. This rainbow that had loved me unconditionally was about to disappear, and her final gift to me was to bring me once more into life. This time it was the life of the present moment.

A world made of rainbows would be a magical, self-liberating world. It is the same world we live in, but seen in a profoundly different light. With this rainbow view of things, our solid material world becomes increasingly spiritual and enlightened. More spirit means less matter. We start out on the spiritual path with material footing, but as we progress along it, the path starts to melt beneath our feet. It's like walking a spiritual plank—at some point we look down and there is nothing there. The world we once knew, everything solid and familiar, is gone.

To melt matter back into spirit means facing our addiction to matter, to ground, and to the sense of reality itself. There may be nothing more liberating than living in a world made of shimmering rainbows, but for the ego there is also nothing more terrifying. In a world made of rainbows, there is nothing to stand on.

❧ Prelude to Emptiness

One of the first discoveries in meditation is that the mind is not as solid and continuous as we think. Prior to meditation, the stream of thoughts that pour through our mind is so constant that it creates the illusion of solidity. One thought flows immediately into the next in a seamless and endless thread. But as we sit in meditation and start to slow down, we discover the discontinuous nature of thought. We begin to recognize the gaps that exist in our mind.

With continued meditation, as the mind slows down even further, we extend this insight and begin to penetrate the nature of external things. We start to realize the gaps in our world. The world out there is just as porous as the one in here, a claim made by science for decades. At the subatomic level, matter is over 99 percent empty space. Meditators do not necessarily see the discontinuous nature of things as described by physicists (although some masters assert that they do), but they feel the discontinuous nature of physical experience altogether. They experience the inner and outer world as empty of inherent existence.

The path, again, does not deny appearance, but it does challenge the status of appearance and point out our addiction to it. Things and thoughts do appear. But they do not exist in any substantial form, as we will see in the next chapter. To deny appearance is to fall into the extreme of nihilism and fosters a dangerous "couldn't care less" attitude. Apathy, skepticism, and indolence are mild symptoms of nihilism; anarchy, suicide, and terrorism are acute manifestations. This is obviously not the attitude one cultivates on the path. But if "couldn't care less" is applied to self-aggrandizement, distraction, entertainment, and the myriad other forms of materialism, than it has its place on the path. As the Indian sage Sri Nisargadatta Maharaj puts it, "It is disinterestedness that liberates."

Trungpa Rinpoche went through a period known as the "CCL" phase; "couldn't care less." Even though he cared more than anything about his students, he didn't buy into their neurotic and solid trips. He saw that we took things and thoughts much too seriously and suffered accordingly. CCL taught us to lighten up.

Nihilism is one extreme, the other is eternalism, or realism. Eternalism is the anti-rainbow view that appearances are real. But as the poet Wallace Stevens phrases it, "Realism is a corruption of reality."[68] If we think the book we are holding truly exists, then we are an extremist, and we are corrupting our world. This is fundamental-ism at the deepest level. We subscribe to this philosophy because it grounds us in a solid world and generates a sense of security within it. Because we are so bewitched by form, so stretched in the direction of eternalism, we need to stretch in the direction of nihilism if we want to be balanced in the middle.

In the end, reality is discovered between the extremes of nihilism and eternalism—between existence and nonexistence—but we need a big dose of emptiness as an antidote to overcome the overdose of eternalism. That is why there is so much cutting along the path and so much devastation to the ego. It is the extreme path to the middle. The path is like putting the ego into a wood chipper. The ego enters the path as a solid, lasting, and independent thing, and comes out the other end as sawdust.

By subscribing to eternalism, we subscribe to suffering because eternalism is not in harmony with reality. Our journey is to bring appearance into harmony with reality, which means we must alter our view of appearance. That requires an understanding of emptiness.

13 🌿

Emptiness

The path is not easier than I thought. It is harder than I ever imagined.

— PEMA CHÖDRÖN

*You must begin by trying to recognize small problems as beneficial,
then gradually, as you become more accustomed to this, you can start
to recognize larger, more serious problems as good, even pleasurable, and
ultimately necessary for your happiness. You will see everything
that disturbs you as essential for achieving happiness.*

— LAMA ZOPA, Transforming Problems into Happiness

EMPTINESS IS one of the most difficult and misunderstood topics in Buddhism. It is also one of the most important. Khenpo Tsultrim Gyamtso Rinpoche says that emptiness is the deepest and most subtle topic one could ever attempt to understand. Buddhism is often called a description of reality, and emptiness is the reality described. This is where the path is headed. To glimpse enlightenment is to glimpse emptiness.

Without an understanding of emptiness, of where we are going, not only is it more difficult to get there, but the challenges in getting there are never understood. The journey to enlightenment is from existence to emptiness, from one end of the spectrum to the other. It is withdrawal from our addiction to ground.

This withdrawal means that solidity, our sense of existence, is being pulled out from under our feet. Things are always falling apart, the world is constantly shifting. Impermanence is therefore a direct expression of emptiness and an immediate experience—from the ego's perspective—of its hardship. Things are impermanent because it is the nature of reality—rainbows are always dissolving—but in my experience, impermanence is heightened along the path because the path is a first-class ticket into emptiness. We are being taught a hard and fast lesson.

It is said that if one is not shocked by the teachings on emptiness, one has not understood them. We do not exist; the world does not exist. If that doesn't disturb us, nothing will. When the Buddha first taught emptiness, five hundred senior disciples suffered heart attacks because everything they knew about themselves and their world was turned upside down.

To complicate matters, we also do not not exist, and the world also does not not exist. Whatever appears neither exists nor does not exist; whatever appears is *beyond* existence or nonexistence. The Second Turning deals with the former problem, that of existence, while the Third Turning deals with the latter problem—that there is "something" out there, but that "thing" is beyond existence or nonexistence, beyond being a something or nothing.

We may not have a literal heart attack when we hear about emptiness, but we may have an intellectual one. On a first pass, emptiness can be stupefying. Our mind may go blank, we may get irritated or elated, we may wonder why anyone should even care. When I first heard about emptiness, I was completely baffled. Then I became nearly manic about it and couldn't get enough. It is difficult to wrap our mind around "nothing," but it is important to try. Understanding these difficult concepts, this description of reality, is a form of necessary hardship. If we want to be free and to remove the source of our suffering, we need to understand and then experience emptiness.

❧ No-thingness

"Emptiness" is the most common translation for a Sanskrit term (*shunyata*) that is also loosely rendered as "openness, freedom, limitlessness, all-encompassing." Emptiness does not mean nothing, for that would be the extreme of nihilism, it means no-thing. It means that when we take a very close look at anything, we will discover there is no-thing there. Things do appear, but that appearance is empty of being solid, lasting, and independent. That "thing" is actually "open, free, limitless, and all-encompassing." On one hand, it is much less than we think; on the other hand, it is much more than we can even imagine. It is free and empty of anything we can say about it.

Let's take the example of a hand. Can we point exactly to where it is? If we remove one finger, is it still a hand? If we remove another finger, and then another, when does the hand become just a palm? The hand is just a conceptual imputation, a convenient label imposed on a collection of parts that themselves have no inherent existence.

Take an apple. Where exactly is it? If we point to the top of the apple, what about the bottom, the right side, the left side? Take a bite out of it. Is it still an apple? Keep taking bites and try to discover when the apple becomes a nonapple. This is not a mere philosophical parlor game—these questions reveal the ground upon which we live our entire lives and the reason why we suffer. We gloss over the empty nature of reality, creating things out of nothing.

The solid world out there is a projection of the ego. Solidity, independence, and permanence are characteristics of the ego, and we unconsciously project these qualities onto a groundless and empty reality, freezing it. We do so because the ego feels protected by the appearance of things as solid, lasting, and independent. These qualities are the ego's security blanket.* Dissolve this world, strip off the blanket, and the ego freaks out.

We are like King Midas, where everything we touch with our senses is transformed into our version of gold, which is the sense of solidity itself. We create, in our own image, the lie of steadfast appearance, and we end up living in that lie and suffering because of

---

* "Relative truth" in Tibetan is *kundzop*, which means "to outfit, or clothe." We unwittingly take naked reality, absolute truth, and dress it up—so that it looks like something it is not. Other renderings of *kundzop* are "all covered, veiled, concealed." We blanket reality with our projections, we pull the wool over our own eyes, and we do so because this blanket keeps the ego snuggly and secure.

it. This is how we unknowingly give power to the world and how the world comes to have power over us. This is how we create duality and become controlled by it. We imbue the world with the qualities of solidity, independence, and permanence, giving it a power it does not inherently have and that power bounces back to control us. We transform a fluid and dreamlike reality into concrete and steel and then wonder why the world is so hard.

This process is so subtle we do not see it. We do not realize that we are the responsible party in our hardship. *Shenwang* is a Tibetan word that means "other-power," and it applies to this process of material imputation, how it is that we invest the world with power it does not inherently possess by reifying it with our projections.

It's like what happens when you fall in love. Your lover didn't have any power over you before you fell in love. They were a stranger, empty of your projections, and therefore empty of any power to influence you. Unless they physically attack you, it doesn't matter what they do. You just don't care. But once that stranger enters your life and you fall in love, they now have tremendous power over you. You project all kinds of qualities onto your lover and unknowingly invest them with power. Now it does matter what they do. The smallest gesture can bring pleasure or pain—a missed phone call or a single word can break your heart. You have endowed your lover with power that they do not inherently have and that power comes back to control you. You have been "shenwanged."

Falling out of love often means that your projections have faded. You wake up one morning, look at your sleeping lover, and realize you don't know this person anymore. The stranger has returned. Your ex-lover emerges truly naked, stripped of your projections, and therefore stripped of their power to control you. You have freed yourself from your own imputations, in this case because they have worn out or have been replaced by a new set of projections onto a new lover. Like Clark Gable at the end of *Gone with the Wind*, you no longer give a damn what they do, and you are free to walk away from the person who once wielded such influence.

In the same fashion, but in a much deeper way, we have been

shenwanged by our love affair with the material world. We have plastered an empty reality full of our material projections, and then matter bounces back to hit us. This is hardship at the deepest possible level, a double entendre of endless repercussions. Every form of hardship is but a secondary expression of this root reification. This is why understanding emptiness is so important and is virtually synonymous with enlightenment itself. Once we get it, every form of hardship evaporates on contact. Every "thing" is seen to be "open, free, and limitless." Everything lightens up.

This is also why humor is so important. "Humor" comes from a root that means "liquid" and implies a sense of fluidity and adaptability. When we "break up" or "crack up" in laughter, we are breaking up the solidity of things, which is a major function of the path. Being serious goes hand in hand with being solid. Humor and seriousness are mutually exclusive; the former melts the world, the latter makes it harder.

Reality is touched through tears and laughter. Whether it is breaking down, or breaking up, the breaking is what is important. On the path we want to liquefy reality, especially our hardship, and the humors of life are a powerful way to do that. When we finally understand emptiness, we realize the whole *thing* is just a big joke. And the real punch line is that we continue to play this bad joke on ourselves.

I was in India a few years ago receiving teachings at the site where the Buddha attained enlightenment. Dzigar Kongtrül Rinpoche was teaching on emptiness. He pointed to a wall and said that the reason we can't get up and walk through that wall is not because the wall is so hard, but because we are. The wall, and everything else in life, is only as solid as we are. Openness is a synonym for emptiness, and when we soften and open, he told us, the world simultaneously softens and opens. When we completely open, we and our world become egoless. At that point everything opens up, and we can walk through solid matter.

The path facilitates this opening and liberates us from our material projections. It allows us to walk away from materialism the way Clark

Gable walked away from Vivian Leigh. We no longer give a damn about "things" and are no longer bewitched by the projective prowess of the ego. As we become more spiritually evolved, we become less materially involved. Matter just doesn't matter anymore. This is the real meaning of renunciation and "CCL." We no longer care about owning a better car, a bigger house, or any "thing."

Tibetans talk a lot about *siddhi*, or psychic power, which comes in absolute and relative forms. Relative siddhi includes the power to read minds, predict the future, and fly through space. Another example is the ability to leave handprints in solid rock. In my travels throughout Asia, I have seen impressive examples of handprints, footprints, and even body prints left in rock by enlightened beings. Relative siddhi, as we have seen, is when we have power over the world.

Absolute siddhi, which is a natural consequence of discovering emptiness, is when the world no longer has power over us. Instead of the ability to make impressions in solid matter, matter is no longer capable of making solid impressions on us. Our love affair with materialism is finally over.

❧ Emptiness, Openness, and Sanity

Psychiatrist M. Scott Peck says: "Mental health is an ongoing process of dedication to reality at all costs."[69] Complete mental health, or total sanity, is one definition of enlightenment, and if enlightenment requires an absolute dedication to reality, it is helpful to know what that reality is. We suffer because we dedicate ourselves to a false reality based upon our solidifying projections and subsequently tell endless lies to ourselves and others based on that primordial mistruth.

The Dzogchen Ponlop Rinpoche says, "Do not worry about shunyata [emptiness]. Try first of all to see your clinging; see how you solidify your relative experiences—how you solidify your pain, your happiness, and joy, and how these experiences become so important to you that you cannot even sleep at night. Our experience is so real, so important, and so bothersome to us that we cannot even have a good night's sleep. This is why the starting point is to try to see how we solidify our experiences."[70] And how we therefore lose contact with the sanity of emptiness.

How do we actually do this, how do we discover emptiness? The entire arsenal of the Second Turning is directed at this project. It is beyond our scope to explore these practices, and there are dozens of books that do so, but one way is to extend the principles of meditation into daily life.

In shamatha meditation, the practice is to recognize the movement of mind and to label that movement as "thinking." By doing so we strip thought of its power and watch the solidity of thought melt into emptiness. As Trungpa Rinpoche writes: "Good and bad, happy and sad, all thoughts vanish into emptiness like the imprint of a bird in the sky."[71] We can extend the spirit of this practice into daily life by recognizing how we constantly freeze an empty reality into solid form and by acknowledging that process as "thinging." This is the practice of illusory form, which is to constantly remind ourselves that the world is made of rainbows and that there are no-things out there. It is reminding ourselves of how things actually are.

When we begin meditation and encounter the solid flow of thought, we constantly label it "thinking" as we work to recognize this movement and liberate ourselves from its undertow. As the mind slows down and we eventually see some space between thoughts, "thinking" lessens. In the same way, when we start the practice of illusory form, we are constantly "thinging." Everything just seems so damn solid and real. But with effort the practice of recognizing our "thinging" takes on momentum, and we start to see the dreamlike nature of things. We start to see the gaps between things and our "thinging" lessens.

"Ego" and "thing" are virtually synonymous, as are egolessness, no-thingness, and emptiness. By labeling things "thinging," we acknowledge how we thing-think. We recognize how it is that we think and perceive in terms of things and how we constantly create hardship by creating something out of no-thing. As with the label "thinking," the act of recognition is the point. In the *Tibetan Book of the Dead* it is stated repeatedly: "Recognition and liberation are simultaneous."

The echo of "thinging" is seeing the world as a dream or an illusion. "Thinging" is like hitting a gong, and the reverberation is resting in the recognition of the dreamlike nature of things. Just strike reality with your brief recognition that it is empty, and then rest in the illusion that is its hum.

When we sit in meditation and recognize thoughts as mere "thinking," thoughts gradually lose their power. We are not swept away and controlled by them because we no longer take their reality so seriously, as Ponlop Rinpoche suggests. Heavy thoughts are replaced with imprints of birds in the sky. In the same way, when we recognize things as "thinging," things gradually lose their power. We are not seduced by shiny objects and controlled by our desire to possess them or push them away. We don't take things so seriously. The world becomes more playful and humorous, and things become more liquid as they melt into emptiness.

The monk Thich Nhat Hanh has made a career teaching about "interbeing," which is his way of talking about no-thingness. It is a lovely way to talk about emptiness as a kind of deep ecology, how it is that everything arises in dependence on everything else. If we could see properly, with the eyes of a buddha, we wouldn't see things, we would see an endless stream of interbeing, which would connect us to our world in an elegant and interpenetrating dance. In a beautiful description of emptiness, Thich Nhat Hanh writes,

> If you are a poet, you will see clearly that there is a cloud floating in this sheet of paper. Without a cloud there will be no water; without water the trees cannot grow; and without trees, you cannot make paper. The existence of this page is dependent on the existence of a cloud. Paper and cloud are so close. Let us think of other things, like sunshine. Sunshine is very important because the forest cannot grow without sunshine, and we as humans cannot grow without sunshine. So the logger needs sunshine in order to cut the tree, and the tree needs sunshine in order to be a tree. Therefore, you can see sunshine in this sheet of paper.

And if you look more deeply, with the eyes of a bodhisattva, with the eyes of those who are awake, you see not only
the cloud and the sunshine in it, but that everything is
here, the wheat that became the bread for the logger to eat,
the logger's father—everything is in this sheet of paper. . . .
This paper is empty of an independent self. Empty, in this
sense, means that the paper is full of everything, the entire
cosmos. The presence of this tiny sheet of paper proves the
presence of the whole cosmos.[72]

People often wonder what happens to the world when one becomes
enlightened, when one really sees emptiness. Does the world disappear, do things vanish? Things, just like thoughts, continue to appear.
What disappears is our perception of things as separate from us. What
disappears is our view of things as solid, lasting, and independent.
It's like what happens when we discover we are dreaming while we
are still dreaming. The dream doesn't stop, but taking it to be real
does.

When we wake up to its illusory nature, the dream is stripped of its
power. That tiger about to attack us can no longer hurt us; the insult
from our dream boss no longer carries any weight. When we attain
enlightenment, we wake up from the nightmarish power of solidity.
Things still appear, but they now appear as the empty forms—the
rainbows—that they really are. The end of the path is not the end of
existence, it is the end of being duped by existence. And if there is
reincarnation, it is the end of being duped into existence and being
compulsively reborn.

❧ Psychological Ground

Ground addiction manifests in one of the most frustrating of all obstacles: the deadly force of habit. With our understanding of ground
addiction, we can talk about habit as the unconscious construction of
psychological ground. Habit is one way we bring form to our world
and are subsequently formed by that world. As we saw earlier, habit

is a form of mass or momentum where each repetition of a habit adds more weight to an already established pattern. The more we do something, the more momentum we add to it, the more influential it becomes, and the easier it becomes to do it again. Habits become so powerful that their momentum sweeps us away, and we become helpless victims of our own inertia. For example, think of those who can't control themselves around alcohol, cigarettes, or sex.

Habit is a ground addiction, and thus the phrase "habit forming" is redundant. We love our habits. They bring form to our lives, and the ego, as the archetype of form, adores them. Habits bring a sense of stability, pattern, and predictability to an otherwise formless world, so we unconsciously generate them everywhere.

If we travel for extended periods, where many habitual patterns are disrupted, we can study how we impose our established habits onto new situations and how we take refuge in the routines—the forms—of our life. For example, instead of releasing my habits and enjoying the formless new situation of being in Bhutan, I often feel an urge when I'm traveling to cut the sightseeing short and return to the routines that keep me safe. I can't wait to go for my run, read my books, or even meditate. I don't see how deep my habits are until I step out of them, and traveling is one way to do that.

Our long-standing bad habit of taking things to be solid and real is so firmly established that it is no longer seen as a habit. Solidity is just the way things are. But it is not the way things are; it is the way we have made things to be. We have projected things to be solid and real for so long that this habit is automatic and sweeps us away in its torrential influence. This is why it is so incredibly difficult to see the emptiness of things and wake up.

By understanding this enemy, habit, which is just a more immediate way to talk about karma, we develop the patience necessary to counteract its effects and deal with frustration along the path. It is not difficult to glimpse emptiness. A breakthrough occurs, and it suddenly seems so easy. But before we know it, the experience fades and we are back in the same old rut. It's frustrating. The tidal wave of habitual pattern crashes in and sweeps us away. The insight is gone, the breakthrough is lost, and we are left wondering what happened.

As we saw earlier, the practice of the path is to replace unconscious habits of confusion with conscious habits of wisdom. To work with the unconscious addiction of seeing reality in terms of things, we engage the conscious practice of labeling things "thinging." It is an endless practice of counteracting our bad habit, and it only seems endless because it is replacing the beginningless practice that got us to this point. "Thinging" acknowledges our unconscious addiction and replaces confusion with wisdom.

One or two flashes of "thinging" won't do it; one or two thousand barely scratches the surface of things. But with effort, the practice of illusory form takes on a momentum that starts to affect the way we see the world. We are using the force of habit in a conscious manner, one that takes patience and diligence, and one that will turn the tide on the deadly habit of taking things so seriously.

14 🍂

The Mistake of the Ego

Ego is no more than this: identification with form . . .
If evil has any reality—and it has relative, not an absolute reality—
this is also its definition: complete identification with form—
physical forms, thought forms, emotional forms.
—ECKHART TOLLE, A New Earth

LIKE EMPTINESS, ego is also one of the most important and misunderstood topics in spirituality. It is accused of being the source of our suffering, the thing we are supposed to either befriend, transcend, or destroy. To progress along the path, we need to come to terms with ego, to face it and discover its essence. Relating inappropriately to the ego is the source of a great deal of unnecessary hardship.

From an absolute perspective, the ego does not exist. This is important to understand because it sets the view and shows us where we are going. In other words, we should never try to get rid of the ego because there is nothing to get rid of. Trying to get rid of the ego ironically reifies it. We are wrestling with an illusion and wondering why we cannot pin it down. So the point is not to get rid of it but to see through it. We may already know better, that destroying the ego is not the point, but we still sit in meditation and try to get rid of our thoughts or banish unwanted experiences. This is the same as trying to erase the ego.

We tend to relate to the ego the way a child relates to a monster in his room. A child wakes up in the night screaming that he just saw a monster. We comfort the child and assure him that no such beast exists, but no matter what we say, he doesn't believe us. To prove our point, we have to ask the child where he saw the monster, go there, and show him that there is nothing there. We show him it is not in the closet, under the bed, or behind the door. Only when he sees for himself, does he finally believe the monster doesn't exist.

In a similar way, in the darkness of ignorance, we believe that we exist. It doesn't matter what others say, we know in our bones that this monstrous sense of self is here. We can feel it. The only way to prove that it doesn't exist is to turn on the light of wisdom and look at where we think it is. Only when we try to find it and discover that there is no ego in the closet, under the bed, or behind the door, do we come to the stark and liberating realization that we absolutely do not exist.

On the relative level, of course, we appear to exist. We each have a body, thoughts, emotions, and perceptions. We relate to other people and we each come to the mutual conclusion that you are out there and I am in here. This conclusion may be mutual, but it is misinformed. Relative truth, remember, is truth from the perspective of confusion. We don't each have our bodies, feelings, perceptions, and thoughts—they have us. They "have" us in the sense that we are so completely identified with them, with these forms, that we forget that we are the formless (empty) awareness that lies beneath all form. We are possessed. We are possessed by that which we feel we possess.

Unraveling the ego on the path is a necessary hardship. Getting to know that which creates such a relative and absolute fuss can help us relate to and remove a lot of trouble. In the next few chapters, we will discover how the illusion of the ego is constructed, and therefore how it can be deconstructed. We will see how that deconstruction is initially felt as frustration, and eventually as panic and fear.

❧ The Five Heaps

In order to arrive at the absolute, emptiness, we have to go through the relative, the ego. In order to discover the truth of our nonexistence and the heart of liberation, we have to examine existence and the heart of entrapment. What is the ego? What is it made of? What does it live on? When Siddhartha sat under the bodhi tree 2,600 years ago, he looked closely at these questions. What he discovered transformed him into the Buddha. He saw that the ego is just a gloss over five aspects of experience, what are called the five skandhas in Sanskrit. *Skandha* means "heap," or "aggregate." The Buddha saw that the ego is one bad and deeply entrenched habit that causes lots of trouble.

He also saw that the difficulty in sharing his insight is that the five skandhas occur so quickly and are so much the fabric of our being that we do not see them. It is like trying to see the insides of our eyelids, which are so close to our eyes that we can't see them. It's time to pull our eyelids back and take a look.*

The five skandhas describe the development of the ego. They are the five building blocks of experience that we glom onto that generate the illusion of self. The five heaps also describe the construction of duality and the process of perception altogether. In other words, by describing the construction of a sense of self in here, we simultaneously describe the construction of the sense of other out there. We can't have one without the other. The illusion of self and other is bootstrapped. They are created simultaneously and interdependently—they lift each other up. Self and other are both constructed perceptions, they are "takes" on reality. In this case they are *mis*takes.

The five skandhas occur rapidly, and until we reach the fourth and fifth skandha, they occur subliminally. Accounts vary, but they flash

---

*The description and use of the five skandhas that follows is not entirely traditional. It follows the inimitable view of Trungpa Rinpoche, who infuses this principally Hinayana teaching with Vajrayana wisdom.

by about once every five-hundredths of a second. They are called heaps because they heap on top of each other to create the final illusion of self and the mistake of duality. It is like a conveyor belt where an item is passed down and progressively assembled until the final product is made. It is a pattern of duality that continually strengthens until the manufactured sense of self and other pops out the other end. This popping out occurs constantly, unconsciously, and rapidly.

Before we go over these heaps, it is important to understand the context within which they arise. Because the first skandha is that of form, it is easy to fall into a materialist, and therefore reductionist, view. ("Form" usually refers to visual forms, but here "form" refers to the contents of all five senses—to whatever we can perceive with our senses.) The first skandha is the only one that corresponds to the external physical world, so it is easy to think that things start from matter (form) and can be reduced to it. But the skandha of form arises out of vast and formless space. It is, in fact, an unconscious reaction to space. In other words, the ego is born out of an inappropriate relationship to the absolute freedom of open space. To appropriate means "to take possession of"; to "*in*appropriate" means to *mis*take, and that is exactly what the ego does to space.

To get a feel for the first skandha, imagine a completely open space. It is unknowable, ineffable, unnamable, and awake. It is prior to existence, but it is not nonexistence. It is freedom, indescribable liberation, infinite and eternal. This is not ordinary physical space, even though that is the best analogy for it, but the space of mind.[†]

[†] Just like outer space, inner space may seem powerless because it can't really do anything. But this space has tremendous power. Space accommodates and holds everything, allowing any action to take place. Space is also indestructible. You can't cut it, bomb it, or burn it. Space cannot be hurt.

Inner space is the same. By opening our heart and mind, we can discover this inner space and accommodate anything that happens, allowing the experiences of our life to take place without resistance or reservation. This receptivity manifests as kindness and compassion, first expressed to ourselves, and then to others. We accept the circumstances of our life and who we are, which is kindness and benefit to ourselves. And we accept others just as they are, which is kindness and benefit to all beings. (*continues on facing page*)

This is the groundless ground of all being and form. It is nirvana, the absolute, a vast openness, emptiness. Trungpa Rinpoche once said that space is the Buddhist version of God.

But we, as the ego, can't stand it. We are afraid of this "God." It is not because this God is too demanding or restrictive. On the contrary, we fear space because it is too open and vast. It is everything we want, and it is the heart of who we are, but it is just too much space. We cannot relate to it because there is no-thing to relate to. So instead of relaxing into this open space, we freeze it. Instead of dissolving into infinity, we contract into something finite. Instead of melting into eternity, we petrify into time. Instead of resting in nirvana, we congeal in samsara. In other words, we panic.

We forget Khenpo Rinpoche's teaching to be "open . . . spacious . . . and relaxed," and we freak out and freeze space. That very reaction to space, that self-contraction, transforms the groundless into ground. Stephen Hodge, in his commentary on the Tibetan Book of the Dead, talks about the experiences of the dead, the formless mind that has dissolved back into this primordial space after death, and his comments apply here: "Unable to withstand the experience of limitless expansion, they may react by curling in upon themselves, and mentally turning away from all that spaciousness in order to shut themselves off from the all-encompassing terror [that is, the truth of their nonexistence]."[73]

❧ The First Skandha

That panic *is* the first skandha, which is form. Form is made of panic, and it is a profoundly inappropriate relationship to the formless. It is an unconscious response to the truth of our nonexistence, a knee-

---

This inner space is also indestructible. Insults pass through us without hitting anything; personal attacks and offenses have no place to land. We allow all movement, but we ourselves remain unmoved. Others can cut, bomb, and burn our body, but our heart and mind remain unscathed. When the Vietnamese monks immolated themselves in protest of the war, they were able to do so because fire cannot harm space.

jerk reaction to the empty space that is the heart of who we absolutely are. This is a critical point, the crux of the entire construction project of the ego: the first skandha, form, is based on fear, bewilderment, and ignorance. It *is* fear, bewilderment, and ignorance taking form.

The ego is therefore conceived from a stunned reaction to space. Trungpa Rinpoche says, "The whole development of the five skandhas [the ego] is an attempt on our part to shield ourselves from the truth of our insubstantiality."[74] If space is the Buddhist version of God, the first skandha is the Buddhist version of original sin. And just like with the ego, from an absolute point of view, "original sin" is also merely a nonexistent delusion. Mathematician George Spencer-Brown probably did not know about the skandha of form, but he describes its spirit elegantly in his mathematical treatise, *The Laws of Form*:

> A universe comes into being when a space is severed or taken apart. The skin of a living organism cuts off an outside from an inside. So does the circumference of a circle in a plane. By tracing the way we represent such a severance, we can begin to reconstruct, with an accuracy and coverage that appear almost uncanny, the basic forms underlying linguistic, mathematical, physical and biological science, and can begin to see how the familiar laws of our own experience follow inexorably from the original act of severance.[75]

One way to glimpse the energy of the first skandha is to look for instances that exaggerate its genesis, this process of panic. Moments of intense self-consciousness provide such a glimpse. If you have ever given a public talk or performed for others, you know the nervous energy that accompanies performance. If you ride that energy, it can infuse your performance with passion. But that energy can transform into panic if it is not managed and can then negatively affect your performance. One aspect of this panic is intense self-consciousness. It's as if all the awareness being placed upon you by the audience somehow draws your own awareness onto yourself. Awareness implodes onto itself, and that implosion gives birth to (an exaggerated sense of) self.

The more self-conscious we are, the more our performance suffers; the less self-conscious, the more our performance shines. This includes any performance on the stage of life. If we are very self-conscious when we meet someone we want to impress, we may fumble for the right word or act clumsily. If we are open, spacious, relaxed, and not self-conscious, then we naturally tend to shine.

As a pianist and public speaker, I have experienced the entire range of self-consciousness. When I am relaxed and in the flow, it almost feels like I am not even the one performing. I feel like a conduit for some higher energy that flows through me. But when I contract in self-consciousness and worry about how I appear, I struggle on stage and my performance suffers. And so it is, to varying degrees, with every action based on the self-centeredness of the first skandha.

The first skandha, in other words, is an intense and continuous form of self-consciousness. (It is represented in the myth of Narcissus, the lad frozen in love with his own image-form.) In this fundamental sense, this level of self-consciousness gives birth to the sense of self altogether. The self becomes conscious—it comes to life—as awareness implodes onto itself. The ego is therefore a constant panic attack, and the panic is the ego's response to the truth of its own nonexistence.

Upon this illusory rock of frozen space, the ego will now build its church. Fear, panic, bewilderment, ignorance, and denial form the ground upon which the ego stumbles into the world. Stephen Hodge summarizes the situation this way:

> Our so-called self, the ego, is a parasitical illusion without any substantial existence, something that has been constructed as a defense mechanism to deal with the experience of impermanence. As it strives to create itself out of empty space and become solid, the ego-self always feels paranoid that it will be discovered for what it is—a hollow illusion.

It works hard to maintain its status of "self-importance" and suffers greatly as the all-encompassing reality of great space continuously dissolves the fabric of its being. Having no basis in reality, the ego-self keeps crumbling away and must be constantly reinvented.[76]

With this ground established, we can now proceed quickly through the remaining skandhas and the constant reinvention of the self. We will then bring the whole enterprise into practical focus around meditation and hardship. The first skandha is the most important because it sets the stage for what is to be built upon it. Once we have broken away from the truth and made the primordial cut of duality (the first skandha), we can rapidly descend into all kinds of deception (skandhas two through five).

It is important to realize that the skandhas did not occur sometime in the hazy past, leaving us now helpless victims under their control. The implosion of awareness that gives birth to self (consciousness) occurs constantly. It is happening right now. The original sin of duality occurs every time we see ourselves as separate from the rest of the world, and it occurs preconsciously. We are not aware of this deeply ingrained and habitual response to space.

Even though we are emphasizing the skandha of form as it manifests most intimately in our physical body, the first skandha extends to encompass anything that can be perceived by the five senses. It includes the environment. The final point is that even though we were born with a body (form), and even though Freud was right when he said, "Ego is first and foremost a body ego," our body is not the problem. It is our relationship to body that is the problem. That relationship is constituted by the next four skandhas.

✤ Skandhas Two through Five

As we go through the remaining skandhas, we need to keep in mind that we are learning about the construction of the ego because the path is about its deconstruction. By studying how the ego is put together, we can better understand why it hurts to take it apart. The ego is the fundamental "thing," and therefore the mother of all things. By dissolving it into no-thing, we start to dissolve everything. We start to realize emptiness, and we do so very personally.

The second skandha is "feeling," and it refers to the way we automatically relate to what we have frozen. We unconsciously reach out and feel these frozen forms, to size them up. Feeling is a reflexive and primitive response to form, before any higher conceptual processes enter in. Feeling is at the level of both body and mind, and it is the link between the two. This early stage of the relationship is one of finding the form either pleasant, unpleasant, or neutral; either supportive, threatening, or neither. This is the precondition of what is called the three poisons, the three most fundamentally inappropriate ways of relating to reality, and these three feelings will take complete birth in the next skandha as passion, aggression, and ignorance.

Relating to form appropriately means relating to whatever arises with equanimity. It is not to judge the form, or always refer it back to ourselves. If we can let forms arise without grasping them, pushing them away, or spacing out, they self-liberate—in both senses. Self-liberation means we don't have to do anything to be free. It is the highest form of liberation, one that we will return to in part 3. The forms liberate themselves, and we simultaneously self (ego) liberate. If left alone, forms arise in our experience and dissolve, like clouds passing in the sky.

As we saw earlier, there is no problem with anything that arises in reality, even the frozen forms of the first skandha—which is *everything* that arises in our physical experience. The problem, again, is one of inappropriate relationship. The three poisons are the essence of all inappropriate relationship, and they are conceived at the level of feeling.

The second skandha is like putting our hand inside a black bag full of all kinds of unknown stuff, all manner of forms. We don't know what these things are yet (skandhas three through five have not yet occurred), but we can feel them. Some forms are soft and fuzzy, and therefore we enjoy feeling them. Others are prickly, so we push those away, and still others are such that we are indifferent to them.

Trungpa Rinpoche writes: "Having already the basic form, something definite and solid to hold onto [the skandha of form], we go a little beyond that to trying to identify that form as friend or enemy, hostile or welcoming. This has the effect of solidifying whatever it is even further as something that defines ego's position by implication."[77] In other words, "One must constantly try to prove that one does exist by feeling one's projections as a solid thing. Feeling the solidity of something seemingly outside you reassures you that you are a solid entity as well." If we are able to define something "out there," the immediate implication is that there must be something "in here"—the witnessing ego. In this unconscious and reflexive way, both self and other are simultaneously brought further into the world.

The third skandha is called "perception," or perception-impulse. "Perception" here refers to receiving information from the world of form, and "impulse" is our further response to that information. This is where the three poisons, conceived at the skandha of feeling, come to rapid maturation as passion, aggression, and ignorance. At the level of feeling, these three poisons were inarticulate, still at a gut level. At the third skandha, we now want some forms more clearly, don't want others, and couldn't care less about still others. It is as if we are now able to feel more completely into the black bag and attach meaning to the things we had only felt before, and as a result, we develop a deeper relationship to these things.

This skandha refers to the process of recognizing an object, recognizing its distinctive characteristics, for example, color, size, male or female, friend or enemy, and it literally affects the way we see. The other night I was walking into my dark garage when I was suddenly struck by a form I saw in the back seat of my car. I had a brief moment of panic as my mind raced to figure out who or what was in my car. In a microsecond I recognized and remembered the large duffle bag I had left propped up in the back seat. My "perception" was now complete, and I was literally able to see the bag more clearly now that I knew what it was. In dealing with the process of perception, the colloquialism, "I'll believe it when I see it," is replaced with, "I'll see it when I believe it." This was a revealing demonstration of what I do constantly as my mind races to figure out my world.

The fourth skandha is called "formations," and its name suggests the increasingly complete formation of a solid world of self and other. This is where our labels, judgments, identifications, and concepts come in to color our world. Francesca Fremantle provides this helpful list of other translations that point to the scope of this large "heap": thoughts, intellect, concept, mental events, mental occurrences, mental factors, mental formations, mental constructions, volition, intention, motivation, impulses, forces, conditions, activities, predispositions, and habitual tendencies.[78] "Formations" are not yet at the level of full-blown thought and emotion, which finally arise at the fifth skandha, but they are what move us into thought and emotion. They are the triggers of fully manifest thought, word, and deed.

The fourth skandha is like a stream of sparks. Up to this point we have been reacting and perceiving mostly at an unconscious level, but with the fourth and fifth skandhas, we finally get into consciousness. The "perception" of the last skandha now triggers action at the level of body, speech, and mind. But once again, if we just related to the perception of the third skandha properly, it would be like a campfire spark that harmlessly disappears into the night sky. The spark self-liberates if we just let it. No action, and therefore no karma, would result.

But instead of making use of another chance at self-liberation, we take the final step into full-blown self-consciousness. The fifth skandha is called "consciousness," and it is here that the ego (self) becomes fully conscious of itself. Instead of letting the sparks of the fourth skandha dissolve into space, consciousness throws gasoline onto them. That gasoline comes in the form of (implosive) attention. The untrained mind pours attention onto the sparks that arise within it and whoosh!—off we go into discursive thought, emotional indulgence, or fantasy.

This happens all the time, and since we are now at the level of consciousness, it is easy to see. Meditators work with this constantly, but anyone who thinks will recognize the display of the fourth and fifth skandhas. For example, we hear the distant sound of a police siren. A tiny spark of perception, already identified and related to at the level of the third skandha, has just popped into our mind. Without even knowing it, our attention pours onto this perception, and we are off into a discursive commentary: "Where is the cop car going? I bet somebody is in big trouble. Better them than me. I hope it's not too serious. This world is a mess. Why are those sirens so loud . . ." A harmless little spark of perception triggers a mushroom cloud of discursiveness. And so we fill our minds, our days, and our very lives with this constant chatter triggered by our perceptions.

Consciousness keeps the whole process of the five skandhas in operation, and therefore feeds the ego to keep it happy. If there is a gap in the process, consciousness patches it up. It's like a radar beam that constantly sweeps across the other four heaps and then plugs up any holes. The fifth skandha is like an aerobics instructor who is always goading us on, shouting "keep it going!" It is like the ego's coach on the sidelines, barking out encouragement to keep us moving, to keep the karma going—to keep the sense of self alive.

This is what the ego is made of. There are endless details and varying interpretations, but the important points are the following: the ego is not a single indivisible thing but a collection of parts glued together by constant movement. The ego was not suddenly created by some big bang in the distant past, but is constantly brought to life moment to moment. The ego is conceived through an inappropriate relationship and is kept alive by discursiveness. All these factors will come into play as we talk below about meditation and the unraveling of the skandhas.

Pay attention to your mind and you will notice these skandhas, especially the fourth and fifth, popping in and out incessantly. If we simply witness them, they provide a harmless display of the natural movement and radiance of the mind. This, of course, is the essence of meditation, to witness whatever arises with complete equanimity. But if we don't, these harmless sparks ignite our worldly actions of body, speech, and mind, and therefore transform into the sparkplugs that drive the engine of samsara. Once again, that which we witness on the meditation cushion is that which runs our life off the cushion. The point of meditation is to start to see this and to develop a proper relationship to it—and to ourselves. We do not have to get rid of the skandhas, we do not have to get rid of the ego, but if we want to get rid of unnecessary hardship, we do have to relate to them properly.

15 ❧
Frustration by Design

*When meditation gets good enough and you start to threaten your
sense of self, you may get more reactive rather than less reactive.
There may be a heightening of vulnerability, a susceptibility to
feeling threatened. You may react more strongly and angrily
to things because you're trying hard to reconstitute the self
that is under pressure and slowly dissolving.*
—HARVEY ARONSON, "Psychology and Buddhism"

ARMED WITH the five skandhas, we now return to the practicalities
of hardship on the path and to a deeper understanding of why hardship occurs. We will approach it by emphasizing the role of meditation in relation to the first and fifth skandhas, the ground and fruit
of the ego. As we will see, space and speed are at the heart of nirvana
and samsara respectively.

❧ Meditation, Frustration, and the Fifth Skandha

We begin where we left off, at the level of the fifth skandha, to see how
meditation works with consciousness. Movement is the heartbeat of
consciousness. As we saw earlier, movement is the "substance" of
the realm of desire. At a physiological level, if we do not move, or if
something in our field of awareness does not move, then consciousness tends to be absent. For example, if you place your hand on your

thigh and leave it there unmoving, you will quickly lose conscious-ness of your hand. Without moving it, you will not be able to tell where your hand ends and your thigh begins. Your hand and thigh have dissolved into a form of nonduality.

If you hold your open eyes perfectly still, you will shortly experi-ence a type of blindness. Our eyes are constantly blinking and darting around, our pupils are always contracting and expanding, and a con-tinuous high frequency tremor, called micronystagmus, is constantly at work to bring forth visual consciousness. Keep it all still, and the visual world disappears. Richard Gregory, dean of the psychology of seeing, writes, "When the image is optically stabilized vision fades after a few seconds, and so it seems that part of the function of eye movements is to sweep the image over the receptors so that they do not adapt and so cease to signal to the brain the presence of the image in the eye."[79]

To enhance states of meditative absorption, it is recommended that you hold your body still, temporarily hold your breath, and quiet the movement of your eyes. Try it and notice the effect on your mind. Eye movement is related to the movement of thought, and neurolinguistic programming even associates the direction of this movement with different thought states. Dream states are marked by REM, or rapid eye movement, which is the stage of sleep where the movement of thought transforms into a dream reality. In the inner yogas, the movement of breath is directly associated with the move-ment of thought. When a meditator enters the deepest meditations, all breathing can stop as all thoughts cease. In short, at every level, movement triggers consciousness.

Mental movement is the heart of consciousness, especially the self-consciousness of the fifth skandha. Our sense of self is kept alive by relentless motion. Meditation faces this movement head on, and it does so by frustrating movement. The first thing we do in medi-tation is nothing. We sit still. We have gone on strike against the corrupt movements of the ego. By sitting still we are boycotting the machinery that generates and sustains the ego. Trungpa Rinpoche says that we have to create chaos in the efficient mechanism of consciousness, and nothing can do that except absolute nothing—which is meditation.

The minute we stop moving, alarms go off at the level of the fifth skandha. Remember that its job is to keep the whole process going, to keep the ego alive by looking for gaps in the "efficient mechanism." When we sit down to do nothing, that is the greatest threat to the life of the ego. We are holding a knife against its throat, and it will do whatever it takes to get us going again. It will tell us that we have better things to do, that this is a waste of time, that we will never be able to meditate. The coach will kick into gear and start barking out motivating thoughts to get us off our ass and into the world.

Meditation, doing nothing, frustrates the mechanism of the five skandhas, and this translates into literal frustration. It really is frustrating to meditate—and it is supposed to be. It is frustration by design; necessary hardship. The litany of complaints from meditators is legion: it's boring, tedious, and irritating. For beginning meditators, or if sessions are kept short, frustration may not arise. We are still window shopping. But if we extend our sessions, meditation will challenge us and expose our addiction to movement.

By sitting still we are starving the motion-craved ego, and the resulting hunger for action can be intense. We can reach the point where we feel that if we do not move, we will lose our mind. The five skandhas are starting to unravel, and this frustration is a good sign. We have entered the stage of hot boredom, which triggers the itch to move. We want to create a mental breeze and cool off, perhaps remembering we need to return a phone call or run to the store. And it is urgent. Doing nothing gives the ego a cardiac arrest.

Sogyal Rinpoche defines two types of laziness. The first is laziness as we usually think of it, the second is what he calls "active laziness," and it is epidemic. It is the constant busyness, the business of samsaric life, that serves to distract us from taking a closer look at things. It creates the gloss that keeps us skimming across the surface of life, never allowing us to plumb its depths. "I can't meditate, I have bills to pay, kids to pick up, food to buy . . ." It is a distraction therapy for the ego, a way to keep it all going and a way to shield ourselves from deeper and uncomfortable truths. All that hard work and ceaseless activity is just laziness in motion.

In the movie *Speed*, a criminal places on a bus a bomb that is set to explode if the bus drops below forty-five miles an hour. It is the desperate job of the bus driver, Sandra Bullock, and the detective hero, Keanu Reeves, to keep the bus moving. They crash through things, roll over others, and generally create a big mess to keep the bus going. Your ego has stuck you with a similar explosive, and it is the desperate job of consciousness, the driver of the five skandhas, to keep you moving. Let your mind drop below forty-five thoughts per minute, or whatever speed limit you have set to maintain your sanity, and it feels like you will explode.

There is a deeper sense of "you" that transcends the ego altogether and does not fear stillness. It longs for it. This is your spiritual essence, that deeper part of you that is fed up with the relative activities of the world and wants out. These two parts of yourself, the relative and the absolute, battle each other initially. Material and spiritual desire go head-to-head as the old habits for self-fulfillment clash with the new passions for self-transcendence. Just knowing that these relative and absolute forces are at work can help you transform this wrestling match into a dance. Instead of fighting with the old passions that move you, you start to understand them and bring them onto your new path. You remember the adage "transcend but include."

Relating properly to movement is critical on the path. By understanding what moves you, why you love to move, and how the path works with motion, you find yourself moving more gracefully and rapidly along the path. And you do so by sitting still.

❧ Meditation, Fear, and the First Skandha

It is important to realize that the path does not just reverse the process of the five skandhas—it is not that clean, simple, or predictable. As always, the map is never the territory, and reality is never so tidy. But we can better understand hardship by looking at how a journey back through the skandhas orients the basic thrust of the path and the tough times we encounter upon it. Sandra Maitri says, "what we have to do to regain contact with our depths is to retrace, in effect, our developmental steps."[80] In other words, we can use the skandhas as a teaching tool to shed light on why the path can be so hard. The skandhas can be used as a map that helps us orient and understand our pain. The path is messy, but the five heaps can help us clean it up.

The fifth skandha is what we first encounter in meditation, and it constitutes the majority of our meditative experience.* We start the path at the top of the heap, where thoughts and emotions are what we see when we begin to look into our minds and when we try to figure out who and what we are. The fifth skandha, after all, is consciousness. The deeper skandhas are mostly unconscious processes and therefore initially inaccessible, but with training we can learn how to feel them. The deeper we go, the more we enter the domain of feeling, and even though "feeling" refers to the second skandha itself, the word also applies to the unconscious panic of the first skandha, which takes place well before the knowable thoughts of consciousness. Panic is not a thought but a gut-level feeling.

When we begin to explore ourselves (the five skandhas), we are greeted by the ego's initial defensive systems, which are still the relatively harmless experiences of boredom, frustration, and irritation. The ego would prefer that we not take a look, for remember, ignorance is ego's bliss, so these annoying experiences are its first "Keep Out" sign. Stay busy, don't bother with this spiritual stuff, we have better things to do.

As we cut through the outer skandhas into deeper territory, the defenses become increasingly formidable and effective. Instead of a "Do not enter" sign, we come up against barbed wire and flam-

---

* It is unclear whether our ordinary experience is just the fifth skandha, or includes some of the fourth. Jeremy Hayward, a physicist and Buddhist scholar, says, "The fifth skandha is not pure consciousness *itself*, but includes what we are conscious *of*, i.e., some of the fourth, which is something similar to the relation between the conscious and the subconscious." E-mail message to author, August 2008.

ing trenches. We go from initial frustration into real fear. When we descend to the first skandha, we are starting to get somewhere, and the forces at work are no longer a joke.

In the following quotation, Sandra Maitri is not writing about the five skandhas, though she very well could be. She is speaking about ego development in the lineage of Claudio Naranjo and A. H. Almaas:

> This layer of fear becomes particularly apparent in the process of retrieving contact with Essence [the open space before the first skandha], as we experientially move beyond the outer strata of the personality [skandhas two through five] and begin getting close to the underlying state of deficient emptiness.[†] It is this layer of fear that is the archetype of signal anxiety, the sense of impending danger that we feel as something stored in the unconscious starts making its way into awareness, and which mobilizes the ego's defensive systems to keep this content sealed off from consciousness. Signal anxiety, then, is a superficial manifestation of this primal layer of fear. It is . . . paradoxically the same fear that catapulted us out of contact with Essence in the first place.[81]

What we are trying to see in this chapter, and with the Second Turning altogether, is that these frightening deeper spiritual experiences are indeed just a joke. There is nothing behind these formidable defenses; they are absolutely empty. It is only when we take the feelings to be real and forget the space that lies beyond them that we suffer. The spikes of fear are not the problem, it is how we relate to the spikes that becomes the problem.

[†] Deficient emptiness lies at the core of her description of the ego and is the result of losing contact with our essential nature. This is not the same emptiness we have been talking about, but a negative state of emptiness, a deficiency, that lies at the heart of the ego.

If we think these defenses are solid, that we really will lose our mind if we continue, then from the ego's point of view it has succeeded in keeping us out. It has duped and distracted us yet again from discovering the truth. But like the end of the *Wizard of Oz*, when Dorothy realizes that the wizard is just a facade, we can finally take the necessary steps directly into our fear and discover the liberating space beyond. We can cut through the panic of the first skandha and rest in open space.

This may seem like a lofty experience, but it can happen at any time. After about five years of meditation, I had my first "close encounter" with emptiness. I was doing an evening meditation session at my local center and was settling into a "good" meditation. My mind was slowing down. Suddenly I felt like I was dropping into a bottomless pit, and my heart started pounding. A surge of panic hit me along with a terrible feeling that I didn't exist.

My first impulse was to run, but I sat in this uncomfortable space until the session was over. My mind would dip into this dark pit of nonexistence, then jump back up into consciousness awareness. I felt like I was a yo-yo bouncing up and down from near terror to relief. I didn't know it at the time, because I did not know anything about the skandhas, but it almost felt like I was cycling through the heaps— from near terror at the bottom of the heap (the panic that is the first skandha), to relief at the top (the fifth skandha).

I was relieved when the session was over and I could finally move, but I also think that if I could have stayed in that space for the entire evening, a breakthrough might have occurred. But I couldn't. I was happy to be actively lazy again.

It is important to realize that if we experience space without reference to the ego, it becomes a breath of fresh air. If we do not try to contain infinity but allow ourselves to dissolve into it, space becomes what it is. It is "God," nirvana. By knowing this we can more readily face the barrier of fear, embrace it, and then walk through it into the space beyond. This is when we really have to follow our fear and go through it.

As we have seen, the skandha of form is created by freezing space (the space of mind). On an absolute level, of course, it is impossible to freeze space, but relatively we generate the illusion of frozen space—the facade of form. It is like the story of the magician who created an illusory lion that then turned around and ate the magician. We are the magicians of our own reality, and by making it real and forgetting that we did so, we fall prey to our own magical powers.

❦ Siddhi and Speed

We talked earlier about siddhi, or psychic power. Siddhi is a testament to the power of the mind, and it seems to be reserved for the highest stages of the path. We have to be pretty advanced to walk through walls and fly through space. But you and I demonstrate a form of samsaric siddhi now, for we are constantly transforming space into solid form. Far from being mystical, for the ego this is a practical and necessary manifestation of its power. It is a miracle that the ego routinely performs to keep itself alive.

How do we freeze space? How do we create the illusion of form out of the reality of emptiness? We do it by relating inappropriately to space through the implosive reaction of panic, and the heart of panic is blinding speed. Speed freezes space. We have seen how motion is the principal "substance" of the realm of desire and that rapid motion is a principal form of substance abuse.

If you extend your hand while sitting still, it can easily move through space. Your hand is free to do what you want. But if you extend your hand out of a car moving at one hundred miles an hour, you quickly discover what speed does to space. Your hand is no longer free to move about. You have to wrestle with the freezing space to move it where you want.‡

Similarly, before I freeze mental space, my mind is open, spacious, and relaxed. It is free. I can do whatever I want. There is no you,

---

‡ This is just an analogy for freezing space, for which we have few. The wrestling here comes from air resistance brought about by movement, but hopefully you get the point.

there is no me, so "I" am free to dance and play. But once I freeze space, I now have to deal with you and me and every other icy form I bump into. I am restricted by the forms I have frozen into reality.

When I took my first sky dive, I was instructed to step out of the plane that was flying at four thousand feet and stand on a tiny platform. As I stepped out, I was stunned by the blast of air and had to grasp tightly onto a rail attached to the wing. It was said that Jesus could walk on water, a truly miraculous feat, but I have seen many barefoot water skiers do the same thing by traveling at fifty miles an hour. All kinds of samsaric miracles occur and forms of illusion arise when speed comes into play.

Look closely at moments of panic or moments of intense self-consciousness and you will discover an initial implosion of awareness followed by a stunning impact. The greater the self-consciousness, the more seemingly solid the space. If we are a bit nervous, then we won't restrict ourselves, and our performance won't suffer, but if we are frozen stiff in self-consciousness, we won't be able to move. Another example is when we are hit with sudden bad news. Out of the blue your spouse tells you she's having an affair and wants a divorce, or you hear that a loved one has been killed. It literally feels like you have been struck, and people can go into shock from the force of this impact.

We are emphasizing the way that the first skandha arises because the discovery of space is one purpose of meditation. The path is about returning to this groundless ground, the space prior to the big bang of the first skandha. The etymology of "religion" (re-ligio) suggests this process: linking back to space. As Deepak Chopra says, "All this effort to learn, when all we have to do is remember." But the ego does not want to remember, and amnesia is a natural consequence of post-traumatic stress disorder, the trauma of constantly hearing the hard truth of our nonexistence. Ignorance really is bliss for the ego.

This primordial amnesia is the root of all subsequent mindlessness. Recall that mindfulness, *drenpa*, means "to remember." At the deepest levels, mindfulness leads us to recall that we are that open space and that we can literally *re*member, or unite, with it.

So where does hardship fit into all this? Remember that some synonyms for the first skandha are "panic," "bewilderment," and "fear." The first skandha is what gave birth to samsara in the first place, and this therefore is what we can experience near the end of the path. As we get closer to the truth of our nonexistence we are getting closer to panic, bewilderment, and fear. Knowing that this might lie ahead on the path is important in understanding and expecting hardship.

Seeing through the skandhas begins with frustration at the level of the fifth skandha and ends with fear at the level of the first. This is what happens *near* the end of the path, but not at the end itself. It can also happen in brief moments at any point on the path. At the end of the path, lying beyond these defenses, are the noble qualities of enlightenment, infinite wisdom, compassion, and power. This is the view that keeps us going forward and that will cut through any panic and fear.

To summarize: we began the worldly path with an insane reaction to space, and we must end the path by facing that insanity. We return to face our samsaric roots. The skandha of form was the ego's first attempt to shield itself from the truth of its insubstantiality, and now it is the ego's last attempt to keep us away from this devastating truth.

When our meditation is boring and frustrating, that is not a bad sign but a good one. We are starting to penetrate the fourth and fifth skandhas and beginning to frustrate their mechanism. When our meditation is starting to freak us out, that is not a bad sign but a good one. We are starting to enter the deeper skandhas and approaching the truth. When we feel like we are about to lose our mind, that can mean we are getting close to gaining real sanity.

16 🌱
Working with the Skandhas

HOW DO WE WORK with the five skandhas? They can seem so abstract and ironically impersonal. The first thing is to become familiar with them. This familiarity applies to both the relative and absolute levels. In meditation we initially become familiar with our relative sense of self; we discover and become familiar with the skandhas. We start with what is most available, which is consciousness itself, the fifth skandha. Trungpa Rinpoche says,

> The practice of meditation is to see the transparency of this shield [of the five skandhas]. But we cannot immediately start with the basic ignorance itself; that would be like trying to push a wall down all at once. If we want to take this wall down, we must take it down brick by brick; we start with immediately available material, a stepping stone. So the practice of meditation starts with the emotions and thoughts.[82]

In meditation we are introduced to the bricks of the ego at the level of the fifth skandha, and we become familiar with how we put all these bricks together. Meditation introduces us to the fifth skandha by providing contrast. If we just look at the ceaseless movement of our mind, we are not meditating. We are indulging, or maybe witnessing, our thoughts. We need the contrast against which our moving mind can be observed, and this contrast is generated by giving the meditator a stable object upon which to focus, usually the breath, body, or some other reference. That reference point then becomes the canvas upon which the moving mind can more easily be seen. By being told to keep our mind still, we more easily recognize its movement. The fifth skandha now stands out.

Meditation is elegant in that it goes directly back to the first skandha, form, as a way to work with the skandhas. We use the root of the ego to uproot the ego. With meditation we are learning how to relate to form properly. Instead of spinning mindlessly out of control from the ground of form and giving birth to the remaining four skandhas, we return mindfully to this ground as a way to work with our unstable mind. The original sin is not the first skandha per se but our pathetic relationship to it.

In the normal operations of the ego, we only touch into the first skandha here and there, just long enough to feel its security. We spend most of the time in our thinking minds, in skandhas two through five. We touch into the forms of the world just long enough to set off a cascade of commentary about them. We perceive something and then run with it into endless judgment and internal gossip.

So the problem is not with the first skandha but our partial experience of it. The first skandha is the ever-present world of form, and this is what we return to in meditation. We literally and figuratively come to our senses, which can perceive only the present world of form. We can't hear the past nor see the future; our five senses are locked into nowness, so we use the natural wisdom of our sensory contact with form as a way to work with the skandhas altogether. This, of course, is the practice of mindfulness, having a mind-full-of-nowness, a mind-full-of-form.

In meditation, the instruction is to be with our body and breath, to be *fully* with form. This is how we frustrate the higher skandhas, especially the endless chatter of the fifth skandha, which like shame-less paparazzi, makes its career out of endless commentary about form. Because of the higher skandhas, we live in our heads and not in reality, but by returning *fully* to the world of form, we boycott the higher skandhas and come back to our roots in direct experience.

Partial experience is what generates the skandha of form in the first place. It is our inability to experience space properly that causes us to freeze it into form, and it is our subsequent inability to experience form completely that causes us to slide into the higher skandhas and into full-blown confusion. If we can be fully present with *whatever* arises—space, form, feeling, perception, formation, or conscious-ness—we will discover that complete experience to be nondual.

This is why the idea of descending back through the skandhas is merely provisional. We do not need to work our way back to the space prior to the first skandha, for if we plunge directly into what-ever experience presents itself, we will discover that space in whatever arises. We start and finish where we are. As Jakusho Kwong puts it, we need a path not to go from here to there but to go from here to here.

Remember that the "absolute experience of duality is itself the experience of nonduality." It is therefore our half-hearted relation-ship to the world of form, not form itself, that is the problem. As Francesca Fremantle puts it, "The skandha of form refers to this inter-face, this sphere of [half-hearted] relationship between subject and object, not to matter or material existence itself. Form is very basic and straightforward: just simple, direct contact between the senses and their objects, without any interpretations, reactions, or precon-ceptions [without the commentary of the higher skandhas]."[83] The way out, again, is to dive in: to return fully to the world of form.

But most of us want out of the world of form; that is why many of us enter the spiritual path in the first place. We long for ascent into heaven not a descent into earth. For the ego, heaven is the culminat-ing head space of the fifth skandha, so it is a rude awakening when the spiritual path turns us directly into the world of form and smack into that which we thought we could escape. It's that nasty u-turn again.

This is where meditators get stuck. The minute we leave our body in meditation and ascend into the false sanctuary of our mind, we are off the path and lost in our head. I know meditators who have been practicing for twenty years, and they are completely lost in mental space. This is not the sacred space prior to the first skandha, but a fabricated and indulged space that creates a ready avenue for escape. They are "spaced-out" in a subtle and sophisticated way. They have become disembodied practitioners, spinning around in their version of what meditation should be.

Instead of synchronizing mind and body, their meditation is about leaving the world of bodies altogether. But successful meditation means a return to form, which starts with a return to our body. Meditation is not an out-of-body experience, which is why every authentic practice begins with, and sustains, some form of mindfulness. Mindfulness is what brings us down to earth, and it is here that we will finally find spirit. We are starting to head into the fruition of the path, (discussed more fully in part 3).

In the last year of my long retreat, I dreamt I was with His Holiness the Seventeenth Karmapa, the head of the tradition I follow. The dream turned into a lucid dream, which meant that I suddenly realized I was dreaming. I was awake in my dream and I asked His Holiness, "How can I serve you?" I expected him to say, "You must write books," or "You must spend your life in retreat." Instead he said, "Change my diapers." His answer came as a real shock, one that woke me up from the dream. It was a command to plunge into the earth. I always held highfalutin ideas of what it means to be spiritual, and the Karmapa slammed me into the ground to wake me up.

❧ Relative Familiarity

We can use the gist of the five skandhas to summarize the entire path. The first half of the path is to become familiar with your relative mind. Get to know your ego, your five skandhas, who you *think* you are. This is not always pleasant. You discover how wild your relative mind is and how hard it is to sit still. Once you settle down and see through the rough movements of mind, the more subtle and repressed elements bubble up. This is also challenging because the reason these elements were repressed in the first place is because you did not want to deal with them. All sorts of junk is percolating beneath the surface of consciousness, and meditation brings it up. As Trungpa Rinpoche puts it: meditation isn't a sedative, it's a laxative.

It needs to come up, and we need to become familiar with it because it is the silent engine that drives our confused lives. Lama Shenpen Hookham says, "At first, the truths we discover about ourselves might be far from comforting. That is why it is important to be committed to truth itself, whether or not it is comforting, if we want ultimate liberation."[84]

This is where meditation meets therapy. Even though all thoughts eventually self-liberate, they can cause unnecessary hurt until they do. A therapist can help us become familiar with the psychic abscesses that are being drained and ease the liberating process.

Typologies like the Enneagram can also help. A good typology is a method for becoming familiar with and befriending every aspect of our relative self. But it's not easy. When I discovered my type in the Enneagram, I was startled by its accuracy and offended by its insight. I'm not special, I'm just a "five." It was like looking into a mirror and seeing the pimples I try to hide.

This is also where intimate spiritual relationships can help. Our lover can provide a powerful mirror that reveals our blind spots—if we are willing to take a look. Short of living with a guru, a deep relationship can strip us down and accelerate our path by exposing our damaging habitual patterns.

These painful revelations are tremendous blessings. Before we can *discover* who we truly are, we have to discover who we are not; before the sun can be revealed, we have to remove the obscuring clouds. The typologies, the neuroses, the painful thoughts and emotions are not who we really are, they are the constructs we have built up to create the facade of our relative self, the face we present to ourselves and the world.

Becoming familiar with the dark clouds and shadows constitutes the first half of the path. As Sakyong Mipham Rinpoche says, before we can become buddha, we have to become human. Before we wake up, we have to realize we are asleep. This level of seeing involves hardship and demands real warriorship. Trungpa Rinpoche writes,

Anyone who is interested in finding out about oneself, and anyone who is interested in practicing meditation is basically a warrior.

We have a fear of facing ourselves. That is the obstacle. Experiencing the innermost core of our existence is very embarrassing to a lot of people. A lot of people turn to something that they hope will liberate them without their having to face themselves. That is impossible. We can't do that. We have to be honest with ourselves. We have to see our gut, our excrement, our most undesirable parts. We have to see them. That is the foundation of warriorship, basically speaking. Whatever is there, we have to face it, we have to look at it, study it, work with it and practice meditation with it.

Once we decide to look at ourselves, we may experience ourselves as wretched. . . . Whatever arises, we look at ourselves, either based on hope or fear, whatever there may be. The important point is looking at ourselves, finding ourselves, facing ourselves, giving up our privacy and inhibition. Once we have done that, we turn to the good side of things. We begin to realize that we have something in us which is fundamentally, basically good—very good. It actually transcends the notion of good or bad. Something worthwhile, wholesome and healthy exists in us. But don't jump the gun and try to get hold of that first. First, let's look. If we actually face ourselves properly and fully, we will find that something else exists there, something beyond facing ourselves.

The starting point is acknowledging that some kind of goodness exists in us. It is necessary to take that arrogant attitude, positively speaking. There is some feeling of upliftedness. We are worthy people, and we have something going for us. We are not all that totally wretched. Of course, we do have the wretched aspect that we have to face and look at. That is absolutely necessary in order to realize the other part. But they don't actually interact as counterparts. It's simply that you go through your clouds, and then you see your sun. That is the basic approach, the basic idea we should take towards the worthiness of our existence. That . . . is the warrior's philosophy of looking at ourselves.[85]

✤ Absolute Familiarity

After you become familiar with your relative self, you see through it and are introduced to your true nature. This is the sun behind the clouds, and it is completely selfless. Becoming familiar with your absolute nature constitutes the second half of the path.

Earlier we introduced the five paths, and the first two paths, the Path of Accumulation and the Path of Juncture, are where we become familiar with who we are not. These are the "cloudy" paths. They purify the clouds and open the way to the sun. Practitioners on these two paths still think that things exist. They have not yet become noble.

The third path, the pivot point in the middle of the five paths, is the Path of Seeing. This is a very short path and constitutes the moment when we finally cut through the clouds and see the sun at our core. It is seeing emptiness. This first stage of recognition is called "Joyous" because seeing who we really are brings great joy. Seeing that all our problems are fundamentally empty is also joyful. This is how we transform hardship into joy at the level of the Second Turning.

When we leave this moment of discovery we enter the Path of Meditation, or Familiarization, the fourth path. Clouds still appear, but for the first time they are really seen as clouds. Thoughts and emotions still arise, and things still appear, but they no longer seduce us. The journey is now to become more and more familiar with our sun. When we completely realize who we are, we enter the fifth Path of No More Learning and become a buddha. There is nothing left to learn about ourselves. We have seen through all the clouds and completely identify with the sun. We wake up to who we are.

Even before the breakthrough into the Path of Seeing, we can glimpse our true nature as the clouds part along the first half of the path. It's still mostly cloudy, but the sun peeks through. Depending on how we relate to that flash of illumination, it can be either liberating or blinding. The light is so bright in contrast to the clouds that it can be terrifying.

This is frightening because the sun is the direct experience of egolessness or emptiness. If we relate to it for what it is, it becomes a moment of joy, but since we are still on the first half of the path, which is based on the ego as the central reference point, we tend to refer this egoless experience to the ego. And the ego has no choice but to relate to egolessness as a death threat. Our heart starts pounding, and we may feel like we are about to go crazy. We are getting warm. We are starting to feel our sun. Liberation is not liberation *to* the self, but liberation *from* the self, and the self responds by trying to pull us away.

Once we really see emptiness and do not merely glimpse it, we can bask in the warmth and joy that is our new (nonreferential) reference point along the Paths of Seeing and Meditation. This can bring about a second level of fear, one that is often surprising. The first level of fear is the shock of our nonexistence, the fear of emptiness. The second level of fear is the fear of our fullness. We are afraid of our luminosity, our brilliance. We are intimidated by our inner wealth and natural resources, the force with which our true nature shines. Abraham Maslow writes that "we are generally afraid to become that which we glimpse in our most perfect moments," and John Welwood comments, "no doubt because our larger being threatens us in many ways." He goes on to say, "If we were to open to it fully, perhaps it would disrupt our cozy little habits and throw our familiar, small identity into question . . . [we] are primitives in regard to our larger being."[86]

We have seen how hard it is to embrace our shadows; it is just as hard to embrace our light. It takes courage to cut through the clouds and discover our sun but also endless bravery to display its radiance. Discovering our larger being, the luminosity within, is our journey through part 3.

Part III

THE THIRD TURNING

We shall not cease from exploration
And the end to all our exploring
Will be to arrive where we started
And know the place for the first time.
—T. S. ELIOT, Four Quartets

The dawn of enlightenment in the Buddhist tradition
cannot take place unless first there is a sense of desolation,
meaninglessness, and being a fool. . . . Then the dawn of
enlightenment can actually take place properly. . . . Such a thing
cannot happen unless there's nightfall and darkness. . . .
We have already understood that there's no me, no self, no ground.
That nonexistence begins to make sense. That nonexistence
of self, of ego, becomes the Star of Bethlehem, and the dawn
of enlightenment begins to take place.
—CHÖGYAM TRUNGPA

AFTER THE DISSECTION and analysis of the First Turning and the ego devastation of the Second Turning, what's left? There is something "after" emptiness, it is just not a thing. Something does "exist," and the Third Turning defines that existence.* So while the Second Turning emphasizes negation, the Third Turning emphasizes affirmation.

With the First and Second Turnings, we might analyze a car into its parts, and then discover that even those parts do not exist. With the Third Turning, we agree that that is all true, but then we hop in the car and go for a joy ride. The Third Turning is therefore celebratory. It is all about rejoicing in the shine of reality, the radiant play of it all. This is where we fully embody and celebrate our lives, our thoughts and emotions, our aging bodies, and this sacred earth. This is where we redeem all things material but without getting stuck in materialism. This is where we joyfully return to matter, and all manifestation, but now in a brand new light.

If emptiness is not "balanced" with form—if the union of form and emptiness is not recognized—emptiness can become dismissive of relative truth and flip into escapism. "It's all empty" can easily be appended with "so who cares?" This is "Advaita-speak." In the Third Turning we avoid this spiritual trap by returning to the world of form and purifying it with our new view of emptiness. This proper view, seeing things as the union of form and emptiness, literally transforms form into luminosity. Form becomes luminous, everything lightens up, and we wake up to a world of shimmering rainbows.

"Luminosity" is the essence of the Third Turning, and it is the "light" in enlightenment. If we relate to luminosity without interference, it becomes a liberating play, a complete delight, but if we get in the way, or get carried away, the play transforms into the tragedies and dramas of samsaric existence.

With the proper lens provided by the Third Turning, we discover

---

*As we have seen, "existence" is a tricky term. The challenging point is to discover that reality is beyond existence or nonexistence. In other words, it is beyond any concept we can apply to it. What is "out there" (appearances) neither exists nor does not exist. The idea is not to get caught up in any concept about reality but to cut through all the concepts that obscure it and finally rest in the direct experience of reality. So while defining "existence" may be intellectually stupefying, reality is experientially accessible. That is what is important.

that everything—even our pain, heartache, depression, and loneli-ness—is made of light. Everything reduces, or more accurately ele-vates, into enlightened joy. In my tradition we recite a liturgy that states: "You teach us the great view of emptiness. You reveal the joy of luminosity." If we can relate to difficulties from a Third Turning perspective, then the darkness in our life turns into light, and we finally transform spiritual hardship into joy.

As we saw in our discussion of "interbeing," when things are dis-covered to be empty of self, they are simultaneously seen to be full of other. This is the secret of emptiness, the basis of compassion, and the fruition of the Third Turning. This is also why we don't need to fear emptiness for it is actually fullness. In other words, as our personal sense of self shrinks and eventually evaporates, our cosmic sense of identity proportionally expands. When we (the ego) finally become nothing, we automatically become everything—we become full of other. The Tibetan master Kalu Rinpoche says, "You live in confusion and the illusion of things. There is a reality. You are that reality. When you know that, you will know that you are nothing and, in being nothing, are everything. That is all."[87]

This transformation from emptiness into fullness has its own set of challenges, for not only are we afraid of the seeming darkness of emptiness, we are just as afraid of our light. We are afraid to let go (Second Turning) and really shine (Third Turning). We are afraid of being who we are.

In First and Second Turning meditations, we were taught to dis-tance ourselves from our thoughts and emotions. In the First Turn-ing, they are seen as problematic; in the Second Turning, they are seen as empty. Here in the final Turning, thoughts and emotions are no longer a problem. We celebrate them; they light us up. We appreciate their color and play, and we inhabit them fully—but prop-erly. Transformation becomes more important than renunciation. We delight in the light and reinhabit all form, mental and physical, with a newfound gusto. As if for the first time.

17 🌿

The Art of Working with Emotions

Hell is not punishment, it's training.
—SHUNRYU ROSHI, Zen Is Right Here

When our neurosis is blatantly in our face—particularly as
Western practitioners—we may feel that we have made a mistake
of some kind. Or we may feel that the practice is "not working"
and stop meditating. Each one of these represents a "wrong view."
—REGINALD RAY, Secret of the Vajra World

HARDSHIP ALONG THE PATH, as in life itself, finally comes down to emotional hardship. In the First Turning, it is emotionally difficult to take the self apart. It hurts when the limbs of the ego are severed. In the Second Turning, it is emotionally challenging to discover that even the parts don't exist. It hurts when the heart of the ego is ripped out.

On a more experiential level, when we sit in meditation and work with our thoughts and emotions, we can usually deal with difficult thoughts, and even physical hardship is workable. It is the charged emotions that are so challenging. What makes anything hard is our emotional reaction to it, the way we poison an already difficult situation and make it into a more difficult one. How can we skillfully deal with emotions themselves? What are they made of?

In their essence, emotions are just runaway luminosity, a term we will define in the following chapters. Luminosity is not easy to understand, but emotions are, so we begin our final ascent into the light by working with its most intimate, and often blinding, play. The Dzogchen Ponlop Rinpoche says, "Even in the moment when you experience the most destructive emotion, such as rage, if you can penetrate to its essence you find tremendous space and energy, luminosity."[88] Learning how to relate to emotions is learning how to properly shine.

A student of Chokyi Nyima Rinpoche shared the following story. Rinpoche, who lives in Nepal, had finished a trip to India and was waiting at the Delhi airport to board the return flight to Kathmandu when the announcement came that the flight had been cancelled. The students traveling with him immediately knew that this meant a grueling forty-eight-hour bus drive along bumpy roads, instead of a one-hour comfortable flight. They were going to have to endure two days of flies, heat, and dusty roads and broke out into a litany of complaints. Rinpoche, on the other hand, simply said, "And so?" and didn't exhibit the slightest sense of irritation. The students quickly realized why they were still students and were humbled by their teacher's appropriate response to an unwanted situation.

Hardship boils down to emotions, and emotions boil down to one of the central themes of this book: proper relationship. If we relate appropriately to something hard, it melts into something soft.

There is a big difference between having an emotion and having an emotional problem. Emotions are the electricity of life. They plug us into life and light us up. Emotions make us human; we never want to get rid of them. Emotional problems, or uncontrolled negative emotions, on the other hand, are when the electricity burns us up. It is when we don't relate to the energy properly. The Dalai Lama says of negative emotions,

> Anyone who practices the Dharma has a duty to do battle with the enemy—negative emotions. . . . In doing so, we may encounter difficulties from time to time. But in ordi-

nary war, the trials and difficulties people go through are accepted and even encourage them to fight harder against the enemy. Moreover, in the ordinary world, a warrior's wounds are considered as signs of bravery, like medals. So as practicing Buddhists fighting this real enemy . . . we should expect difficulties, and treat them as signs of victory.[89]

To "battle with the enemy" is to engage the enemy, to work with our negative emotions instead of being worked over by them. So even though we will begin by engaging our negative emotions as an enemy, we will end up making friends with our enemies and discovering the scintillating joy that lies at their heart. In these next two chapters we will explore proper engagement with emotions and the origin and cessation of hardship at an emotional or luminous level.

❦ Sensitivity

When the repressive mind is peeled back in meditation, all kinds of emotions, many of them unwanted, come bubbling up. As we have seen, when our heart opens through spiritual practice, we become more sensitive, like an exposed nerve. Until we learn how to relate to this heightened sensitivity, it is often experienced as heightened touchiness. Things get to us. We laugh and cry more easily, or we may feel emotionally fragile, like a crystal vase. We literally feel more, and if these feelings are handled improperly, they easily escalate into emotional upheaval and instability.

Being sensitive, open, and tender is the promise of the path; being touchy and irritable is its peril. Ken Wilber says that as we progress along the path, things hurt more but they bother us less. Things bothering us less means discovering skillful ways to handle what we increasingly feel—in both senses.

We can sit in the controlled atmosphere of meditation and attain lofty states of realization, but when we leave the cushion and have to relate to the world, our realization often dissolves. Someone sparks an emotional outburst and we lose it. The meditation is gone, our spiritual practice is history, and we are back to where we were before we ever started the path. It is disheartening, epidemic, and unnecessary.

"Going into the marketplace" after meditation is a traditional test for meditative stability. If we can hold our seat and not be swayed by the events of the world, then we have passed the test. If we are thrown by the marketplace and find ourselves reacting to people and situations, then it's back to the cushion. This immovability is what transformed Siddhartha into the Buddha. As he sat under the bodhi tree, he did not move as inner and outer forces attacked him. Demons, seductive maidens, and arrows all turned into flowers because the Buddha wasn't moved by them. He held his seat. We face the same demons, seductions, and arrows every day, but they move us like a pinball in a video arcade.

The Buddhist tradition offers many instructions on how to deal with emotions properly. Part of the problem is that there are so many instructions that we do not know which one to apply or when to apply it. Do I avoid a negative emotion, destroy it, breathe into it, bring an antidote to it, transform it, offer it to my guru, let it self-liberate, or just forget about it? Each of these approaches has its place, the trick is to discover that place.

In the lifetime of an emotion, different instructions can be applied, depending on the force of the emotion. If we apply a gross remedy to a subtle emotional problem, it's like shooting a bazooka at a mosquito. It's overkill. If we apply a subtle remedy to a gross emotion, it is like trying to stop a tank with a flyswatter. We will get squashed as the tank rolls over us.

What follows is a summary of instructions on how to work with negative emotions and when to apply them. When we talk about "working with it," which is common parlance in spiritual communities, we are talking about how to work with the energies without repressing or inappropriately expressing them. In other words, how to engage the enemy properly. The following instructions are one way to shrink the treasury of teachings into pocket-sized advice so that we can carry them with us into the marketplace. It is like taking our meditation cushion with us—we will never lose our seat.

❦ The Four ARTS

The four ARTS are four progressive approaches to poisonous emotion, going from gross to subtle, and are the pith instructions from each of the three yanas. The fourth instruction is the heart of the Mahamudra and Dzogchen approach to emotion, which is part of the Vajrayana.* The four ARTS for handling a difficult emotion are: 1) Abandon it, 2) Remedy it, 3) Transmute it, 4) Self-liberate it. They are easily remembered with the acronym: ARTS.

The first approach represents the spirit of the Hinayana. At this level, emotions are a problem, an enemy, and the best way to deal with the enemy is to avoid it. Difficult emotions are pests. If they haven't approached your neighborhood, keep them away; if they are already in your house, get rid of them. Isolation is a central theme. We don't want any part of the emotion, and if something tends to spark one, then keep that thing away. This approach is visible in countries where the Hinayana is emphasized. For example, in some Southeast Asian countries, monks are instructed to avoid females. They sit isolated on buses, or stand aside when a woman walks by. Celibacy is stressed, and walled-off monasteries are a potent metaphor for this sequestered approach. Monastics are constantly building external and internal fences to keep infecting emotions at bay.

Buddhism describes five primary emotional energies—passion, aggression, ignorance, jealousy, and pride—and at this level each of these energies wants to see a specific aspect of an object. Passion wants to see the positive aspect of an object and will repress or ignore other aspects as it extracts the pleasurable. Aggression sees the negative aspect; jealousy sees the aspect that is better than us or that puts us down; pride sees the aspect that is not as good as us or that lifts us

---

* Some scholars put Mahamudra and Dzogchen in their own vehicle, the Sahajayana, or the vehicle of co-emergence—"being born (*ja*) together with (*saha*)."

up; and ignorance, which is the most difficult because it is the most insidious, does not really care.

These five emotional poisons are the five primordial colors from which every other emotion arises. Frustration, disappointment, anxiety, or any other feeling is a blending of these five "colors." They are like an artist's palette that we dip our brushes into as we paint our countless emotions onto the world and bring color and calamity to our lives.

Any object or person can be subjected to this poisoning, and this accounts for the wildly disparate perceptions people have of the same thing. I can lust after the same person someone else loathes, envies, puts down, or ignores. These five energies are not recognized as energy at this level but only as poison. (The energy will be revealed and skillfully engaged in the higher ARTS.) They poison the objects they contact, so the best approach is to avoid the poison by avoiding the triggering object.

Another method that fits into this level is also object oriented, but in this case *you* become the object. The instruction is that when you feel under emotional attack and cannot handle it, visualize yourself as an inert object, like a piece of wood. Freeze. Remain motionless. Do not talk back (either to yourself or to another) and let the emotions crash over you like waves on a rocky shore. Letting the emotion run its course and exhaust itself is a last-resort approach, and crude, but it is better than lashing out when you feel you are about to lose it. You may be denying, repressing, and altogether ignoring the situation, but at least you are holding your seat. The bottom line: do not move; do not allow yourself to be moved.

Abandonment is the most dualistic approach. There's me and my emotions, keep the two apart. Abandonment is also the only approach that works with the objects that trigger the emotions; the remaining three methods work with the emotions themselves. Emotional upheaval cannot operate without an object, so get rid of the object. It is easy to ridicule this approach, but it is where we start, and we employ it more than we think. It's the "pull the blankets over your head and go to sleep" approach at the end of a hard day. It's the "I need a drink," "I need a vacation," "I need a tranquilizer," or "Get me out of here" approach.

Meditators use abandonment from the outset. When we enter a quiet meditation room and isolate ourselves on the cushion, we are stepping into a walled environment and abandoning daily distractions. It is a powerful initial approach to create some sense of space between ourselves and the objects of the world. We try to control our minds by controlling our world, and by walking into a shrine room, we are entering a highly controlled world.

This initial approach is effective but eventually sterile. The protective container is helpful, but it can become like a sterilized operating room. When meditation first slices us open and our heart is exposed, it does help to keep infecting viruses out, but we can't live in an operating room. It does no good to create an antiseptic cocoon out of secluded meditation. No matter how disinfected it is, it is still a cocoon, and it restricts full participation in life. Sooner or later we have to get dirty. We have to enter the contagious world of others and plop directly into the grease and grime. That is what the Mahayana is for and that is what the world is for. We may evolve into pristine states in the germfree climate of isolated meditation, but the marketplace still awaits us.

❧ Remedy It

The second approach is more refined because it starts to work with emotions themselves. Instead of trying to get rid of the object that ignites the emotion, we work directly with the emotion by applying a remedy to it. There is still a sense that the emotion is poisonous, so we work with antidotes, but at least we are starting to relate to emotions. Instead of isolation, replacement is a central theme. When we find ourselves seething with hate, replace the hate with feelings of love. Replace pride with equanimity, and jealousy with joy in the fortune of others. Replace passion with appreciation, and ignorance with accommodation. Or we can replace these poisonous emotions with objects of meditation. For example, passion for someone can

be replaced with meditation on their ugliness (imagining their intes-
tines, or feces, for instance), and anger can be replaced with meditation on patience.

The *lojong* or "mind training" slogans of Buddhism are the heart
and practical application of this second approach. Most of the fifty-
nine lojong slogans are applied as antidotes to difficult situations
or emotional upheaval. For example, if we are feeling picked on,
"Be grateful to everyone"; if we are feeling self-righteous, "Drive
all blames into one"; if we're feeling unlucky, "Always maintain only
a joyful mind"; when we're feeling competitive, "Don't try to be
the fastest"; and if we are wishing ill upon others, "Don't wait in
ambush."

Lojong blends into the next approach of transmuting emotional
upheaval, but the slogans are primarily an antidote or replacement
approach. It is not as dualistic as abandonment, but it is still dualistic.
We may not be getting rid of the object that triggered the feeling, but
there is still a sense of getting rid of the feeling or replacing it. We are
no longer avoiding the object, as in the previous approach, but we are
not yet embracing the emotion itself, as in the next approach. There
is mutual exclusivity at work at this level—we cannot experience both
the poison and the antidote at the same time.

To demonstrate the subtlety of these slogans and to see how they
blend into both the earlier and later levels of working with emotions,
let's look at the slogan: "Three objects, three poisons, and three
seeds of virtue." This slogan recommends that when we are in the
midst of an emotional eruption, drop the object that sparked the
emotion. If we are enraged over what our boss did, drop the boss and
just be with the rage. On one level, we are getting rid of an object,
though at this level it's an object of thought, the thought of the boss
(not a physical object, the physical boss). By getting rid of this object
(the spirit of the first approach), we are left with the emotion itself
(the spirit of the third approach).

Normally, when we have an object of aggression, we direct our
anger toward it, but if we drop the object, there is nothing to feel
angry toward, and we are left with the anger itself. We start to relate

to the emotion directly. Engage the real enemy, which is not out there. I use this frequently when I'm driving. When someone cuts me off and sparks my anger, I used to race ahead to give the driver a dirty look and feed or justify my anger. Even though I still have that urge, now I make an effort not to look. This cuts the hook and allows me to own and process the energy itself.

If we do not drop the object, we keep the emotion alive by bouncing it off the object. It's like emotional tennis. If we have someone or something (like a practice wall) on the other side of the net, the tennis ball that we strike will keep coming back, and the game will be kept alive. But if we remove the object on the other side, then no matter how hard we hit the ball, nothing will come back. Sooner or later we just exhaust the energy. This is helpful if we find ourselves in an unworkable emotional situation with someone. If we can remain silent and not strike the ball back, the game ends because there is no one to play or fight with.

This remedial approach is powerful and the most applicable of the four approaches for most practitioners.[†] Most of us cannot wall ourselves off from the world, as in the first approach, and many do not practice Vajrayana, as in the latter two approaches. Lojong is a fruitful place to concentrate our efforts when handling unwanted circumstances. Even for Vajrayana practitioners, the wealth of resources from this level is inexhaustible.[‡]

❁ Transmute It

The third approach of transmutation is based on the principle that wisdom is the essence of any emotion; medicine can be found within poison. "Transmuting" is an alchemical process and is more subtle

---

[†] There is another "R" aspect to this second approach and that is to *recognize* the emotion as being empty, in the true spirit of the Mahayana. We will explore this under "self-liberation" below. Recognition and liberation are simultaneous if the emptiness of the emotion can be seen.

[‡] Two good books on lojong are: *Training the Mind*, by Chögyam Trungpa; and *Start Where You Are*, by Pema Chödrön.

and refined than "transformation." "*Trans*formation" implies turning something into something it is not, like apples into oranges, and leans toward the essence of the remedy approach. "Transmuting" is finding wisdom right there in the confusion, seeing the diamond in the heap of coal.

Of the five principal emotions described above, each can be transmuted into its associated wisdom: passion is transmuted into discriminating wisdom, aggression into mirror-like wisdom, pride into the wisdom of equanimity, jealousy into all-accomplishing wisdom, and ignorance into dharmadhatu wisdom. (Ignorance as an emotion refers to the way we respond to a situation by zoning out.) These five wisdoms are five aspects of enlightened energy and are the heart of Vajrayana Buddhism.[§]

Instead of getting rid of the object that ignites the emotion or applying an antidote to it, at this level we fully embrace the emotion. We go directly into it and flip the confusion into wisdom. It is a far cry from the Hinayana monastic who sits across the aisle from a female and who may be ignoring, denying, or repressing the energy of passion. At this level we have intercourse with that energy. The great yogi Gotsangpa put it this way in a verse from one of his songs (*klesha* is the Sanskrit word for conflicting emotions):

> When kleshas get me going and their heat has got me burning,
> I try no antidote to set them right,
> Like an alchemistic potion turning metal into gold,
> What lies in kleshas' power to bestow
> Is bliss without contagion, completely undefiled,
> Kleshas coming up, sheer delight![90]

This advanced approach to emotions is based on a thorough grounding in the previous two approaches and a strict training in the

---

[§] It is beyond the scope of this book to explore these wisdoms, but many books are available that do so. See Chögyam Trungpa, *Journey without Goal* and Irini Rockwell, *The Five Wisdom Energies*.

methods of transmutation. The instruction is to dive into the emotion but armed with the proper tools. Uniting with whatever arises in a skillful way is the essence of Vajrayana or tantra. This is why tantric iconography depicts deities in sexual, or nondual, union.

There is a reason why this practice of emotional nonduality is reserved for more advanced stages. If we plunge into the currents of passion or aggression without adequate training, we are going to drown. The energy will sweep us away, and we will be lost in samsaric "nonduality." If we unite with the energy unskillfully, instead of transmuting the emotion, we end up indulging it.

Self-deception is a real problem at this level. Thinking that we are capable of graduate school when we have barely finished preschool can get us into trouble. Instead of heightened wisdom, we get heightened neurosis, which is common among Vajrayana practitioners. There are Vajrayana meditators who rationalize their emotional indulgence in just this dangerous fashion, feeling it is okay to boldly express their anger or passion and that by doing so they are being "tantric." Emotional release is not tantra, it is supersamsara. While emotions are fundamentally luminous emptiness, without the proper preparation (relationship), that luminosity can be blinding.

But for one who is properly prepared and equipped, transmutation is a potent way to engage emotional upheaval. It is the gasoline that fuels the "quick path" of the Vajrayana, for whatever arises is fully embraced and brought onto the path, accelerating the path's accomplishment. Contemplative psychotherapist Rob Preece shows us how the tantric approach invites and then works with hardship:

> Spiritual practice often brings to the surface aspects of ourselves that are extremely painful. We have a deep reservoir of emotional wounds and patterns that may be hard to accept in ourselves, and which we have consequently often ignored or denied. This forms a powerful "Shadow," to use Jung's term. As we begin to develop some aspects of tantric practice, these repressed emotions will be resurrected from the underworld of our psyche. This enables

the energy bound up in them to then be addressed and potentially transformed. This can sometimes be an uncomfortable process, and it is important to accept and value ourselves even though we feel dreadful, or are frightened of or disgusted with what we see. When we practice Tantra, the dark aspects of our Shadow will almost certainly be evoked, and it requires great courage, honesty, and humility to face and transform them. . . . In this willingness to face unconscious habits we also need compassion towards ourselves as we pass through periods of struggle and discomfort in our practice. Through a genuine love, self-acceptance, and sense of humor about ourselves, we can potentially uncover even the darkest inner monsters. . . . While traditional teachings speak of insights and realizations experienced on the spiritual path, it is seldom made clear that these often come through pain and turmoil.[91]

❧ Self-Liberate It

The last approach is the most subtle. At this level we do not get rid of the emotion, we do not apply an antidote to it, and we don't even transmute it. We just look directly at it, recognize its emptiness, and let it be. If we can rest in its luminous nature, the discursive commentary that transforms a pure emotion into a poisonous emotional upheaval evaporates on the spot. Self-liberation doesn't mean erasing the energy; it means erasing the chatter that transforms the luminous energy into indulged emotional drama. To give it a double entendre, the technique of self-liberation liberates the energy from the commentary provided by the self, which is a spin on the energy that generates the very sense of self. In other words, self-liberation is virtually synonymous with ego-liberation—on the spot.

Doing nothing is the hardest thing to do, and the challenge of this approach is evident when we try to apply it. Unlike the process of transmutation, where we might not know what to do, the instructions for self-liberation are easy. We just cannot do it. We can't let things self-liberate. The energy of the emotion then tosses us around like a leaf in an autumn windstorm. We get caught up and blown away.

The way to work with this level—which is the level of recognizing and resting in the perfection and emptiness of whatever arises—is to develop an appropriate relationship to whatever arises. By studying how we constantly alter reality, how we poison it with our passion, aggression, and ignorance, we can release our urge to perfect our emotions and rest in their innate purity. We learn the art of leaving things alone. Whatever arises then self-liberates back into emptiness. In twenty years of being around meditation masters, I am struck by how often they employ this method in dealing with others. They seem to ignore a situation, or a person, which can feel frustrating. It is as if they don't care, but "couldn't care less" is a branch of self-liberation.

Seeing the purity in our emotions is recognizing their emptiness. We stain things when we take them to be real. By seeing their empty nature, we are purifying them of existence and simultaneously freeing ourselves from the suffering that ensues from that imputation. The emotion still appears, but we don't take it to be real and solid. Instead of being hit with a baseball, we are struck by emotions now transformed into snowballs. Because they melt on contact, they don't sting as much. When the emotion is purified, what we are left with is pure energy, luminous emptiness.

One can argue that all emotions eventually self-liberate. A fit of anger eventually ends, a broken heart gradually mends. Emotions do fizzle out, but they tend to leave a heap of rubble in their wake. That form of self-liberation is like a Mack truck freeing itself as it blasts through the side of your house. That is not the self-liberation we are talking about, which is when an emotion arises and dissolves simultaneously.

In the second year of my group retreat, we were thrown into several weeks of turmoil. We had been in silence for five months and the pressure cooker was building steam. When it finally erupted, the emotional energy released was far from meditative. In an effort to work with the energy, we met weekly to process the events. At the end of one intense session, a retreatant said something that stopped the rest of us in our tracks. We had spent the last hour caught in our own painful story lines, and after listening quietly, she said, "At one level, this entire affair is nothing but 'thinking'."

We didn't say anything, but most of us were thinking the same thing: but what about my feelings? What about the insult from . . .? She was referring to the simple instruction from basic meditation: whenever anything distracts us from following our breath, we label it "thinking" and then return to our breath. "Thinking" pops the bubble of involvement in the distraction and gets us back on track.

Even though it is an entry-level instruction, it comes from the highest levels. What she was saying is that the entire blow-up was irreducibly nothing but "thinking" and that we could let the drama self-liberate with this simple insight. But as with any form of self-liberation, easier said than done.

Several years ago I was doing couples therapy, trying to work through some blind spots in a relationship. My therapist was offering a number of methods for working with emotions, and at the end of one session, he said that while all these methods can be beneficial, the greatest benefit comes from taking the painful emotion, bringing it into our heart, and melting it into emptiness.

What a liberating thought! No matter what arises, no matter how painful or intense, it all reduces into "thinking" and evaporates into space. We may not be able to apply this lofty teaching while in the midst of an emotional outburst, but it provides the view that is at the heart of self-liberation—and real freedom.

❧ Do Not Disturb

The Dzogchen Ponlop Rinpoche says that fundamentally emotions don't bother us—we bother them. If we let them blaze without our interference, they are luminous. The idea of "disturbing emotions" takes on an entirely different meaning in this light. Do not try to be free of your emotions—let your emotions be free of you. Be free of your inappropriate relationship to the emotion, just let the energy be. At these highest levels, emotion is pure energy, raw and rugged light, so do not act or suppress the energy and do not indulge. The next time you get angry, put a "do not disturb" sign on the anger and watch it transmute into the energy of clarity.

Stay with the emotion and stay in the present. If we do that, we don't feed the emotion, and it dies a natural death—it self-liberates. If we stay in the present, then there is no time. There's no time to add on all the commentary or rationalizations that feed the emotion.

The problem with negative emotions stems from an unrecognized reprimand in the origin of the emotion itself. The first issue, therefore, is that we often spank ourselves for becoming emotional. In other words, there are two stages of inappropriate relationship in a full-blown negative emotion, there are two major "add-ons." The first stage is that the negative emotion is usually generated out of an initial inappropriate reaction to some event. For example, we get angry when someone cuts us off on the road. The energy has been ignited.

At this point, once we are angry, we can't do anything about the trigger, or at least we should not. Let the trigger go, release the object that ignited the emotion. By doing so we are now free to focus on the emotion itself. As practitioners, we often feel bad that we have become emotional, and it is this reprimand that we need to drop. Subtract this first add-on. If we don't, it is like being burned a second time.

The key once the emotion is in full swing is to relate to the emotion itself, not the trigger, and to not beat ourselves up for being emotional. The energy is now what is happening, and contrary to what we might think, this energy is not bad. It only becomes disturbing to us, and therefore bad, when we start to disturb the emotion itself, especially when we think we need to get rid of it.

So the first stage of inappropriate relationship comes when we relate inappropriately to an event, something that triggers the emotion. The second stage of inappropriate relationship comes when we relate inappropriately to the emotion itself. We may have been unskillful when we got angry, but when the emotion is raging relate to the energy that is happening, not to what has happened. Subtract all the other add-ons. If you do so and relate to emotion purely, it becomes pure.

Proper relationship will not get rid of the emotion; it actually allows you to feel it more fully. Emotion becomes more vivid and radiant when it is left undisturbed. It becomes more luminous.

❦ Meeting the Buddhas

In Tibetan Buddhism each of the five principal emotions is associated with a buddha, who represents the inherent wisdom in the emotion. This means that if we can relate to these five emotions properly, they can wake us up. We will discover that respective buddha as the heart of the emotion itself and wake up in the midst of confusion.

If we relate to anger properly, we will meet the luminosity of the buddha Akshobhya, and he will wake us up in the midst of our rage. If we relate to pride skillfully, it transforms into the light of the buddha Ratnasambhava. If we look into our passion, we will find the radiant buddha Amitabha, waiting to wake us up in the heat of our desire. If we dive into our jealousy without acting out or suppressing it, it turns into resplendent buddha Amoghasiddhi, always there to arouse us when we are green with envy. If we remain with our delusion, we will encounter the incandescent buddha Vairochana.

We tend to think that spiritual people should not display emotion and that being emotional is not being spiritual. Uncontrolled emotion is not spiritual, but blazing pure emotions are—they are the luminosity of our sun. These teachings are not telling us we should never get angry or display intense passion. Emotion is the juice of life, and becoming emotionally whitewashed is not the point. Every human feels passion; that's not the problem. Being blinded by its luminosity is the problem.

Part of the fear of being who we are is the fear of expressing what we think and feel. We don't know how to let go and properly shine, so we deny our energy or express it poorly. To properly inhabit our emotions is the way to celebrate them, to ride their energies without being thrown by them. If we just express whatever we think and feel, that isn't skillful. That's childish. We can cause damage by leaking all the contents of our hearts and minds. Children can get away with it, but we cannot.

If we repress everything, that too isn't skillful and can lead to all kinds of neurosis. That's puritanical. We do need to contain and express ourselves—but properly. The container should not be too tight nor too loose. It is not always easy to be who we are and to shine properly. Understanding the luminous nature of thoughts and emotions, what they really are, can help us shine.

One reason I enjoy spending time with spiritual masters is to watch how they express their emotions. It is hard to generalize, but in my experience they do not repress or express the way we do. For example, I have seen masters express anger in a seemingly unspiritual way. But when something is truly wrong, they will respond in a truly right way, which can require a seemingly negative emotion.

Two things are different in the way a master works with difficult situations. First, they relate appropriately to an inappropriate situation. When someone is about to hurt another or himself or herself, an immediate tough-love response may be in order. Second, when the anger flashes, it doesn't linger. Anger can explode onto a situation, but then it melts, hence their second-order relationship, this time to the emotion itself, is also appropriate.

Let's now turn to when these ARTS can be applied in the lifetime of an emotional upheaval.

18 ✤
Applying the Four ARTS

The more profound the practice, the more profound the demons.
—PATRUL RINPOCHE, The Words of My Perfect Teacher

ANY OF THE FOUR ARTS can be applied to any emotion, but one way to organize their application is to look at the lifetime of an emotion and the momentum behind it. In other words, which of the ARTS we apply depends on how energized the emotion is. We will start with the most advanced approach.

When an emotional upheaval is first born, it manifests as a mere thought with no established thrust. It's a helpless infant, completely dependent on us for further life. If we can let it be and not feed it with our attention, emotions at this level disappear on their own. They are born and they die simultaneously. They self-liberate—if we let them.

This approach requires tremendous awareness. We have to be able to detect the emotion when it first flickers up. If we can "catch and release" at that first instant, then we can apply the art of self-liberation, and like a campfire spark, it's there and gone in a flash. But most of us do not even realize that emotions start out as harmless sparks of thought, and by the time we catch on, the emotion has already taken on a life of its own, and we have left the domain of self-liberation. The harmless spark ignites a flash fire of energy. Instead of catching it, we get caught up in it and are often burned.

This approach is difficult because having thoughts is the daytime version of falling asleep. In other words, discursive thought is the way we go unconscious throughout the day and is a form of lack of awareness. Thoughts arise in a flicker of mindlessness, and we tend to catch on after the thought has already gathered a head of steam and is well on its way to either a daydream or an emotional outburst.

The level at which self-liberation can be practiced is so subtle that we are not usually aware that thought itself is already tinged with emotional overtones and is ripe for inflation. Every thought is already colored by one of the five principal energies. We can see this by observing how a tiny thought can be fed till it becomes a full-blown fantasy. If the thought is "red," the energy of passion, before we know it, we might find ourselves lost in a sexual fantasy. If the thought is "green," it carries us off into flights of envy; if it is "blue," into daydreams of anger or revenge; if it is "yellow," then images of pride sweep us away, and if a thought is "white," we might space out or drift into reverie. Emotion is energized thought. Just how energized it is dictates which of the four ARTS to apply. Most of us are incapable of applying self-liberation, and in the flicker of an eye, we have left the moment when the fourth of the ARTS can be successfully applied and are tumbling into the domain of the remaining three.

The Dzogchen teachings speak of the "lion's gaze." If we throw a stick at a dog, the dog chases the stick, but if we throw a stick at a lion, the lion chases us. It doesn't get seduced into following the projection, but keeps its gaze on the projector. We have the gaze of the dog and constantly chase after our projections. We lose sight of where emotions come from because we take our mind's eye off the projector and get lost in the emotion itself. We get carried away with the charged movements of mind. Dilgo Khyentse Rinpoche, quoting Milarepa, says,

> Thoughts are the play of pure awareness. They arise within it, and dissolve back into it. To recognize pure awareness as where your thoughts come from is to recognize that your thoughts have never come into existence, remained, or

ceased. At that point, thoughts can no longer trouble your mind. When you run after your thoughts you are like a dog chasing a stick: every time a stick is thrown, you run after it. But if, instead, you look at where your thoughts are coming from, you will see that each thought arises and dissolves within the space of that awareness, without engendering other thoughts. Be like a lion, who, rather than chasing after the stick, turns to face the thrower. One only throws a stick at a lion once.[92]

Self-liberation is the domain of the realized ones. They still have thoughts and emotions, but they relate to them in a profoundly different way. Thoughts still pop up, but they don't grow up. They are recognized and liberated on the spot. They are "stillborn," in both senses of that phrase: buddhas still feel things, they just don't feel them the way we do. They feel things completely, and then they let go completely. Remember that Dzogchen is also translated as the "great completion," and great completion suggests this art of complete feeling and release.

Unlike the buddhas, we relate to emotions in a funny way. Instead of feeling it completely and releasing it completely, we imprison ourselves by feeling it partially when it first arises, and then we attempt to keep feeling it after it should have dissolved. Suzuki Roshi says, "When you do something, you should do it with your whole body and mind . . . you should do it completely, like a good bonfire. You should not be a smoky fire. You should burn yourself completely. If you do not burn yourself completely, a trace of yourself will be left in what you do."[93] We talked earlier about the relationship of pain to suffering: pain is just a good fire; suffering is its smoke.

Instead of burning the emotion, we glom onto it and force feed it with our attention, keeping it alive and smoking. Instead of getting mad and burning the anger out, for example, we often smolder over an event, or we cap our emotions, which drives them back into our mind and body, where they are stored as dirty seeds. These seeds of improper expression or repression are buried within us and manifest as symptoms of neurosis. Instead of letting the emotion flow properly through us and burn purely, which processes the energy and releases it, we repress it or express it improperly and sow the seeds of emotional suffering.

Remember that it is disinterestedness that liberates and that in this case we should lose interest in the emotion after we have fully experienced it. But most of us are far from being disinterested in our thoughts and emotions. We are very interested in the entertainment they provide and the way they support our egos. We like to smoke.

We simply don't want them to self-liberate, so we allow ourselves to get swept away by the energy, and through self-righteousness ("I deserve to be mad!"), indignation ("How dare he say that to me!"), or any of the infinite rationalizations born of habitual pattern, we indulge the emotion by paying attention to it. We mull it over, keep it alive by repeating the scene in our minds, or keep justifying our outburst. And so the tiny spark ignites a rocket as we are shot up into the subsequent phases of an emotional disturbance.

We can try to apply self-liberation at any point in the life of an emotional upheaval, but the momentum of full-blown emotion tends to squash this technique like a tank rolling over a pea-shooter. The three remaining ARTS are better equipped for dealing with momentous emotions. The practice of self-liberation may seem inaccessible to mere mortals, but knowing about it provides a view of where emotions come from and to what we can aspire.

⚜ The Final Three

So before we know it—and precisely because we do not know it—the thought has grown up into a full-blown emotional upheaval. We have fed it with our attention, and it has taken on life. This force feeding often happens in a flash. The tiniest provocation escalates into an instantaneous emotional outburst. Some jerk cuts us off on the road, and we explode in anger; an attractive man or woman walks by and he or she ignites our passion. The remaining three ARTS can now be applied. The order is not fixed, and often a combination of approaches is useful, but for consistency we will continue to follow our scheme of subtle to gross.

Unless we can apply the next technique of transmutation early in the life of an emotion, or unless we are well practiced in the method, the momentum of a raging emotion will probably sweep us away. As we often say when the dust settles, "I got carried away, I lost it." Applying transmutation to a full-blown emotional upheaval can cripple the outburst, partly because we have taken our attention away from indulging and therefore feeding the emotion, but unless we are proficient in this art, it may not fully handle the energy. The instruction for transmutation is to plunge directly into the emotion, which in my experience is more easily accomplished when the emotion is still developing.

Tulku Urgyen Rinpoche speaks about Vajrayana transmutation from the point of view of someone accomplished in this technique: "The stronger and more forceful the disturbing emotions are, the greater the potential for recognizing our original wakefulness." This is true, but for most of us, it is almost a theoretical statement because of the difficulty in applying this technique, which even Tulku Urgyen acknowledges: "If we can remember [to apply the technique], difficult as it may be . . ."[94] Unless we are well rehearsed, we won't remember. Transmutation can be applied at any point, but plunging into a gentle stream is easier than diving into a roaring river.

If you can catch the energy, then transmute it, but if not, then you reach the point in the life cycle of the emotion when it is best to employ either a remedy or practice abandonment. When emotion is raging out of control, then the best you can hope for is a flash of awareness that triggers the memory of abandonment or a remedy. This is why practicing the lojong slogans in advance is so helpful, for they can pop up in the middle of an outburst like a lifesaver tossed into the river. But without practicing the slogans beforehand, there is no chance they can come to rescue you. You have to work with them before they can work with you.

This means that without practicing the remedies the only approach left is abandonment, and that is what most of us apply—if we apply anything at all. It is better than nothing. The emotion is boiling, but we are not willing to give in. Playing deaf and dumb, or walking away, is still better than acting out. The reason it is better not to act out is because acting out creates karma, and karma creates habitual patterns that predispose us to act the same way again. If you lose it once, it is easier to lose it again; if you hold your seat once, it is easier to hold your seat again. It may not be so skillful to turn yourself into a log, but it's even less skillful to throw one.

These final three approaches can be applied in almost any order to a full-blown emotional upheaval. We can also apply all these techniques to a single emotional episode. Perhaps we start with abandonment and weaken it, then bring in a remedy for the remaining energy or work with transmutation. A key to dealing with emotional upheaval is just do something different. Don't give in to the emotion and fall into the same old ruts. Even if you are trying to decide which approach to apply, that in itself is helpful because you interrupt the momentum behind the emotion. By pulling your attention away from the emotion, you have stopped feeding it.

❧ The Grand Scheme

All four stages of an emotion and a visual guide for the application of the four ARTS to it can be symbolized by an inverted triangle, or the letter "V." We used this model earlier in summarizing the three yanas, starting with the lowest yana at the base. Here we start with the highest yana at the base, which is the technique for self-liberation.

The point where the two lines join at the bottom is the most nondualistic. Self and other, me and my emotion, are united at the point when thought and emotion first arise. At this level, thought and emotion are recognized to *be* awareness (awareness taking on the form of thought and emotion), hence they are self-liberated *as* awareness. And as we will see, awareness is one way to talk about luminosity. When the emotion takes on more life, it appears to emerge and diverge from awareness. It only appears to, for in reality emotion at any level is always and only awareness, but we just don't see it that way. In theory, self-liberation can therefore be applied at any level, but in practice it is more difficult to apply once the emotion has left the "point." Emotion becomes progressively more dualistic as it takes on momentum and escalates up the "V." The emotion becomes more energized, more substantial, and more of an object as it goes up the scale.

At the "point," subject and object are one, but then the split begins, and duality between me and my emotion is born. This is why the central teaching of the first level out from the point, that of transmutation, is to dive back in. Dive directly into the emotion. You are trying to reunite with it in a skillful way, to "plunge straight into their essential point," as Gotsangpa put it in the song above. Return to the nondual point, which is the point of energy, and recognize emotion as awareness (luminosity) by jumping directly into it. If you do, then the emotion is transformed (recognized) into pure energy, and you are liberated. The fracture is instantly healed.

If you do not, then the energy of the emotion will rip you apart, creating the false sense of "me" and "my emotion." In other words, if instead of looking into the emotion, you look away from it, at either the object that triggered it or your rationalization for indulging in it, then you are heading away from the "point" instead of down into it. If you look in as a nangpa (insider), you will be freed in energy; if you look out, you will be imprisoned in emotion. Turn around and plunge directly into the emotion, and you will return to, and be liberated in, the nondualistic source; look away toward the object, and you will be carried away and trapped in increasingly dualistic domains. With the former, the emotion lights you up, with the latter it can burn you up.

If you can't transmute it by diving into it, then you can step up the scale into the next technique, the more dualistic relationship of applying a remedy. This is not as dualistic and fully "object" oriented as the final technique of abandonment, but it is not as nondualistic as the approaches of transmutation and self-liberation. The remedial approach is "object" oriented in that you are trying to replace one "object," a bad emotional response, with another one, a good alternative response.

The final stage of abandonment is the most dualistic and the most object oriented. You are no longer dealing with the emotion directly, but with the objects that trigger it. There is no attempt at intercourse, at uniting nondualistically with the emotion (the Vajrayana, or tantric approach, is all about this kind of sacred "intercourse") because the momentum has carried you way past that point. Abandonment is used when there is the greatest sense of me and other and when I create offensive and defensive strategies in response to the threat of other. This is when I feel the most under attack by external forces, the world at large, and take no ownership in my emotions or how they are triggered by my inappropriate response to the world. I take no responsibility at this level; I am always the victim playing the blame game. It's never my fault, the world is always against me. My anger and bitterness are justified as *self* defense.

I take no ownership at this level because the sense of subject and object is the greatest. What I am supposed to own up to, my emotions, are too far across on the "other" side. They are so far away (from being me) that I don't see them properly. I have taken my eye off the projector (the point, the mind that gives birth to everything), have fully bought into the projection (the energized emotion), and see only sticks flying around. I have the gaze of a dog.

To summarize: the left line of the "V" represents self, and the right line represents "other." The lines tip away from each other as they ascend, symbolizing the increasing sense of self and other, proceeding from nonduality at the base to complete duality at the top. At the bottom, object is recognized as subject; at the top, subject and object could not be farther apart. Momentum increases as emotion takes on life and escalates up the scale. Fed by our indulgence, it becomes increasingly forceful and difficult to deal with. Karmic repercussions increase because momentum is another word for karma. No karma is generated if a thought is self-liberated, which is why buddhas don't create karma with their thoughts and emotions. Total karma is generated if the thought reaches enough steam to be expressed in speech or deed.

At the bottom, applying the nondualistic technique of self-liberation is apt; at the top, applying the dualistic approach of abandonment is apt. Relationship is the most intimate and appropriate at the bottom; relationship is the least intimate and inappropriate at the top (which is how emotion made its way to the top—by being inappropriately related to at the bottom). Awareness is highest at the bottom, where thought and emotion first arise; awareness is lowest at the top, where emotion rages out of control. Buddhas live at the bottom; we live near the top.

❦ A Fighting Chance

A few months ago I got into a big fight with my girlfriend. She was angry about something I did and started shouting at me. I stayed with her anger, trying to relate to her point of view, and could feel my own anger starting to surge. I could almost see myself leaving the "point" and starting to spike up the spectrum. I tried to hold the energy, catching myself just as I was about to give in to it, and for a few minutes I was able to control it, dipping back down into the brilliant clarity that is the energy of anger before it explodes. I was working with the tantric approach of diving back into the essential point and was able to catch a few glimpses of the brilliant buddha Akshobhya. When I was able to do it, everything was crystal clear, sharp, and penetrating. The expression on her face was so vivid, her words were crisp and vibrant.

But at a certain point, when I felt she had crossed the line, I lost it myself and started to shout back. At that point, once I caved in, I had a hard time controlling myself. I tried to recite a mantra, which is another way to work with the remedy or antidote approach, and it helped because it brought me out of my blinding rage and helped me stay centered. But when she physically pushed me, I lost it again and almost pushed her back. At that point, realizing the energy was out of control, I turned myself into a log. I sat there and let her unload on me, not responding to anything she said. After some time, with no one to engage with, she stormed away.

I was left alone, fuming mad. I tried to "drop the object" and not think about her and turned my attention directly to the energy. It was difficult because I wanted to lash *out*, but I held my seat and worked with the raw emotion. Because I wasn't feeding the emotion by going out with it, I was able to slowly reapply a mantra (*om mani padme hum*), then a slogan ("Drive all blames into yourself"), and finally I just rested in the crackling energy. It was uncomfortable, like sitting on a hot stove. I kept wanting to move out, to get back at her, to show her how wrong she was. My anger eventually settled back down, and I was able to be fully present with what was happening without reacting to it, and it faded away. It eventually self-liberated, but it took twenty minutes to do so.

This is more or less the way I work with the four ARTS. It is clumsy and messy but eventually effective in working with emotional upheavals. I can't apply a strict order, and often fumble about till one of the ARTS clicks in. It's also not easy, but it keeps me from getting into trouble and prevents a great deal of negative action (karma). The more I apply these ARTS, the easier it becomes, and the more I am able to stay centered around the "point." I don't lose it nearly as often.

The four ARTS may initially seem one-sided, even selfish, because we're just dealing with emotions as they arise within us and not as they arise within others. But the emotional reactions in others are often based on the emotions we present to them, so by learning how to handle our emotions more skillfully, we can bring clarity and control to our own minds, more accurately present ourselves to others, and therefore relate to them better. When we are blinded by rage, for example, we can't really see what is happening with others, and we aren't really relating to them. Exploding is usually not the best way to contact someone. To see more clearly what is happening with another person, and to better understand his or her emotions, we have to start with ourselves. Otherwise we plaster the other person will all kinds of unrecognized projections and transferences and feed emotional outbursts instead of abating them.

Turning into a log also doesn't mean I can't walk over and give my girlfriend a big hug, which may be exactly what she needs. It means I let her angry words crash over me without getting to me, without reacting adversely. By not moving, I can sometimes see through her rage, contact her underlying goodness, and even invite it out of her. And I do so by not saying a thing.

One of the biggest problems with emotional outbursts is that we lose possession and control of our emotions. We get all tangled up with the energy of the other person, lose any sense of clarity, and often just escalate emotional upheavals. Learning how to relate to our own emotions, and taking proper ownership of them, has the effect of helping others do the same.

We have presented a number of maps in this book, and while maps are very useful, the map is never the territory. Even when we literally travel, some of our greatest adventures occur when we get lost, when we drop the map and explore uncharted terrain with spontaneity and delight. The point with these ARTS isn't to cram our rich emotional lives into a sterile template or to strip ourselves of these energies. The point is to learn how to shine without scorching ourselves or others. Feel your emotions, fully experience the energies of being human, but don't get overwhelmed and sucked into damaging situations when the energies start to sizzle.

❦ Awareness Lost

When we "lose it" in an emotional upheaval, what we have lost is awareness. When we are possessed by anger or passion, for example, we lose any sense of environmental awareness. We are so focused on ourselves or the object of our emotion that we are unaware of what is happening around us. If we are madly in love with a person, a job position, or an object, we are going after it come hell or high water, and we don't care what happens to those around us or how our obsession inflicts pain on others. At a deeper level, when we "lose it," we have lost the awareness that the emotion is pure energy and that that energy is our deepest "self."

The key in all skillful approaches to emotion is therefore to recapture awareness. If the problem is "losing it," the cure is to regain it. When we are in the midst of an emotional upheaval, one trick is to click into something in the environment, to reestablish some sense of panoramic awareness, which gets us out of ourselves and our indulged energy. A friend told me that he was recently in a shouting match with his wife. He picked up a vase and just as he was about to hurl it against the wall, he caught a glimpse of his cat sitting on the couch yawning. This brief contact with his environment, punctuated by the absurd contrast, brought him to his senses. His anger ventilated, and he started to laugh, recapturing his awareness in the nick of time.

Awareness controls thought and emotion and dictates the application of the four ARTS: the greater the awareness, the more refined the approach. With complete awareness, thought and emotion take care of themselves—they self-liberate. With progressive loss of awareness, thought and emotion require our care—we apply the three remaining ARTS. With these four ARTS, negative emotions can be recognized and liberated into pure luminosity, and a great deal of unnecessary hardship can be prevented.

19 ❧

The Blessing and Curse of Deep Meditation

If you've had a good meditation or a bad meditation,
you haven't had meditation. —TULKU URGYEN

Don't believe in the reality of good and bad experiences;
they are like today's ephemeral weather, like rainbows in the sky.
Wanting to grasp the ungraspable, you exhaust yourself in vain.
As soon as you open and relax this tight fist of grasping,
infinite space is there—open, inviting, and comfortable.
—LAMA GENDUN RINPOCHE

ACHIEVING MEDITATIVE STABILITY is a challenge for any spiritual practitioner. This is especially true for long-term meditators, who even after decades of meditation often express frustration about the fragility of their practice: "The meditation just doesn't seem to be working." "I'm just as confused as ever."

The first issue is that when we practice, what are we actually doing? Just because our body is planted on the ground doesn't mean our mind is planted in our practice. Our body might assume a meditation posture, but our mind may be in Hawaii. In a moment of refreshing candor, a friend who has been meditating for thirty-five years told me that when he meditates he's mostly hanging out. So the first thing is to assess the integrity of our practice. In order to develop stability, we have to practice it—a half-hearted practice gives us half-hearted results.

The second issue is that in order to gain stability in meditation we have to cultivate stability in our life. Instability derives from a disintegrated relationship between life and practice. If we separate our life from our meditation, which most of us do until we reach advanced stages, then it is hard to attain stability. If we think we can tuck our meditation into a corner of our life while we engage in a sloppy lifestyle, then stability will forever elude us.

The Sanskrit word for meditative absorption, the fruit of stability, is *samadhi*. Samadhi means to "establish, make firm" or "putting together." It is also translated as "to get yourself together," and it implies the gathering of attention. Samadhi is being focused one-pointedly on an object of meditation, becoming so immersed that one virtually becomes the meditation.

The conditions required to attain samadhi extend far beyond what happens on the cushion. In order to attain stability, we have to gather not only our thoughts but all the disparate elements of our life. We have to realize that at the deepest levels our life is not different from our practice and has a profound impact upon it. In order to achieve samadhi, we have to get our act together.

During my last trip to India I asked His Holiness the Seventeenth Karmapa about stability. He replied that this was an important point and talked at length about the need for family values, and how love and warmth are critical for stability in meditation. His Holiness said it was important not to get swept up in the allure of technology and that cell phones, computers, and electronic gadgets often make us run around faster, resulting in what he called "bloodless metal people."

The Karmapa spun a web of teachings that I had a hard time tracking because the web was so wide. He seemed to touch on everything. At the end of his reply, His Holiness said that stability was connected to one's attitude and one's conduct in life. In other words, a *dis*-integrated life leads to disintegrated practice.

These teachings made me take a closer look at my life. Where was I cutting corners? When was I kidding myself? Where was I cheating? Trungpa Rinpoche says we should look to see if there is a difference between what we do in public and what we do in private. I pondered the Karmapa's answer for months and then remembered the doctrine upon which I think it was based.

❧ The Three Trainings

The Buddha taught three principal trainings, the *trishiksha*, three disciplines that constitute the core of his teaching. They are a condensation of the famous "eightfold noble path," which is itself the essence of the fourth noble truth—the path leading to the cessation of suffering.*

These three trainings are progressive and interdependent; they build on each other and simultaneously depend on each other. The first training is in moral discipline, or ethics. The term in Sanskrit is *shila*, and it means "habit, custom, conduct, disposition, character, and moral conduct." The second training is in meditative concentration, or samadhi, which is our main topic, and the third training is wisdom, or *prajna*, which is seeing the nature of reality.

Prajna depends on samadhi, which depends on shila. Prajna is the fruit of the Second Turning, for prajna is what sees emptiness, and the texts of the Second Turning are called the prajnaparamita sutras, the sutras of transcendent wisdom. We will focus on the relationship between samadhi and shila and the foundation these two trainings lay for prajna.

The three trainings help us with stability because they reveal its foundation. In other words, we forget that stability depends on

---

*The eightfold noble path is: right view, right resolve, right speech, right conduct, right livelihood, right effort, right mindfulness, and finally right concentration— or right samadhi. It suggests that the first seven create the foundation for, and culminate in, the eighth.

morality. The power of our meditation will stand or fall on our integrity, honesty, and virtue. Author Sam Harris writes,

> The connection between spirituality and ethics becomes inescapable. A vast literature on meditation suggests that negative social emotions such as hatred, envy, and spite both proceed from and ramify our dualistic perception of the world. Emotions such as love and compassion, on the other hand, seem to make our minds very pliable in meditative terms, and it is increasingly easy to concentrate under their influences. It does not seem surprising that it would be easier to free one's attention from the contents of thought, and simply abide as consciousness [samadhi], if one's basic attitude toward other human beings were positive and if one had established relationships on that basis. Lawsuits, feuds, intricate deceptions, and being shackled and brought to The Hague for crimes against humanity are not among the requisites for stability in meditation.[95]

If we are still lying to others or cheating on our taxes, if we gossip or engage in the countless forms of misconduct, then upon this shaky foundation we will build a shaky meditation.

Buddhism reduces misconduct into ten principal unvirtuous actions. Three are related to body: killing, stealing, and sexual misconduct; four are related to speech: lying, slandering, gossiping, and idle talk; and three are related to mind: greed, hatred, and wrong views. With this ancient check list, we can evaluate our modern lifestyle. If we can get our act together around these ten actions, our meditation will get itself together.

The First Turning teachings which govern monastic life, the Vinaya, are often skipped by lay people. But the Vinaya is associated with ethics, and lay practitioners who strive for stability would do well to study this doctrine. It takes looking at themselves honestly for practitioners at any level to realize the need for First Turning homework.

There are other reasons for instability in meditation: poor effort, the force of habitual patterns, and improper technique, to name just a few, but morality and ethics are at the core.

❧ The Danger of Samadhi

Sooner or later a meditator will experience samadhi, which is a time of rejoicing and a time for concern. Meditative absorption, as coveted as it may be, is not the point of the path, for we are not trying to create a state of mind that we then label as "spiritual." The point is to be receptive to any state of mind, even those we deem unspiritual. Because our normal mind is so frantic, the experience of samadhi is easily mistaken for a grand realization. The contrast is so dramatic that we think samadhi is it.

When I stumbled into my tiny samadhi during my first meditation instruction, it was both a blessing and a curse. It was a blessing because I tasted the power of meditation and the bliss of a pacified mind. I had no idea this dimension of experience was even possible, and a new world opened before me. I spent the next few years trying to recapture that state. I was hooked. This hook is initially healthy because it pulls us toward the spiritual path, but at a certain point this hook must be cut. Any hook, no matter how sweet, eventually leads us astray. Sogyal Rinpoche says,

> Bad experiences, if you do not become trapped by them, are actually blessings in disguise. In my life, really, difficulties have been my greatest teacher. They really helped me to transform. When you're really on the path, really true, then whatever obstacles arise they can become a blessing. Good experiences are more dangerous. You may become proud, or complacent, or attached—then they become traps.[96]

There are three classic meditation experiences waiting to snare the more evolved or lucky meditator. They get us because they feel so good. These are the experiences of bliss, clarity, and nonthought, the by-products of meditative absorption. They are the purest honey covering the sharpest hooks. Traleg Rinpoche nails the problem when he says, "The main cause of misperceptions regarding meditation experience is that, after the loss of the initial fervor, we may forget to focus on the essence of meditation and its purpose and instead place more and more emphasis on the underlying meditative experience itself."[97]

Bliss, clarity, and nonthought are delicious states of mind, and they are partial experiences of enlightenment. Bliss is the experience of everything and every thought as heavenly. We delight in whatever occurs. We may feel like we have transcended all conflicting emotions, and we might express our rapture through song and dance. Bliss easily trips us into believing we have soared into the highest states of realization.

Clarity is perceiving whatever arises as pure, sharp, and brilliant. Phenomena are lucid and diamond-like, and it is possible to even see light emanating from objects. Our sense perceptions are heightened and acute, we are more impervious to torpor, and everything seems awake and vibrant. We are also able to more readily grasp and understand things.

Nonthought, or mental spaciousness, is the cessation of discursive thinking. It is utter stillness, like diving below the surface of a stormy sea. We are able to rest our mind in whatever state it is in.

These experiences can arise alone or in combination. Nonthought, for example, is blissful and gives birth to clarity. These three experiences are like mental candy, and a taste is okay, but feasting on these sweets will make your meditation sick.

If these temporary experiences, called *nyam* in Tibetan, are not understood, they poison even the most advanced meditator. They are sophisticated traps that may arise at any point but tend to occur at higher levels. They are common and very dangerous. Khyentse Rinpoche says, "Meditators who run after experiences [nyams], like a child running after a beautiful rainbow, will be misled. When you practice intensely, you may have flashes of clairvoyance and various signs of accomplishment, but all they do is foster expectations and pride—they are just devilish tricks and the source of obstacles."[98]

I have seen many "enlightened" teachers, mostly Western, who are hooked by the experience of samadhi and its progeny of bliss, clarity, and nonthought. They often extol the extraordinary and ecstatic aspects of meditation and easily snag others just as they themselves have been snagged. Their experiences sound so delectable, so "spiritual," that it is tempting to follow their bliss. This is another instance of why it is not always best to "follow your bliss."

There is nothing inherently problematic with these experiences, the problem is one of improper relationship. Because they feel so good, we get addicted. Like the endorphin released in a "runner's high," these nyams are the "meditator's high," and like any long distance runner, long distance meditators also want more of this buzz. But as we have seen, the point is not to feel good but to get real. These experiences can indicate that we are doing the right thing, for they are glimpses of the nature of the enlightened mind and can point the way. But we will lose our way if we try to repeat them. They are by-products of meditation. The problem is that we think they are the final product of meditation.

A rule about obstacles is that the more subtle they are, the more guileful and dangerous. Nyams can be serious obstacles, and we can get stuck in them for years or an entire lifetime because when we are in a nyam there is no sense of obstacle. We think our meditation has finally come together. This is why it is so important to understand the blessing of having obstacles in our life and that feeling good can be an obstacle. Samadhi is the success story of the spiritual path, and remember that there is no tyranny as great as the tyranny of success.

My teacher Khenpo Rinpoche would have us stand up and dance in the middle of his talks and then sit us back down to resume the talk. At first I could not understand why, it felt like an interruption. But he was showing us how to mix meditation and postmeditation and teaching us not to take our formal sessions so seriously. He was also removing any sense of interruption to our spiritual practice—

showing us that *everything* should be practice. In my own meditation, when I feel like I'm settling down into a "good" session, I will
sometimes intentionally move around or stand up. I still find it hard
to do this for I would much rather hang out in the blissful space,
locked into my version of an ideal meditation and of being spiritual.
But this isn't breaking my meditation—it is enhancing it.

The point with the nyams is first become aware of them. Second,
realize that they can be markers of progress or just dumb luck. Third,
relate to them properly, which means let them go. Khenpo Rinpoche
says, "Nurture your samadhi by destroying it." Patrul Rinpoche
writes, "The yogin's meditation improves through destruction. . . .
When experiences of stillness, bliss, and clarity occur and feelings
such as joy, delight or pleasant sensations arise, you should blast this
husk of attachment to experience into smithereens."[99]

Do not try to repeat the experience or sustain it, just let it come
and let it go. Return without expectations to whatever meditation
you were doing when it arose and carry on but carry on without it,
otherwise it becomes a burden. These experiences can transform into
the three root poisons: bliss becomes passion; clarity flips into aggression; and nonthought transforms into ignorance.[†]

Someone stuck in a nyam is just stroking his or her ego with a very
light touch. It is hard to characterize "masters" stuck in nyams, but
they often appear very "spiritual," in a subtle negative sense, and can
project an aura of the nyam itself. They might convey a seductive
spirit of bliss, or a magnetizing clarity, or an alluring nonconceptual-
ity. One such Western master I saw entered a lecture hall with blissful
music playing and tried so hard to be holy. In an angelic voice, she
proclaimed the love and light aspects of her awakening. To me, she
appeared to be stuck in the nyam of bliss.

[†] They also form the basis for the three realms of existence, as introduced in chapter
11. If you are attached to bliss, that will hurl you into the realm of desire, clarity
will throw you into the realm of form, and nonthought will lead you into the
formless realm.

I began my spiritual journey in the New Age, and there is much that is honorable about it, but the New Age tends to be nyam oriented. It is predisposed to making one feel good, and for many of these teachers, bliss, clarity, and nonthought is what they market—and why they sell.

If you are an advanced meditator or one of the new "enlightened" Westerners, it is hard to turn to your adoring students and tell them that you have been seduced into a nyam for the past decade and that it is time for them to find a real teacher. This would be a sign that this student might yet become a genuine teacher. It is easier to remain locked in overt and covert levels of spiritual codependence, thinking that everyone is being lifted up when in fact everyone is being dragged down.

Genuinely spiritual people are those who are completely ordinary. They are who they are without pretense. At the highest levels, practitioners no longer have any preference for samsara or nirvana. They don't try to act spiritually but simply relax in an uncontrived naturalness that is the heart of enlightenment itself.

One of my favorite lamas is Chokling Rinpoche. He is a dazzling teacher and a master of Tibetan ritual, but what impresses me the most is his fearlessness in being who he is. He doesn't sit quietly or speak slowly and softly when he teaches. He talks at breakneck speed, gesturing wildly, and makes no apology for how he manifests. He has expanded my version of what it means to be spiritual.

We can learn by his example. So much angst comes from trying to be other than what we are. The heart of spirituality is relaxation. Don't try to be spiritual, just be who you are, with your foibles and your folly. Don't be afraid of your shine, and avoid the urge to compare it to others. My friend Rabbi Ted Falcon says that his greatest concern is coming to the end of his life and having this regret: "Why was I not Ted Falcon? Why was I always trying to be someone else? Why was I always trying to be somewhere else?" Don't try to be special, and you may find yourself being truly special. Your light is unique. Do not be afraid to turn it on.

❧ Great Bliss and Ordinary Mind

In Tibetan Buddhism and other traditions there is much traffic with the phrase "great bliss." Enlightenment is associated with such bliss, and samadhi is often defined by it. Great bliss is easily misunderstood and ironically can become the source of great hardship. Because we don't know what it is, we have no choice but to refer to the word "bliss" with our limited experiences of it.

People assume that great bliss must be like an eternal cosmic orgasm, but an orgasm, or any blissful experience in the material world, is "small bliss." Eating a great meal, winning the lottery, buying your first house, and getting that dream mate are all instances of small bliss. Small bliss is conditional, and when the conditions that brought it about are exhausted, so is the bliss.

Great bliss, on the other hand, is unconditional. That is what makes it great. It is not based on causes and conditions and when realized is discovered to be inexhaustible. Great bliss is great because it can be applied to everything. What is the secret to such bliss, and how do we attain it?

Great bliss is the result of seeing the emptiness in things. Jamgon Kongtrul Lodro Thaye says, "In the beginning, [realization of] emptiness purifies, then great bliss arises from emptiness. Such bliss can purify every habitual pattern. Of bliss and emptiness, emptiness is the initial purifier and great bliss the principal factor [in the process of purification]."[100] Purification, in this absolute sense, again refers to purifying reality of existence. When we purify the world of our imputation of solidity, the result is the experience of great bliss—and the evaporation of any form of hardship.

Dzigar Kongtrül Rinpoche says that great bliss is relating to the world without grasping and fixation, which is the natural relationship of perceiving it to be empty. You can't grasp onto a rainbow. Great bliss is similar to the small bliss of an orgasm in that both are defined by great release and great relief. Both are experienced by letting go. The discovery of emptiness is marked by this sense of deliverance.

It is a relief to realize that on an absolute level nothing can hurt us because as it says in the *Tibetan Book of the Dead*, "Emptiness cannot harm emptiness." It is a relief to realize the egolessness that lies beneath the ego and to wake up from the nightmare of solidity. Enlightenment is being enlightened from the heavy load of taking things to be real. The burden of existence is finally lifted.

But the secret is that while the initial experiences of emptiness can be dramatic because they contrast with the solid world in which they arise, emptiness itself is very ordinary. And therefore the experience of great bliss is ordinary. It is the ultimate letdown. Because it is so ordinary, we constantly miss it. A Buddhist maxim says:

> It is so obvious we don't see it.
> It is so simple we don't believe it.
> It is so easy we don't trust it.

We are striving for a Hollywood experience, whereas it's more like a Kansas experience. Suzuki Roshi once said that enlightenment was his greatest disappointment. If we open our eyes, great bliss is right in front of us. It is always already present, but our search for it paradoxically obscures it. Striving is the obstacle, relaxation is the access. At the highest levels we need to release even the path itself and self-liberate any antidote.

In my tradition, we try too hard to be Buddhists. We get hung up on our path and forget that the Buddha wasn't a Buddhist. He was just a man who woke up to the ordinary, and we could emulate him without getting caught in the trappings that followed him.

The last stage in the Mahamudra tradition is called "nonmeditation," which is the point where everything is released, even meditation. The path is gone, ambition and expectation are gone, and the result is a descent into the ordinary, which is no result at all. And that is the point. From the ego's point of view, enlightenment is a downer.

Dr. Tsewang Rinpoche, a lama who is also a Tibetan doctor, says that great expectations in meditation create subtle "wind" disorders that can manifest as headaches, sleep problems, and psychological disturbances. The best approach to meditation, he says, or to spirituality in general, is the middle way. Not too tight; not too lose. This middle way balances the humors (wind, bile, and phlegm) of Tibetan medicine and promotes physical and psychological health. We have to exert some effort in our practice, otherwise it is not a practice, but if we are too ambitious, we can retard our path.

20 ❧
The Origin of Confusion

*The creative energy of the alaya [ground of being] became
so strong that it broke away and became avidya [ignorance],
just as a light may become so bright that it dazzles and causes
confusion, or someone may be so overintelligent that he sees
difficulties where there are none, or so overimaginative
that he creates fearful illusions where none exist.*

— CHÖGYAM TRUNGPA AND RIGDZIN SHIKPO, "The Bardo"

WITH THE FIVE SKANDHAS we discovered the complex development of the ego. They helped us understand the sophisticated processes that give birth to confusion and the patience necessary to remove it. In this chapter we will explore a more definitive teaching on the origin of confusion from the Third Turning. We finally unpack luminosity.

This view on the birth of confusion shows us how intelligent confusion actually is. As we will see, ignorance is made of the very fabric that weaves intelligence, and by understanding this process, we can develop the perseverance necessary to overcome it. We can relax and realize it will take time to remove our confusion.

We can also bring a sense of humor onto our path and delight in the irony of just how smart our stupidity really is. Again, this is not the simple ignorance of not knowing about a topic but is the primordial ignorance that forms the basis of our entire samsaric lives.

Instead of relating to this ignorance as an enemy, which only makes it solid, we should befriend our confusion and marvel at its brilliance in giving birth to the ego and an entire world. It is miraculous that out of nothing our confusion has managed to create everything. Instead of trying to get rid of confusion, as embodied in the ego, we can explore its sophisticated play. Then instead of freaking out over something that seems so real, we might chuckle at the recognition that confusion has pulled its magic tricks on us yet again.

Until you soften your antagonistic relationship to the ego, it only continues to get stronger. Become familiar with your ego and make friends with it, for only then will it evaporate into the light it really is.

❧ Luminosity

In part 2 we introduced emptiness, in many ways the heart of Buddhism. As challenging as emptiness is, there is still one more step to go. Emptiness melts the solidity of appearances, which is where all our suffering comes from, but if we take it too seriously we slip from one extreme to another and go from eternalism into nihilism.

Not all schools accept the teachings on luminosity. Some argue that it was taught for those who can't handle the rigors of emptiness. Having nothing to hang our hat on is too much, so they assert that luminosity was taught as a way to appease the fainthearted. But most teachers maintain that luminosity is a more complete description of reality, and that emptiness is not the entire story.

Luminosity is not easy to define. This is partly because there is nothing that is not luminosity. We therefore do not have any contrast that enables us to see it, yet it is that which sees and that which is seen. We cannot hear it for it is that which hears; we cannot touch it for it is that which touches.

First of all, luminosity does not refer literally to light. Although light is analogous to luminosity, luminosity is something even more subtle. It is the light of the mind. But the analogy of light is helpful for a number of reasons. Light is the most subtle form we can imagine, even sound has more form than light. Light is not quite as formless as space, which serves to contain light, but it is almost formless. We cannot touch it, though it touches us, like when a beam of sunlight strikes our skin.

Light is also that which illuminates and allows us to perceive, and therefore know. We "light up" with a thought, or turn on a physical light to illuminate a room. That the word "light" is enveloped in the word "enlightenment" suggests its fundamental role in waking up. While we can say that emptiness is *like* space and luminosity is *like* the light that saturates space, they are still rough analogies.

The Buddha taught that while reality is empty by nature, it is luminous by expression. In other words, if we look closely at anything or any thought, we find that while there is nothing essentially there, there is a knowing. So one way to define luminosity is that it is cognition, the raw capacity to know. Luminosity is awareness.

We can see why the term "luminosity" is used in this first definition, because light is nearly a synonym for awareness. We see when darkness is illuminated by light. We say things like, "Now I see," "A light went off in my head," "I get the picture," or "Now it's clear to me." Even though we associate luminosity with visual light, our use of the term implies that each sense faculty is similarly illuminated or "turned on." When we feel, smell, taste, or hear, we are experiencing luminosity, awareness, mediated by a physical sense faculty. In Buddhism the mind is referred to as the sixth sense, so the mind experiences, or rather expresses, luminosity. Even a blind man can say, "Now I see it," and we know what he means.

The other definition is that luminosity refers to appearance. Anything that appears *is* luminosity. Anything we can think of, anything we can taste, smell, see, feel, or hear is luminosity. The page of this book is luminosity, as is the chair you are sitting on, or the thought you are having.

These may seem like irreconcilable definitions. On one hand we are saying that luminosity is cognition, on the other hand we are saying luminosity is appearance. There is a way to bring these two definitions together and that leads to a profound and duality-shattering conclusion. The way to bring these two definitions together, to unite self and other, thought and thing, and to taste nonduality, is to proclaim that appearance knows itself. Appearance is aware of itself. Appearance is self-reflexive cognition.

❧ Thought Experiment

This may seem like a numbing proclamation, and one that is completely bewildering. If it were easy to understand, we would all be enlightened. While it is difficult to grasp intellectually, it can be known experientially. Indeed, that is the only way it can be known. To get a feel for it, try this exercise. Close your eyes. Sit still for a minute and pay attention to your mind. Don't do anything, don't try to stop your thoughts, just watch your mind. Sooner or later thoughts will appear. When they do, it seems like you are sitting in a theater watching thoughts play out on the screen of your mind. It is like being at the movies. A thought pops up on the screen, and you view it. You may not have thought about it this way before, but it really feels like there is someone in the back of your head or the back of your mind that is watching thoughts arise and cease. This is akin to what philosopher Daniel Dennett calls "the Cartesian Theater," after Rene Descartes, the philosopher of mind-body dualism.

But if you take a close look, you will discover that this is a dualistic illusion. Try to find the looker, the thinker, the viewer. Can you find anything? If you do this thought experiment, it leads to a startling discovery, but you have to really try it in order for it to deliver its punch. If you try to locate the thinker, you will discover that there is no one there. You will not find the looker. There is no thinker or viewer to be found anywhere in this theater of mind. And there is no screen upon which thought is projected. It's an empty house. If you are not jolted by what you "find," you have not looked hard enough. This is a taste of emptiness, the emptiness of yourself.

This is the first half of the experiment, the part that relates to the Second Turning. The Third Turning part of the experiment is this: if you really do look and can't find anything, you will notice that there is still something there. There is still a sense of knowing, of being aware, even if you are aware of nothing. That awareness of emptiness, that knowing, is a taste of luminosity.

This may be too subtle, so let's turn up the voltage and bring in more light. To do this, take a look at your thoughts. Instead of looking back into your empty mind trying to find the projector, look out at the thoughts that are seemingly being projected. Now ask yourself, who is aware of these thoughts? You just discovered, if you completed the first part of this experiment with rigorous honesty, that nothing is aware of these thoughts— emptiness is aware of these thoughts. In other words, and to return to our initial proclamation: thoughts know themselves. That's self-reflexive cognition.

Thoughts arise without a thinker; projections appear without a projector. Thoughts, as the appearances of our mind, are self-aware. They are reflexively aware. We do not need a perceiver, a self, or a thinker to be aware of thought. Indeed, there isn't one. We tried to find the thinker and none could be found. It is not because we didn't look hard enough and that someday we will find the thinker. It is because there is no thinker. There is just thought knowing itself.

Another example is dreams. Who is it that perceives a dream? It feels like there is a viewer, a dreamer watching the dream unfold, but the dream images are self-aware. There is no dreamer, there is just the dream aware of itself. There is no object out there, nor a subject in here. There is just the nondual reflexively aware dream. Dreams provide a good example that can help us to understand nondual perception or cognition, and they are sometimes referred to as the example dream, which implies that the "real" dream is our so-called waking life.

There is one final step in our experiment. It is best if this entire contemplation is done as a guided meditation, where someone leads you through the investigations. But if you are doing this alone, now open your eyes and gaze upon whatever is in front of you. Apply what you just learned on the inside to the outside. Look at the wall, for example. Who is aware of the wall? It may seem like you are aware of the wall, but again, who and where is this "you?" It may seem like your eyes or your brain are aware of the wall. We can cascade through a lengthy list of possible recursive sources for this cognition, but the bottom line is that the wall is aware of itself. The wall lights up itself. Just like there is no thinker, there is no perceiver. We need the eye, the brain, the body, the neurons, and the neurotransmitters for visual perception, but the essence of perception and cognition transcends material mediation.

The point, and the conclusion of our experiment, is that while perceptual channels may differ, there is no fundamental difference in cognition. There is no fundamental difference between the way we know a thought, a dream, or the seemingly external world. Appearance knows itself. This is luminosity. And understanding it provides the entry into discovering a sacred world. A sacred world is made of heart-mind-spirit, not lifeless matter. This magical world knows itself and transcends the pathetic error of subject and object.

This thought experiment is an exercise in nonduality, a touch of enlightenment. It is one way to summarize the Second and Third Turnings, and through it we can glimpse emptiness and luminosity.

❧ The Irreducible Description of Reality

We are trying to develop an understanding of why it is so hard to wake up and to discover the tools that help us deal with the brilliance of the ego. By doing so we can develop the endurance and humor to keep us on this path of illumination.

Earlier we defined Buddhism as a description of reality. Buddhism offers many such descriptions across the spectrum of the three turnings, and the most subtle description is that reality is the union of luminosity and emptiness. In the famous Heart Sutra, which gets to the heart of the matter, this is referred to as the union of form and emptiness: "form is emptiness; emptiness also is form. Form is no other than emptiness; emptiness is no other than form." In other words, the Buddha described reality as the union of the doctrines of the Second and Third Turnings.

This can be formulated in a simple equation: R = L + E. Reality, everything that appears, is Luminosity united with Emptiness. Don't take this equation too literally; it is just a like a finger pointing to the moon. In Tibetan lore, it is said that one should not mistake the pointer for the object that is being pointed to. There is no transcendental mathematics that describes ultimate reality, nor does there have to be an exact percentage of luminosity and emptiness. The issue is one of unification and balance.

With this caveat in mind, we can still use this pointer to emphasize the essential ideas. When this equation is balanced we have the nondual experience of enlightenment. But most of us are not enlightened, so we skew the equation in one of two ways to create duality. If L and E are not in harmony, if luminosity and emptiness are not equal, we fall into one of the two extremes of eternalism and nihilism. We become extremists.

If there is too much L and not enough E, that gives rise to eternalism. In other words, if luminosity is greater than emptiness, we have the appearance of the world as we know it. We discussed eternalism earlier, the common view that things really exist. For us, existence is a cold hard fact.

If there is too much E and not enough L, that gives rise to nihilism. In other words, if emptiness is greater than luminosity, we have the view that nothing really exists or matters. While some people can slip into this view, most people tend toward the extreme of eternalism. Ironically, most of us are blinded by too much light and not by excessive darkness.

Eternalism, and therefore suffering and confusion, is born when there is too much luminosity and not enough emptiness. When the equation isn't balanced and we do not see the openness in things, we take appearances to be real. Instead of seeing empty forms, the union of form and emptiness, which is the ideal way to perceive things, we simply see forms. So in order to see things more accurately, we need to add emptiness to every thing—we need to *see* the emptiness in everything. When we see the essence (emptiness) and the display (luminosity) simultaneously, the result is self-liberation, which is said to be like writing in water. Writing in water means that whenever something appears, the "thingness" of it immediately disappears—it self-liberates. The solidity, the "selfness," of things disappears.

We can facilitate this perception by adding emptiness to every noun, to every thing. We need to replace "car" with "car-emptiness," "chair" with "chair-emptiness," "house" with "house-emptiness," ad infinitum. This is one way to extend our practice of illusory form or "thinging" that we introduced earlier.

It doesn't feel like there is anything empty about the chair I am sitting on. This chair exists. It does not feel like my thoughts and emotions are empty. They can really hurt. This is why the Second Turning is devoted to melting eternalism. External things like chairs and internal things like thoughts, emotions, and the ego just seem so damn real. This is all due to the blinding effects of luminosity unchecked by emptiness.

❧ The Irreducible Description of Duality

This view of the union of luminosity and emptiness applies to our very sense of self and other. It is an intimate portrait of who we think we are and what we think the world is. The birth of duality—which is *not* reality—arises when we mistake emptiness to be the self and luminosity to be other. This is the irreducible description of duality. It is one way to talk about original sin from a Third Turning perspective.

When you performed the first half of our experiment and looked inward for the knower, you could not find anything. There was no self to be found. This is a glimpse of the emptiness of self. But no matter what you saw or rather did not see, you still believe you exist. This is the mistake of taking emptiness to be your self. You don't care about the experiment or what anybody says; you know that you exist. That certainty is a mistake, and it is the *internal* source of all your suffering.*

But who, or what, is doing the looking? Who makes the discovery

---

* Earlier we explored the open space from which the first skandha arose. We saw that the ego is born out of an inappropriate relationship to the freedom of open space and that this appropriation, this *mis*take, forms the basis for the remaining skandhas. Here we see the confluence of this First Turning teaching with the Third Turning doctrine. The problem, at whatever turning, is freezing space.

that there isn't a who? There is something that makes this discovery, something that knows. There is a cognition, a clarity, a light that is aware. That is luminosity.

When you then performed the second half of the experiment and looked out at a thought or an external thing, who was it that was aware of that thought or thing? No one. There was just the thought itself, or the thing itself, aware of itself. That is awareness, luminosity, *mis*taking itself to be a thing. That is the mistake of taking luminosity to be other. You do not care about the experiment; you know that things out there exist and that they exist independently of you. That certainty is a mistake, and it is the *external* source of all your suffering.

So now we have the bottom-line equations or descriptions for both samsara and nirvana: when emptiness and luminosity are equal, when self and other are equal, that is the irreducible description of reality. When emptiness and luminosity are not equal, when self and other are not equal, that is the irreducible description of duality.

❧ Runaway Luminosity

We are finally ready to understand why ignorance is so smart and why it takes patience and perseverance to see through it. Reality fractures into duality, samsara is born from nirvana, and everything arises out of no-thing whenever luminosity breaks away from emptiness. This is the birth of ignorance, and it is literally a brilliant process, one so dazzling that it blinds us. Trungpa Rinpoche says, "As for ego's type of ground . . . that arises when the energy which flashes out of the basic ground brings about a sort of blinding effect, bewilderment. That bewilderment becomes . . . basic ground of ego."[101] Thrangu Rinpoche describes it this way:

> The idea of the realization of mahamudra [nonduality] is basically emptiness, but the emptiness also has the other aspect of great clarity or luminosity. When one forgets the emptiness aspect, or one does not recognize or does not

identify emptiness, the clarity aspect could be said to get
more and more strong, more and more developed until we
have actual appearances. And then we regard appearances
as real, forgetting the emptiness aspect. . . . Where the
source of bewilderment comes is the loss of the emptiness
aspect and the development or proliferation of the clarity
aspect into actual appearances. . . . The clarity aspect is
almost the cause of ignorance, or confusion. For instance,
if we have a television that is so vivid and so clear we begin
to think the things we see are really there. A person appears
to really be there because it is so clear and perfect. It is the
very clarity aspect itself that lends itself to confusion. . . .
[Similarly] we begin to actually perceive things [separate
from ourselves] by thinking that they are actual appearances [that they are real], not recognizing them as merely
the clarity aspect of mind.

Thrangu Rinpoche uses the example of the dream:

When you first begin to fall asleep there is no dreaming,
and then there is some kind of movement of mind and
thought. That thought gains clarity and as it becomes more
and more clear, it finally manifests as something visible.
You then think the things in your dream are separate from
you, an object, and then you develop liking, disliking, fear
or whatever about it. This is the same process that comes
about arising out of the very nature of mind itself. Generally when we think of the word "ignorance," we think of
some dark, some kind of obscure thing. But in fact ignorance actually comes from clarity. It comes from the progressive projection of mind, due to its own clarity.[102]

In other words, as Rinpoche suggests, our ignorance is made of
the fabric of cognition, of that which knows. Ignorance is born from
too much luminosity. This is why it is so hard to see through it.

There are personalities that we can call "solid types." These are very intelligent people who are blinded by their own light. They are so bedazzled by their brilliance that they just can't see past their solid noses. "Solid types" are helpful examples of runaway luminosity. It is always easier to see in others what we cannot see in ourselves, so studying "solid types" can expose that tendency within us.

Solid types are often the most cognitively gifted of luminaries, our scientists and scholars. People who really shine. Being blessed with luminosity, if not tempered with an equally strong dose of emptiness, becomes their curse. They are addicted to clarity and are often stuck in the world of reason, logic, and mathematics. They lust for proof. They are happy when things are made real for them and when their world seems especially solid. Often very serious, they tend to lack any sense of liquidity or humor. There are very few philosophers, for example, that display humor in their writings.

We are often just as dazzled, and sometimes blinded, by their brilliance as they are by their own. Luminaries really stand out. We look up to these brilliant people, often intimidated by their light. And so we unwittingly become members of their cult, the blind leading the blind.

Most of us are "semi-solid types," perhaps not so completely blinded by our cognitive prowess as the solid types. But if we think things really do exist, our luminosity is still running away with us. Our shine is out of control. We may not lust for proof, reason, and mathematics, but we still rejoice whenever we can stand on something physically or psychologically.

Earlier we saw how emotional upheaval arises when we "lose it," when we lose our luminosity-awareness and are carried away (out) by its energy. Now we can see that emotions are just runaway luminosity occurring at the level of feeling.

Khenpo Tsultrim Gyamtso Rinpoche summarizes the situation this way:

> How does confusion occur? When one does not recognize
> the essential nature of consciousness as being empty, one

misunderstands or mistakes the empty aspect of consciousness for a self. Clinging to a self, clinging to an essential entity, is a mistaken apprehension of the emptiness of consciousness. Then by not recognizing the luminous or radiant aspect of the essence of consciousness, one takes that to be an external object. Basic duality arises by mistaking emptiness as a self and clarity or radiance as an object, or "other." An example is what happens with visual perception. When a visual form is first perceived, there is no experience of anything other than the [clarity of] visual consciousness itself. In other words, one does not experience the existence or nonexistence of an object. What is experienced is completely within the realm of visual consciousness itself. But the clarity or radiance of the experience is mistaken to be an outside object, and the emptiness aspect of the experience is mistaken as the organ of the eye.[103]

21 ❦

Hardship as Loss of the Feminine

It became feminine, and then it became mother principle.
And it made love to its own expressions. Therefore it produced
a buddha—as well as samsara, of course, and all the rest of it.
— CHÖGYAM TRUNGPA, Glimpses of Space

LUMINOSITY AND EMPTINESS can be related to masculine and feminine principles respectively, which afford us another opportunity to penetrate these difficult concepts. Emptiness is associated with the feminine principle. Even in Buddhist cosmology, ladies come first. The feminine is also associated with space, which as we have seen is the closest "physical" analogy to emptiness. Like space, emptiness is nothing in itself, but it gives birth to and accommodates everything. It is the womb of reality. Emptiness is the mother of all things.

Emptiness is also associated with the Tao, which itself is compared to a "mysterious female." The Tao is the mother who gives birth to and nourishes "the ten thousand things" (all phenomena). It is that from which everything arises and to which everything returns. Women, as physical representatives of this metaphysical principle, embody space and emptiness in their reproductive organs. The womb and vagina represent space. They are receptive, accommodating, generating, holding, and nurturing.

Out of this groundless ground, this empty space of the primordial mother, comes the itch to play. This is the ineffable urge toward manifestation, birth, and the genesis of all manifest reality. This is the "aggressive" expression of emptiness, a word that derives from roots meaning to "walk toward, step forward." "Aggression" has been unfairly loaded with a negative connotation that was not part of its original meaning. There is a difference between stepping out and lashing out. The deepest meaning of "aggression" is formlessness stepping forward into the world of form, light starting to fill space. This luminosity that emerges as the expressive power and play of emptiness is the male principle. Luminosity is reality turned on, emptiness on display. Male genitalia represent this extended form and action that fills space and moves within it.

Luminosity and emptiness are the parents of reality. While it may seem that emptiness comes first, both luminosity and emptiness are completely inseparable and arise simultaneously. As it says in the *Tibetan Book of the Dead*, "The emptiness and the luminosity are not two separate things, but the nature of emptiness is luminosity, and the nature of luminosity is emptiness."[104] The male and female principle are always and forever in union, constantly giving birth to reality. To become enlightened is to realize this primordial unity.

But we do not see the world this way. We divorce luminosity from emptiness, and this separation gives birth not to reality but to duality. Luminosity becomes too aggressive, excessively male, as it steps too far forward and away from its primordial mate. Confusion and suffering arise when the male principle dominates reality. That this process is mirrored in our aggressive political and patriarchal world is no surprise since it merely reflects this cosmological imbalance.

When the male principle gets out of control, we become overly involved in the world of form and matter. We lose the maternal embrace of emptiness and become lost in the display of (her) form. When the primordial mother holds us, we melt into her arms in nondualistic great bliss; when she releases her caress, we freeze the world into duality.

According to Judith Simmer-Brown, an epithet for the Buddha is "Bhagavan." *Bhaga* is the Sanskrit word for "vagina," so an esoteric interpretation of "bhagavan" is someone who is united with the

wisdom of the vagina, the wisdom of the feminine. A bhagavan is
someone who is blessed with the union of emptiness and looks at the
world through the eyes of the primordial female. Dr. Simmer-Brown
writes, "He has been blessed with union with the vast and limitless mind of the feminine principle, without which enlightenment
is impossible."[105] A bhagavan is engaged in constant union with the
phenomenal world and experiences the endless great bliss that is the
result of that mating.

While women may represent the feminine principle, like most men
they too are caught up in the male principle. Just because you have
a bhaga doesn't mean you are a bhagavan. If you get caught up in
thinking the world is real and seduced into believing your thoughts
truly exist, you are stuck in a patriarchal world view just like the rest
of us.

If the problem is too much masculine principle, the solution, at
least initially, is to emphasize the feminine. Once again we take the
"extreme path to the middle." The path can therefore be seen as a
journey into what we might cautiously call spiritual feminism. On
a provisional level, the worldly path emphasizes the masculine; the
spiritual path, at least initially, emphasizes the feminine: spirit melts
matter. In order to wake up, we have to unite with the bhaga. We
have to melt form back into emptiness by initially overemphasizing
emptiness. We need to become primordial feminists, which is why
the Second Turning is about the great mother Prajnaparamita, who
is depicted as a golden female deity.

❦ Union of Male and Female

The ultimate goal is neither feminine nor masculine, but their nondual (tantric) union. This is the "middle" that the extreme path to the
middle leads us to. The "middle" is the balanced equation of reality,
the union of luminosity and emptiness, male and female. This is what
sex ultimately represents and why we crave it. It is noteworthy that,
after sex, men tend to feel empty and women tend to feel full. Sexual
union serves to temporarily balance the equation.

PRAJNAPARAMITA

At the deepest levels, we lust for another because we want to dissolve the sense of other, the sense of duality. We want to remove the inequity that we feel within ourselves, a tension that gets distorted into self-serving sex instead of self-transcending sex. Self-transcending sex is about unifying opposites, going beyond the duality of self and other. This is perhaps what Goethe was referring to when he wrote in his poem "The Holy Longing":

In the calm water of the love-nights,
where you were begotten, where you have begotten,
a strange feeling comes over you
when you see the silent candle burning.

Now you are no longer caught
in the obsession with darkness,
and a desire for higher love-making
sweeps you upward.

This is also represented in the thangkas, or sacred paintings, depicting deities in physical union. During my last trip to Nepal, I visited my favorite thangka shop where the dealer proceeded to show me some of the recent work of his artists. Emptiness is depicted by a few female deities, and as he was showing me a number of thangkas, I was struck by how unbridled these celestial ladies are. They really get around.

These few female deities were in union with dozens of cosmic males. And they are supposed to be. The problem of eternalism arises when the male deities, which are the archetypes of the male principle in its many guises, become bachelors. The feminine principle, emptiness, needs to join with everything that appears, the masculine, or we will have all the physical and metaphysical problems of materialism.

One advanced meditation practice is that of *tummo*, which translates as "fierce woman." This esoteric practice has received lots of press because of its extraordinary physical by-product. Through visualization and breath control, a psychophysical fire is ignited within the meditator's body that produces real heat. Practitioners are tested by going out unclothed in winter. They sit on the snow, and icy wet blankets are draped over them. This is something that would kill most people, or at least generate severe hypothermia. The blankets start to steam and are slowly dried by the tremendous heat put out by the burning inner body. Dr. Herbert Benson, a professor at Harvard Medical School, has documented these remarkable physiological changes.[106]

SAMANTABHADRA IN UNION WITH SAMANTABHADRI

As impressive as this is, the true miracle is what happens within the body-mind of the meditator. The inner fire burns away all the delusive mental states and allows one to perceive the world as the play of bliss and emptiness. It is a bliss that results from the experience of emptiness. The principal delusion is that of duality, along with the sense of existence, and tummo scorches these solid states of mind. Remember that the mind leads all things, so by incinerating the states of mind that freeze reality into self and other, self melts into other in nondual great bliss. All the icy things we have frozen into reality melt back into the water (no-thingness) that is their essence.

Tummo is considered a forceful method of liberation. It is almost as if the feminine is raping the masculine, melting form back into emptiness. This is where we can return to Jamgon Kongtrul's amazing statement with a new level of insight: "In the beginning, [realization of] emptiness purifies, then great bliss arises from emptiness. Such bliss can purify every habitual pattern. Of bliss and emptiness, emptiness is the initial purifier and great bliss the principal factor [in the process of purification]." The fierce woman penetrates the ego and ejects space into it, forcefully liberating the solid world with her bliss.

☙ Happening Now

Because we are describing this process from a cosmological perspective, it may seem that this primordial divorce between luminosity and emptiness occurred in the distant past, and like the traumatized children of a broken home, we are irreparably stuck in duality. But this process is occurring right now.

In the bardo teachings, one of the most haunting images is what is called the union of the mother and child luminosities. This refers to the final moment of death, when the ego dissolves into emptiness, the great mother. (It gets technical, but in the bardo literature emptiness is also referred to as luminosity. The point for us is that "mother luminosity" refers to emptiness.) If we have some experience of emptiness during life, that is called the child luminosity. When we die, the child returns to the lap of the mother, and if the child recognizes its mother and can rest in her embrace, enlightenment is attained. It's like a drop of water merging back into the ocean.

We are sitting in the lap of the mother, emptiness, at this very moment. We don't have to wait till we physically die to unite with her. But because she is "behind" us, we do not see her. To make matters worse, we leap out of her lap in an effort to find her. We long to reunite with her, to lose ourselves in her embrace, to release this painful separation from reality, and so we move away from her in a paradoxical attempt to find her. This metaphysical doctrine is physically represented when we "leap" out of our mother's lap—her womb—at the moment of birth. We end up looking for love in all the wrong places. And we do it every time we follow a shiny thought.

Instead of turning around and directing our gaze deep within ourselves to find what we are really looking for, we look away. The child only has to turn around to see that the mother is always holding her. What the child so desperately seeks is always already right here. She is sitting in the lap of the bliss she seeks. But because she cannot see the mother, the emptiness that holds her, she looks away. Instead of being a nangpa (insider) she becomes a *chipa* (outsider), gives birth to duality, and starts to chase her own projections. Birth is always a separation. In this case it is the birth of samsara, an aggressive divorce from the emptiness that we will then so ironically spend the rest of our lives trying to find.

The trick, and the saving grace, is that no matter how far the child seems to get away from the lap of the mother, from emptiness, it is impossible to leave her. We cannot actually leave the mother, for luminosity and emptiness can never truly be separated. It is the aggressive gesture of moving away, of looking out, that creates the illusion of duality. And because we have been looking away for so long, this illusion seems very real. Our dogged external gaze is focused and fixed. Duality is rock solid, and liberation from it seems a million miles away.

We have run away from home so long ago that it feels like the return is hopeless. But we only have to stop, take a look within, and discover that which we truly want.

But we do not believe it. We do not feel our mother's warm embrace. So we continue to look for her outside. It is only after we wear ourselves out from looking so hard that we eventually just give up. We have not been able to find her in money, sex, drugs, cars, homes, books, or any of the infinite substitute satisfactions that drive the endless wheel of samsara and our infatuation with frozen light. We have not been able to find what we are looking for in any *form*. When we finally collapse from our efforts and stop looking out, it is then, and only then, that we will find our mother, the formless emptiness that we truly long for, within.

That our mother is "behind" us, holding us, is something we can feel when we do our thought experiment. Remember that the original sin of duality is that we mistake emptiness for the self and luminosity for other. We feel that there is something "behind" our experience, that there is a primordial audience in this Cartesian Theater. We feel that if we just look hard enough into the back rows of this theater, the darkest recesses of our mind, we will eventually find the viewer, the thinker, the witness—the self. But no matter how hard we look, and this time we are looking in the proper direction, we will not find anything. Seeing that which cannot be seen is the ultimate seeing. We will find nothing. And that's precisely it. No-thingness is the emptiness that we mistake for a sense of self. We have not found our self, and we never will. But we have found our mother—the origin of our sense of self—and the origin of all things.

❧ Don't Buy It

What we are discussing is one final way to summarize the entire trajectory of the worldly and spiritual paths and our journey through this book. This is an irreducible expression of the whole shebang. The worldly path of hardship begins when we jump out of our mother's lap and start the frantic and futile search for her outside. On an outer level, this happens every time we chase after an object; on an inner level, this happens every time we chase after a thought. It happens every time we run after our luminous projections, which are nothing but shiny sticks.

This search is sustained because at the moment of acquiring some material thing, there is a fleeting moment of happiness, a temporary release. Because we associate the release with the newly acquired thing, we think more things will bring more release, when it brings only more attachment to the acquired things. Hence we stuff our garages, closets, and shelves full of endless things. We long to feel full, but it is emptiness that we actually crave.

And lest the intellectuals think they are free from this trap, we only need to replace the word "thing" with "thought" to realize the subtle nature of this snare. It is easy for scholars to look down in disdain at the masses clamoring for endless material possessions and be blind to how possessed we are by our endless sparkling thoughts. Acquiring a great idea or philosophy can bring just as much initial release and just as much subsequent attachment as any great thing. Whether we fill our minds with thoughts or our world with things, what we are really looking for is the release from the longing itself. We are looking for no-thing.

On the worldly path, these tiny orgasms, the fleeting moments of happiness, occur whenever we get what we are looking for. We think it is the thing that brought (bought) the release, hence we continue to stumble on the worldly path looking for more thoughts or things, but it is actually the release that arises at the moment we get what we want that is the "thing" we are really after. As we have seen, and this cannot be overstated: we confuse the satisfaction of want with its temporary transcendence.

The irony, and what keeps this dreadful joke of samsara alive, is that we feel the fullness that we covet at the moments that we experience emptiness. That's when we feel "free, limitless, all-encompassing." When we finally let go and rest in the release of not wanting, which we only get in the material world when we get something we want, then we are happy.

The worldly path continues as long as we allow ourselves to be duped into thinking that things and more things will make us happy. Being on the worldly path means we are not looking for mom yet but are still being seduced by her glittering material progeny. Sooner or later we realize that all these things are just substitutes for what we really want. We stop looking out and start looking in. This is renunciation and the birth of the spiritual path. Now we are looking for love in all the right places. We have developed the lion's gaze.

Because we don't identify with emptiness, it takes time to become familiar with what we "find" when we look within. We are so stuck on identifying ourselves with the forms of this world and the forms of our mind that, even when emptiness is finally pointed out, we do not identify with it—partly because there is nothing to identify with and partly because we have such a powerful habit of looking out. It takes time to become familiar with ourselves as nothing—as form-less awareness, luminosity-emptiness. We still get swept away by the things that arise in space and cannot relate properly to space itself.

At a certain point, we even have to stop looking within. We stop any form of looking and just give up. We surrender even the spiritual path and self-liberate any antidote. When we finally give up and relax into the present moment, we will melt back into the arms of the mother we so desperately seek.

In other words, at the deepest levels, what we are longing for is this primordial mother. I have spent many precious hours with dying people. I am struck by how many people start to cry out for their mother as they near death.˙ When I was with my own mother, just hours before she died, she would call out in her feeble voice, "mama, mama." This may well be an expression of longing for her literal mother, a physical source of refuge in a time of crisis. But it may also reveal a profound longing to return to the source of all being, the primordial womb of emptiness. In Buddhism, we arise from the great mother at birth and return to her at death. The crying out for mother at death might therefore be anticipating the impending return to her arms, just moments away. Perhaps they are even seeing this emptiness since many who speak her name are semicomatose and uttering nearly archetypal sounds.

❧ Divine Play

If birth is the separation from the womb of emptiness, death is our consummate reunion. As we have seen, in order to reunite with our mother, the ego—every "thing"—has to die. This puts us in that painful double-bind: we want to unite with emptiness, but we fear its unity. For the ego, it is death.

The spiritual path leads to that death and our liberation from everything—from identifying with form. By "dying" and returning to the primordial mother, we not only dissolve into her, but we become her. We then give birth to all the things of our world and the thoughts of our mind as empty forms, the children of luminosity (form) and emptiness. We give birth to rainbows, children of illusion. Everything still arises, but not as solid and independent things. We

---

˙ It is said that as fighter pilots are just about to crash, the last thing many say is "mom." In listening to voice recorders recovered from crash sites, researchers found that the pilots tried to pull the plane up right until the last moment – they kept fighting. But just before the crash, the last thing many cried out was "Mom!" My hospice worker friends say that dying people utter "mom" more than they do "God," which at this level may be the same.

are no longer fooled by appearances. The inner and outer world is no longer so real or aggressive, and every form of hardship melts into space and light—and therefore into joy.

As the feminine comes to embrace the masculine, the world is defined by play and not by hardship. This is *lila* in the Hindu tradition, the divine play of the manifest world; it is *rolpa* in Tibetan, the delight of the dance of form; and it is *maya*, the world of illusion. It is joy.

But those who live in this playful and magical world do not hang out there. We still experience a marvelous form of suffering—one that never ends. Because we have become one with everything, the suffering of others now becomes our own. By becoming empty of self we become full of others. So we descend from our heavenly realization into the world of form to liberate those still stuck within it. We have gotten the punch line in this bad joke of solidity, and we want to share it with others. We realize the unnecessary hardship that is samsara, and our compassion drives us to remove the suffering of others because we realize there is no other. Their pain is our pain, and we want to get rid of it.

Earlier we discussed the three poisons and the three yanas, which we can now relate to each other. Each yana specializes in transforming a poison, and a trajectory of the entire path is sketched out when all three poisons are transformed. The Hinayana works with establishing a proper relationship to the heat of passion, transforming it into the warmth of compassion. The Mahayana helps us relate to aggression, transforming it into clarity, precision, and insight. And the Vajrayana works with ignorance, transforming it into wisdom. This threefold transformation inscribes an upward arc that culminates with wisdom. This wisdom is the heavenly benefit for *oneself*, which is the realization that there isn't one. It is the discovery of no-self (selflessness, egolessness, emptiness).

If we were to get stuck at this "point," we would be trapped in the limitation of the arhat. In other words, we are only halfway there. Wisdom is just the point at the top where we take the infamous u-turn, which is finally discovered to be a "you-turn." "I" return to help "you." The arhat transforms into a bodhisattva and drops back down to earth.

From the peak of wisdom, from the viewpoint of emptiness, we begin the descent back into form. We jump back into the play of light and start to help others. We leap back into the luminous form of our thoughts, emotions, bodies, and every other thing imaginable, to benefit those still stuck in their exclusive identification with form. We use our wisdom (ignorance transformed) to "walk towards, step forward" (aggression transformed) with compassion (passion transformed). The wisdom of emptiness takes on compassionate form, and every action becomes truly selfless. This inscribes a downward arc that culminates in compassion, the earthly benefit for *others*.

With this upward and downward arc, we complete the circle of the path, which is the ultimate benefit for self and other. We come full circle and return to reinhabit the world of form that we once left—as if for the first time. But completing this circle is only the beginning. It may be the end of our personal hardship and confusion because once we reach the top, we have transcended any sense of being a separate person. Our samsara ends. But helping others who have not come to this point and who still experience personal hardship is endless. Samsara is endless. In this sense, the path is eternal. Compassion, "suffering with" others and enduring their hardship, continues till the end of time.

In the "end," for those who have reached this point, samsara is seen as a bad dream, a rotten joke, and any form of personal hardship breaks up into laughter and light when we finally get it. After all the relative tools have loosened the grip of hardship, the absolute final step is to bring it into our heart and dissolve it. Then we step back into the world and express our wisdom with compassion. We reenter everything we have renounced and inhabit every thing and every thought with fearless gusto, and we delight in the luminous play. Our experience then becomes one of eternal bliss, and our activity that of endless compassion.

Bibliography

Almaas, A. H. *Facets of Unity: The Enneagram of Holy Ideas*. Boston: Shambhala, 1998.

Anam Thubten. *No Self, No Problem*. Ithaca, N.Y.: Snow Lion Publications, 2009.

Aronson, Harvey. "Psychology and Buddhism," *Buddhadharma Magazine* 6, no. 2 (2007).

Baker, Ian. *Heart of the World*. London: Penguin, 2004.

Balsekar, Ramesh S. *A Net of Jewels: Daily Meditations for Seekers of Truth*. Redondo Beach, Calif.: Advaita Press, 1996.

Barasch, Marc Ian. *Field Notes to a Compassionate Life: A Search for the Soul of Kindness*. Emmaus, Penn.: Rodale, 2005.

Brown, G. S. *The Laws of Form*. New York: Julian Press, 1969.

Brunton, Paul. *A Search in Secret India*. New York: Samuel Weiser, 1977.

Chödrön, Pema. *The Places That Scare You: A Guide to Fearlessness in Difficult Times*. Boston: Shambhala, 2001.

Chögyam Trungpa. *Glimpses of Abhidharma*. Boston: Shambhala, 1975.

———. *Glimpses of Space: The Feminine Principle and Evam*. Halifax, N.S.: Vajradhatu Publications, 1999.

———. *Journey without Goal: The Tantric Wisdom of the Buddha*. Boston: Shambhala, 2000.

———. *Myth of Freedom*. Boston: Shambhala, 1976.

———. *Sadhana of Mahamudra*. Translated by Nālandā Translation Committee. Halifax, N.S.: Nālandā Translation Committee, 1968.

————. *The Sanity We Are Born With: A Buddhist Approach to Psychology.* Boston: Shambhala, 2005.

Chögyam Trungpa, and Rigdzin Shikpo. "The Bardo." In *The Collected Works of Chögyam Trungpa,* vol. 6. Boston: Shambhala, 2004.

The Dalai Lama. *Essence of the Heart Sutra.* Translated by Thupten Jinpa. Somerville, Mass.: Wisdom Publications, 2002.

————. *For the Benefit of All Beings: A Commentary on the Way of the Bodhisattva.* Translated by Padmakara Translation Group. Boston: Shambhala, 1997.

————. *A Policy of Kindness: An Anthology of Writings by and about the Dalai Lama.* Ithaca, N.Y.: Snow Lion Publications, 1990.

The Dalai Lama, Herbert Benson, Robert A. F. Thurman, Howard E. Gardner, Daniel Goleman, and the participants in the Harvard Mind Science Symposium. *Mindscience and East-West Dialogue.* Boston: Wisdom Publications, 1991.

Dilgo Khyentse Rinpoche. *Zurchungpa's Testament.* Ithaca, N.Y.: Snow Lion Publications, 2006.

Dilgo Khyentse, and Padampa Sangye. *The Hundred Verses of Advice: Tibetan Buddhist Teachings on What Matters Most.* Translated by Padmakara Translation Group. Boston: Shambhala, 2002.

Dzigar Kongtrül. "The Haunted Dominion of the Mind." *Buddhadharma Magazine* 3, no. 4 (2005).

————. *It's Up to You: The Practice of Self-Reflection on the Buddhist Path.* Boston: Shambhala, 2005.

Dzogchen Ponlop. "How to Work with Emotions." *Buddhadharma Magazine* 6., no. 4 (2008).

————. *Mind Beyond Death.* Ithaca, N.Y.: Snow Lion Publications, 2006.

Eliot, T. S. *Four Quartets.* Orlando: Harcourt Books, 1943.

————. *The Wasteland.* New York: Barnes and Noble, 2005.

Fremantle, Francesca. *Luminous Emptiness: Understanding the Tibetan Book of the Dead.* Boston: Shambhala, 2001.

Fremantle, Francesca, and Chögyam Trungpa. *The Tibetan Book of the Dead: The Great Liberation through Hearing in the Bardo.* Boston: Shambhala, 1976.

Goethe. "The Holy Longing." In *News of the Universe: Poems of Twofold Consciousness*, edited by Robert Bly. San Francisco: Sierra Club Books, 1995.

Gregory, Richard L. *Eye and Brain: The Psychology of Seeing*. 4th ed. Princeton: Princeton University Press, 1990.

Halifax, Joan. *Being with Dying: Cultivating Compassion and Fearlessness in the Presence of Death*. Boston: Shambhala, 2008.

Harris, Sam. *The End of Faith: Religion, Terror, and the Future of Reason*. New York: W.W. Norton, 2004.

Hodge, Stephen, and Martin Boord. *The Illustrated Tibetan Book of the Dead*. New Alresford, Hants: Goldsfielp Press, 1999.

Jamgön Kongtrul. *Creation and Completion: The Essential Points of Tantric Meditation* Boston: Wisdom Publications, 1996.

Jung, Carl. *Collected Works of C. G. Jung*. Translated by R. F. C. Hull. Bollingen 20, 2nd ed. Princeton: Princeton University Press, 1973.

Kapleau, Phillip. *The Wheel of Life and Death: A Practical and Spiritual Guide*. New York: Doubleday, 1984.

Kornfield, Jack. *After the Ecstasy, the Laundry: How the Heart Grows Wise on the Spiritual Path*. New York: Bantam Books, 2001.

———. *A Path with Heart: A Guide through the Perils and Promises of Spiritual Life*. New York: Bantam Books, 1993.

Lama Shenpen Hookham. *There's More to Dying Than Death: A Buddhist Perspective*. Birmingham: Windhorse Publications, 2006.

Lama Yeshe. *Introduction to Tantra: A Vision of Totality*. Somerville, Mass.: Wisdom Publications, 1987.

Lama Zopa Rinpoche. *Transforming Problems into Happiness*. Somerville, Mass.: Wisdom Publications, 2001.

Levine, Stephen. *A Year to Live: How to Live That Year As If It Were Your Last*. New York: Bell Tower, 1997.

Madal, Fabrice. *Chögyam Trungpa: His Life and Vision*. Translated by Ian Monk. Boston: Shambhala, 2004.

Magid, Barry. *Ending the Pursuit of Happiness: A Zen Guide*. Somerville, Mass.: Wisdom Publications, 2008.

Maitri, Sandra. *The Spiritual Dimension of the Enneagram: Nine Faces of the Soul*. New York: Tarcher, 2001.

Maslow, Abraham. "Back from the Dead." *Time Magazine*, October 6, 1986.

McLeod, Ken. *Wake Up to Your Life: Discovering the Buddhist Path of Attention.* New York: HarperCollins, 2001.

Mukpo, Diana J. *Dragon Thunder: My Life with Chögyam Trungpa.* Boston: Shambhala, 2006.

Nālandā Translation Committee, trans. *Rain of Wisdom: The Grand Songs of Lord Marpa.* Translated by the Nālandā Translation Committee, under the direction of Chögyam Trungpa. Boston: Shambhala, 1979.

Ngawang Zangpo. *Sacred Ground: Jamgon Kongtrul on "Pilgrimage and Sacred Geography."* Ithaca, N.Y.: Snow Lion Publications, 2001.

Nyoshul Khenpo. *Natural Great Perfection,* trans. Lama Surya Das. Ithaca, N.Y.: Snow Lion Publications, 1995.

Ostaseski, Frank. "You Mean I'm Going to Die Too?," *Buddhadharma Magazine* 7, no. 3 (2009).

Pagels, Elaine. *The Gnostic Gospels.* New York: Vintage Books, 1989.

Patrul Rinpoche. *The Words of My Perfect Teacher.* Translated by the Padmakara Translation Group. New York: HarperCollins, 1994.

Patrul Rinpoche, and Vidyadhara Garab Dorje. *Lion's Gaze: A Commentary on "Tsig Sum Nedek."* Introduced and explained by Venerable Khenchen Palden Sherab Rinpoche and Venerable Khenpo Tsewang Dongyal Rinpoche, translated by Sarah Harding, and edited by Joan Kaye. Boca Raton: Sky Dancer Press, 1998.

Peck, M. Scott. *The Road Less Traveled: A New Psychology of Love, Traditional Values, and Spiritual Growth.* New York: Touchstone, 1978.

Pettit, John W. *Mipham's Beacon of Certainty: Illuminating the View of Dzogchen, the Great Perfection.* Somerville, Mass.: Wisdom Publications, 1999.

Piver, Susan. "My Views" *Shambhala Sun Magazine* 16, no. 6 (2008).

Preece, Rob. *The Psychology of Buddhist Tantra.* Ithaca, N.Y.: Snow Lion Publications, 2006.

The Random House Dictionary of the English Language. 2nd ed., unabridged. New York: Random House, 1987.

Ray, Reginald. *Secret of the Vajra World: The Tantric Buddhism of Tibet.* Boston: Shambhala, 2001.

———. *Touching Enlightenment: Finding Realization in the Body.* Boulder: Sounds True, 2008.

Ricard, Matthieu. *Journey to Enlightenment: The Life and World of Khyentse Rinpoche, Spiritual Teacher from Tibet.* New York: Aperture, 1996.

Rilke, Rainer Maria. "The Man Watching." In *News of the Universe: Poems of Twofold Consciousness,* edited by Robert Bly. San Francisco: Sierra Club Books, 1995.

Roberts, Bernadette. *The Experience of No-Self: A Contemplative Journey.* Boston: Shambhala, 1982.

Roethke, Theodore. *The Collected Poems of Theodore Roethke.* Garden City, N.Y.: Anchor Press, 1975.

Shaw, Miranda, "Working with Sense Pleasures." *Buddhadharma Magazine* 2, no. 1. (2003).

Shunryu Suzuki. *Zen Is Right Here: Teaching Stories and Anecdotes of Shunryu Suzuki.* Edited by David Chadwick. Boston: Shambhala, 2007.

———. *Zen Mind, Beginner's Mind: Informal Talks on Zen Meditation and Practice.* New York: John Weatherhill, 1985.

Simmer-Brown, Judith. *Dakini's Warm Breath: The Feminine Principle in Tibetan Buddhism.* Boston: Shambhala, 2001.

Smith, Huston. *The Forgotten Truth: The Common Vision of the World's Religions.* New York: Harper Collins, 1976.

Stewart, Jampa Mackenzie. *The Life of Gampopa: The Incomparable Dharma Lord of Tibet.* Ithaca, N.Y.: Snow Lion Publications, 1995.

Thich Nhat Hanh. *Being Peace.* Berkeley: Parallax Press, 1987.

Thrangu Rinpoche. *A Commentary on the Song of Lodro Thaye.* Boulder, Colo.: Namo Buddha Publications, 1990.

Tolle, Eckhart. *A New Earth: Awakening to Your Life's Purpose.* London: Plume, 2005.

Traleg Kyabgon. *Mind at Ease: Self-Liberation through Mahamudra Meditation*. Boston: Shambhala, 2003.

Tulku Thondup. *Enlightened Living: Teachings of Tibetan Buddhist Masters*. Boston: Shambhala, 1990.

Tulku Urgyen. *Rainbow Painting*. Kathmandu: Ranjung Yeshe Publications, 1995.

Walsh, Roger. "Meditation Research: The State of the Art." In *Paths beyond Ego: The Transpersonal Vision*, edited by Roger Walsh and Frances Vaughan. Los Angeles: Tarcher, 1993.

Welwood, John. "Intimate Relationship as a Spiritual Crucible." *Shambhala Sun Magazine* 17, no. 2 (2008).

———. *Journey of the Heart: The Path of Conscious Love*. New York: HarperCollins, 1990.

Wilber, Ken. *No Boundary: Eastern and Western Approaches to Personal Growth*. Boston: Shambhala, 1979.

Wilber, Ken, Jack Engler, and Daniel P. Brown. *Transformations of Consciousness: Conventional and Contemplative Perspectives on Development*. Boston: Shambhala, 1986.

Yongey Mingyur Rinpoche. *The Joy of Living: Unlocking the Secret and Science of Happiness*. New York: Harmony Books, 2009.

Notes

Introduction

1 Paul Brunton, *A Search in Secret India* (New York: Samuel Weiser, 1977), 304–5.

2 R. M. Bucke, quoted in Ken Wilber, *No Boundary: Eastern and Western Approaches to Personal Growth* (Boston: Shambhala, 1979), 2.

3 Marpa Lotsawa, quoted in Nālandā Translation Committee, trans., *The Rain of Wisdom: The Grand Songs of Lord Marpa*, trans. Nālandā Translation Committee under the direction of Chögyam Trungpa (Boston: Shambhala, 1989), 135.

4 Anam Thubten, *No Self, No Problem* (Ithaca, N.Y.: Snow Lion Publications, 2009), 58.

5 Padampa Sangey, quoted in Ian Baker, *Heart of the World* (London: Penguin, 2004), 161.

6 Barry Magid, *Ending the Pursuit of Happiness: A Zen Guide* (Somerville, Mass.: Wisdom Publications, 2008), 70

7 Eckhart Tolle, *A New Earth: Awakening to Your Life's Purpose* (London: Plume, 2005), 102.

Chapter 1

Epigraph drawn from Roger Walsh and Francis Vaughn, *Paths beyond Ego: The Transpersonal Vision* (Los Angeles: Tarcher, 1993), 61.

Chapter 2

First epigraph drawn from Dzigar Kongtrül, *It's Up to You: The Practice of Self-Reflection on the Buddhist Path* (Boston: Shambhala, 2005), 79; second epigraph drawn from Achaan Chah, quoted in Jack Kornfield, *A Path with Heart: A Guide through the Perils and Promises of Spiritual Life* (New York: Bantam Books, 1993), 42.

8 Yongey Mingyur Rinpoche, *The Joy of Living: Unlocking the Secret and Science of Happiness* (New York: Harmony Books, 2009), 21.

9 Dilgo Khyentse Rinpoche, *Zurchungpa's Testament*, trans. Padmakara Translation Group (Ithaca, N.Y.: Snow Lion Publications, 2006), 59–60.

10 Dzogchen Ponlop, *Mind Beyond Death* (Ithaca, N.Y.: Snow Lion Publications, 2006), 257.

11 A. H. Almaas, *Facets of Unity: The Enneagram of Holy Ideas* (Boston: Shambhala, 1998), 54.

12 Elaine Pagels, *The Gnostic Gospels* (New York: Vintage Books, 1989), 281.

13 T. S. Eliot, *The Wasteland* (New York: Barnes and Noble, 2005).

14 Reginald A. Ray, *Touching Enlightenment: Finding Realization in the Body* (Boulder: Sounds True, 2008), 136.

15 Ringu Tulku Rinpoche (talk, Boulder Shambhala Center, May 2005).

16 Fabrice Madal, *Chögyam Trungpa: His Life and Vision*, trans. Ian Monk (Boston: Shambhala, 2004), 157.

17 Miranda Shaw, "Working with Sense Pleasures," *Buddhadharma Magazine* 2, no. 1 (2003), 32.

CHAPTER 3

Second epigraph drawn from Diana J. Mukpo, *Dragon Thunder: My Life with Chögyam Trungpa* (Boston: Shambhala, 2006), 366.

18 The Dalai Lama, *Essence of the Heart Sutra*, trans. Thupten Jinpa (Somerville, Mass.: Wisdom Publications, 2002), 23–24.

19 Traleg Kyabgon, *Mind at Ease: Self-Liberation through Mahamudra Meditation* (Boston: Shambhala, 2003), 38.

20 John Welwood, "Intimate Relationship as a Spiritual Crucible," *Shambhala Sun Magazine* 17, no. 2, (2008), 112. Rilke quote is from "The Man Watching," in *News of the Universe: Poems of Twofold Consciousness*, ed. Robert Bly (San Francisco: Sierra Club Books, 1995).

21 Sakyong Mipham Rinpoche (talk, Shambhala Mountain Center, July 22, 2007).

22 Dzigar Kongtrül, "The Haunted Dominion of the Mind," *Buddhadharma Magazine* 3, no. 4 (2005), 29.

23 Jampa Mackenzie Stewart, *The Life of Gampopa: The Incomparable Dharma Lord of Tibet* (Ithaca, N.Y.: Snow Lion Publications, 1995), 83.

24 Matthieu Ricard, *Journey to Enlightenment: The Life and World of Khyentse Rinpoche, Spiritual Teacher from Tibet* (New York: Aperture, 1996), 108.

25 Thomas Aquinas, quoted in Marc Ian Barasch, *Field Notes to a Compassionate Life: A Search for the Soul of Kindness* (Emmaus, Penn.: Rodale, 2005), 13.

26 Barasch, *Field Notes to a Compassionate Life*, 13–14.

CHAPTER 4

First epigraph drawn from Theodore Roethke, *The Collected Poems of Theodore Roethke* (Garden City, N.Y.: Anchor Press, 1975), 231; second epigraph drawn from Patrul Rinpoche, quoted in Tulku Thondup, *Enlightened Living: Teachings of Tibetan Buddhist Masters* (Boston: Shambhala, 1990), 93.

27 Sandra Maitri, *The Spiritual Dimension of the Enneagram: Nine Faces of the Soul* (New York: Tarcher), 26.

28 Mukpo, *Dragon Thunder*, 367.

29 *The Random House Dictionary of the English Language*, 2nd ed., unabridged (New York: Random House, 1987).

30 Chandrakirti verse translated by Ari Goldfield.

31 John W. Pettit, *Mipham's Beacon of Certainty: Illuminating the View of Dzogchen, the Great Perfection* (Somerville, Mass.: Wisdom Publications, 1999), 416.

32 Francesca Fremantle, *Luminous Emptiness: Understanding the Tibetan Book of the Dead* (Boston: Shambhala, 2001), 68.

33 Guru Rinpoche (Padmasambhava), quoted in Baker, *Heart of the World*, 161.

34 Wilber, *No Boundary*, 85–86.

35 Dzigar Kongtrül, *It's Up to You*, 104.

36 Frank Ostaseski, "You Mean I'm Going to Die Too?," *Buddhadharma Magazine* 7, no. 3 (2009), 45.

37 Patrul Rinpoche, quoted in Tulku Thondup, *Enlightened Living*, 93–94.

38 James Pagel, "Dreaming: Research Makes Gains." *Denver Post*, July 3, 2005.

39 Khenpo Karthar Rinpoche, "Teachings on Marpa Guru Yoga" (talk, trans. Yeshe Gyamtso, Karma Triyana Dharmachakra, July 4, 1992).

40 Tenga Rinpoche, "Clearing Away Obstacles" (talk, trans. Elizabeth Callahan, Halifax, N.S., June 1998).

41 Joan Halifax, *Being with Dying: Cultivating Compassion and Fearlessness in the Presence of Death* (Boston: Shambhala, 2008), 199.

42 Welwood, "Intimate Relationship as a Spiritual Crucible," 63.

43 Anam Thubten, *No Self, No Problem*, 59, 62–63.

44 Chögyam Trungpa, *Glimpses of Abhidharma* (Boston: Shambhala, 1975), 101.

CHAPTER 5

First epigraph drawn from Ben Franklin, quoted in M. Scott Peck, *The Road Less Traveled: A New Psychology of Love, Traditional Values, and Spiritual Growth* (New York: Touchstone, 1978), 50; second epigraph drawn from Sakyong Mipham Rinpoche, quoted in Susan Piver, "My Views," *Shambhala Sun Magazine* 16, no. 6 (2008).

45 Pema Chödrön, *The Places That Scare You: A Guide to Fearlessness in Difficult Times* (Boston: Shambhala, 2001), 27.

46 See studies documented in Ken Wilber, Jack Engler, and Daniel P. Brown, *Transformations of Consciousness: Conventional and Contemplative Perspectives on Development* (Boston: Shambhala, 1986), 250–51.

47 Huston Smith, *The Forgotten Truth: The Common Vision of the World's Religions* (New York: Harper Collins, 1976), 42.

48 Ibid.

49 Peck, *The Road Less Traveled*, 16.

50 Francesca Fremantle and Chögyam Trungpa, *The Tibetan Book of the Dead: The Great Liberation through Hearing in the Bardo* (Boston: Shambhala, 1976), 42.

51 Stephen Levine, *A Year to Live: How to Live That Year As If It Were Your Last* (New York: Bell Tower, 1997), 43.

52 Carl Jung, *Collected Works of C. G. Jung*, trans. R. F. C. Hull, Bollingen 20, 2nd ed. (Princeton: Princeton University Press, 1973).

CHAPTER 6

First epigraph drawn from Chögyam Trungpa, quoted in Chödrön, *The Places That Scare You*, 89; the second epigraph drawn from Lama Zopa Rinpoche, *Transforming Problems into Happiness* (Somerville, Mass.: Wisdom Publications, 2001), 3.

53 Lama Yeshe, *Introduction to Tantra: A Vision of Totality* (Somerville, Mass.: Wisdom Publications, 1987), 52–53.

CHAPTER 7

54 Traleg Kyabgon, *Mind at Ease*, 156.
55 The Dalai Lama, *A Policy of Kindness: An Anthology of Writings by and about the Dalai Lama* (Ithaca, N.Y.: Snow Lion Publications, 1990), 83–85.
56 Welwood, "Intimate Relationship as a Spiritual Crucible," 63.

CHAPTER 8

First epigraph drawn from Dzigar Kongtrül, *It's Up to You*, 79; second epigraph drawn from Reginald Ray, *Secret of the Vajra World: The Tantric Buddhism of Tibet* (Boston: Shambhala, 2001), 252.

57 Milarepa, quoted in Patrul Rinpoche, *The Words of My Perfect Teacher*, trans. Padmakara Translation Group (New York: HarperCollins, 1994), 56.

PART TWO

Epigraph drawn from Ramesh S. Balsekar, *A Net of Jewels: Daily Meditations for Seekers of Truth* (Redondo Beach, Calif.: Advaita Press, 1996), meditation for April 12th.

CHAPTER 9

First epigraph drawn from Chödrön, *The Places That Scare You*, 10; second epigraph drawn from Ray, *Touching Enlightenment*, 235.

58 Goethe, "The Holy Longing," in *News of the Universe: Poems of Twofold Consciousness*, ed. Robert Bly (San Francisco: Sierra Club Books, 1995), 70.
59 Kabir, quoted in Levine, *A Year to Live*, 10.

CHAPTER 10

First epigraph drawn from Bernadette Roberts, *The Experience of No-Self: A Contemplative Journey* (Boston: Shambhala, 1982), 43; second epigraph drawn from Guru Rinpoche, quoted in Baker, *Heart of the World*, 268.

60 Almaas, *Facets of Unity*, 22.
61 Chögyam Trungpa, *Journey without Goal: The Tantric Wisdom of the Buddha* (Boston: Shambhala, 2000), 111.
62 Ibid.

63 Verses by Friedrich Klopstock, translated by Steven Ledbetter.
64 Abraham a Sancta Clara, quoted in Phillip Kapleau, *The Wheel of Life and Death: A Practical and Spiritual Guide* (New York: Doubleday 1984), 47.

CHAPTER 11

Epigraph drawn from Mukpo, *Dragon Thunder*, 360.
65 Jamgön Kongtrul, *Creation and Completion: The Essential Points of Tantric Meditation* (Boston: Wisdom Publications, 1996), 31.

CHAPTER 12

Epigraph drawn from Chögyam Trungpa, *Journey without Goal*, 112.
66 Tolle, *A New Earth*, 73, 76.
67 Abraham Maslow, "Back from the Dead," *Time Magazine*, October 6, 1986.
68 Wallace Stevens, quoted in Baker, *Heart of the World*, 268.

CHAPTER 13

Second epigraph drawn from Lama Zopa Rinpoche, *Transforming Problems into Happiness*, 6.
69 Peck, *The Road Less Traveled*, 50.
70 The Dzogchen Ponlop Rinpoche, "Vast Heart, Profound Mind" (talk, Nalanda West, Seattle, March 2005).
71 Chögyam Trungpa, *Sadhana of Mahamudra*, trans. Nālandā Translation Committee (Halifax, N.S.: Nālandā Translation Committee, 1968), 19.
72 Thich Nhat Hanh, *Being Peace* (Berkeley: Parallax Press, 1987), 45–47.

CHAPTER 14

Epigraph drawn from Tolle, *A New Earth*, 22.
73 Stephen Hodge and Martin Boord, *The Illustrated Tibetan Book of the Dead* (New Alresford, Hants: Goldsfielp Press, 1999), 155.
74 Chögyam Trungpa, *Myth of Freedom* (Boston: Shambhala, 1976), 23.
75 G. S. Brown, *The Laws of Form* (New York: Julian Press, 1969), v.
76 Hodge and Boord, *The Illustrated Tibetan Book of the Dead*, 47.
77 Chögyam Trungpa, *Glimpses of Abhidharma*, 21.
78 Fremantle, *Luminous Emptiness*, 101.

CHAPTER 15

Epigraph drawn from Harvey Aronson, "Psychology and Buddhism," *Buddhadharma Magazine* 6, no. 2 (2007), 52.
79 Richard L. Gregory, *Eye and Brain: The Psychology of Seeing*, 4th ed. (Princeton: Princeton University Press, 1990), 66–67.
80 Maitri, *The Spiritual Dimension of the Enneagram*, 35.
81 Ibid., 32.

CHAPTER 16

Epigraph drawn from Jack Kornfield, *After the Ecstasy, the Laundry: How the Heart Grows Wise on the Spiritual Path* (New York: Bantam Books, 2001), 27.

82 Chögyam Trungpa, *Myth of Freedom*, 23.

83 Fremantle, *Luminous Emptiness*, 96.

84 Lama Shenpen Hookham, *There's More to Dying Than Death: A Buddhist Perspective* (Birmingham: Windhorse Publications, 2006), 7.

85 Chögyam Trungpa, "Warriorship in the Three Yanas," talk 1 (seminar, Rocky Mountain Dharma Center, August 22, 1978).

86 John Welwood, *Journey of the Heart: The Path of Conscious Love* (New York: HarperCollins, 1990), 63.

PART THREE

First epigraph drawn from T. S. Eliot, *Four Quartets* (Orlando: Harcourt Books, 1943), 59.

87 Kalu Rinpoche, quoted in Ken McLeod, *Wake Up to Your Life: Discovering the Buddhist Path of Attention* (New York: HarperCollins, 2001), 382.

CHAPTER 17

First epigraph drawn from Shunryu Roshi, *Zen Is Right Here: Teaching Stories and Anecdotes of Shunryu Suzuki*, ed. David Chadwick (Boston: Shambhala, 2007); second epigraph drawn from Ray, *Secret of the Vajra World*, 252.

88 The Dzogchen Ponlop Rinpoche, "How to Work with Emotions," *Buddhadharma Magazine* 6, no. 4 (2008), 53.

89 The Dalai Lama, *For the Benefit of All Beings: A Commentary on the Way of the Bodhisattva*, trans. Padmakara Translation Group (Boston: Shambhala, 1997), 38.

90 Gotsangpa's song translated by Jim Scott and Ann Bucardi.

91 Rob Preece, *The Psychology of Buddhist Tantra* (Ithaca, N.Y.: Snow Lion Publications, 2006), 14.

CHAPTER 18

Epigraph drawn from Patrul Rinpoche, *The Words of My Perfect Teacher*, 189.

92 Dilgo Khyentse and Padampa Sangye, *The Hundred Verses of Advice: Tibetan Buddhist Teachings on What Matters Most*, trans. Padmakara Translation Group (Boston: Shambhala, 2002), 96.

93 Shunryu Suzuki, *Zen Mind, Beginner's Mind: Informal Talks on Zen Meditation and Practice* (New York: John Weatherhill, 1985), 63.

94 Tulku Urgyen, *Rainbow Painting* (Kathmandu: Ranjung Yeshe Publications, 1995), 24.

CHAPTER 19

Second epigraph drawn from Lama Gendun Rinpoche, quoted in Nyoshul Khenpo, *Natural Great Perfection*, trans. Lama Surya Das (Ithaca, N.Y.: Snow Lion Publications, 1995), 12.

95 Sam Harris, *The End of Faith: Religion, Terror, and the Future of Reason* (New York: W.W. Norton, 2004), 220.

96 Sogyal Rinpoche (lecture, San Francisco, November 8, 2000).

97 Traleg Kyabgon, *Mind at Ease*, 198.

98 Ricard, *Journey to Enlightenment*, 108.

99 Patrul Rinpoche and Vidyadhara Garab Dorje, *Lion's Gaze: A Commentary on "Tsig Sum Nedek,"* introduced and explained by Venerable Khenchen Palden Sherab Rinpoche and Venerable Khenpo Tsewang Dongyal Rinpoche, trans. Sarah Harding, ed. Joan Kaye (Boca Raton: Sky Dancer Press, 1998), 88–89.

100 Ngawang Zangpo, *Sacred Ground: Jamgon Kongtrul on "Pilgrimage and Sacred Geography"* (Ithaca, N.Y.: Snow Lion Publications, 2001), 58.

CHAPTER 20

Epigraph drawn from Chögyam Trungpa and Rigdzin Shikpo, "The Bardo," in *The Collected Works of Chögyam Trungpa*, vol. 6 (Boston: Shambhala, 2004), 552.

101 Chögyam Trungpa, *The Sanity We Are Born With: A Buddhist Approach to Psychology* (Boston: Shambhala, 2005), 96.

102 Thrangu Rinpoche, *A Commentary on the Song of Lodro Thaye* (Boulder, Colo.: Namo Buddha Publications, 1990), 41, 46, 54.

103 Khenpo Tsultrim Gyamtso Rinpoche, "The Essential Points of Creation and Completion," (talk, trans. Sarah Harding, Boulder Shambhala Center, October 1995).

CHAPTER 21

Epigraph drawn from Chögyam Trungpa, *Glimpses of Space: The Feminine Principle and Evam* (Halifax, N.S.: Vajradhatu Publications, 1999), 4.

104 Fremantle and Chögyam Trungpa, *The Tibetan Book of the Dead*, 77.

105 Judith Simmer-Brown, *Dakini's Warm Breath: The Feminine Principle in Tibetan Buddhism* (Boston: Shambhala, 2001), 103.

106 The Dalai Lama, Herbert Benson, Robert A. F. Thurman, Howard E. Gardner, Daniel Goleman, and participants in the Harvard Mind Science Symposium, *Mindscience and East-West Dialogue* (Boston: Wisdom Publications, 1991), 44.

Index